Country Careers
Successful Ways to Live and Work in the Country

Country Careers
Successful Ways to Live and Work in the Country

_____   _____

Jerry Germer

John Wiley & Sons, Inc.

New York ▪ Chichester ▪ Brisbane ▪ Toronto ▪ Singapore

In recognition of the importance of preserving what has been written, it is a policy of John Wiley & Sons, Inc., to have books of enduring value printed on acid-free paper, and we exert our best efforts to that end.

Library of Congress Cataloging-in-Publication Data

Germer, Jerry, 1938–
    Country careers : successful ways to live and work in the country / Jerry Germer.
        p.   cm.
    Includes index.
    ISBN 0–471–57583–6 (cloth) — ISBN 0–471–57582–8 (paper)
    1. Career changes—United States. 2. Quality of work life—United States. 3. Urban-rural migration—United States. 4. United States—Rural conditions. I. Title.
    HF5384.G47 1993
    650.1—dc20   93–18820

Printed in the United States of America

10 9 8 7 6 5 4 3 2 1

*To Lucie, for 25 years of love, support, and
a rich life—wherever we were.*

Preface

This is a book about change and choices—choices in the workplace and economy and the choices they open to you for a more rewarding career; changes in cities and suburbs and your choices for better places to live and work.

The idea for the book began when Neal Maillet, an editor at John Wiley & Sons, speculated that millions of professionals dream, from time to time, of trading their fast-track urban jobs for a more fulfilling one in a greener setting. My agent, Julian Bach, saw me as one who had actually made the trade and suggested I undertake the project.

As an architect and writer on building topics, I was hesitant to undertake a project such as this at first. The enthusiasm of the people I interviewed for this book quickly warmed me to the idea. Except for a few I made up to illustrate a particular point, all of the examples presented are the stories of real people, many of whom are corporate or urban refugees. But all of them demonstrate how it is possible to forge a career of one's own design in a place one chooses to live. Their accounts will, I hope, inspire you in your own quest for the good life.

And now, a word about words. I use *outland* to refer to any location outside of metropolitan and suburban areas. I had trouble finding a word that could equally refer to husband, wife, significant other, and life-partner. *Spouse* is what I settled on, for better or worse.

This is a "how-to" book. A series of worksheets supplements the text to help you make the decisions you'll need to make if you are planning a country career. I realize that most of life's decisions are made not by worksheets, but I hope, nevertheless, that they will be useful and maybe even fun. The worksheets are not intended to give you hard and fast answers (I am not a social scientist) but rather to prompt your thinking and imagination. Hopefully you and your spouse will both fill them out to arrive at a consensus.

Special attention for help and support in putting this book together is due the following: the people whose lives I wrote about, for patiently co-operating in one or more telephone interviews; Barbara Blackburn and Gil Gordon, two of the aforementioned folks, for their additional insights in special areas; Neal Maillet, my editor at John Wiley & Sons, for suggesting the idea for the book and helping me steer it through the publishing process; copyeditor Greg Everitt; Mary Ray, who coordinated production; Julian Bach, my agent; my writers group in Keene, New Hampshire, for their helpful comments along the way; Laurence and Lucie Barber, for their encouragement; and Lucie, Max, and Lucinda—for being the pillars of my life.

Contents

Part One

Shady Lane, the Street of Dreams

Introduction

Americans are starting to trade down. They want to reduce their attachments to status symbols, fast-track careers and great expectations of Having It All. Upscale is out; downscale is in.

Janice Castro, *Time*[1]

Mark stares into the mauve fabric of the office partition that separates his cubicle from his neighbor's. Slurping his first cup of coffee, he boots up his computer and tries to get his head into another workday.

This early September morning should have been the start of a pleasant time of year. But, as he joined the usual crowd of impatient workers on Route 128 for his daily commute into Boston, the heavy, humid air held the smell of auto exhaust. By the time he got to the Mass Pike, the morning rush had turned into a crawl, stretching his normal 45-minute commute from Dedham to over an hour—and stretching his nerves as well. The smog that hovered over the traffic made the drivers surly; they showed it by driving more aggressively. "Am I just losing patience as I get older," he wondered, "or is this traffic really getting worse each year?"

And why is it getting harder for Mark to work up any zeal for each day's tasks? His initial enthusiasm for the project he is working on has subsided. What remains is a mountain of tedium—checking details for consistency, making sure all contingencies are covered. He knows from other recent projects that whatever strokes might come from the client will go to his department head, leaving the people who did the real work—Mark and the team he manages—with only follow-up problems to attend to.

At 42, Mark makes good money as the project manager of a five-member computer software–writing department of a medical equipment manufacturer. He can afford the material rewards accorded this income

3

level, but the commitment required to keep up with his job keeps him from enjoying them. If he's lucky, he might get two back-to-back weeks for vacation. But whether he and his wife, Diane, will be able to schedule their vacations at the same time is even more a matter of luck.

After years of teaching music in elementary schools, Diane is burned out. She doesn't care if she never sees another kid with a cornet. None of the three schools where she teaches can afford a full-time music teacher, forcing her to spend part of her workday shuttling between them. Like Mark, she has wearied of commuting.

Two years ago, realizing that the most she had to look forward to was more of the same, Diane enrolled in a graduate program at Northeastern University leading toward a degree in school administration. She doesn't know where this might take her but hopes that making the effort will open the door to other opportunities.

Mark thinks back on how little time he and Diane have had together in the past few years. He especially regrets not spending more time with his daughter, Jennifer, now 15 and growing up much too quickly. A bright kid, Jennifer has distinguished herself in drama and is a star soprano in the school choir. How many times has he or Diane had to skip one of her plays or concerts because of work?

As Mark finishes his coffee and turns toward the list of phone calls to be returned, it occurs to him that he faces a never-ending stream of workdays that leads nowhere except to retirement, if the company doesn't ax him before then.

As he checks the day's appointments on his wall calendar, the picture on it catches his eye. A white clapboard church steeple rises above the roofs of a New England village. Buildings are mirrored in the placid pond in the foreground. Crimson and gold trees recede into the low hills beyond the village. The scene sparks memories of his childhood in a town of about the same size on the Hudson River. Life was slower there. He had time to think. The chirping of crickets was the only sound he heard at night, except for the occasional horn blast summoning the volunteer fire department to an emergency. Toward morning, when even the crickets slept, the distant rumble of a train coming into town broke the silence. He could take comfort knowing that he had another hour before he had to get up to start the day; he breathed in some of the fresh, clean air coming through the open window and then went back to sleep.

In the suburb where he now lives, each night brings a continuous din of traffic interrupted only by sirens.

Mark often dreams about returning to a place like the calendar picture, where life would be less frantic, less noisy, and less crowded; a place where people cared about each other. But how could he or Diane make a living in a place like that?

Redefining the American Dream

I invented Mark and Diane to illustrate what's happened to many of the baby boom generation in pursuit of the American Dream. If your life doesn't fit their model exactly, then, it probably overlaps. Folks like Mark and Diane know something is out of whack in their lives but don't know just how to articulate it. Is there something amiss with the dream itself?

When I was in first grade, our teacher told us, "Anyone can grow up to become president." My succeeding teachers repeated this message in some version or other. Somewhere around eighth grade civics class it got watered down to this: If you get a good education and work hard, you may not become president, but you will get a rewarding job, a car, and a house, and you will be able to send your children to college. This was pretty much the theme of my high school commencement speaker, with something or other thrown in about public service.

Thousands of immigrants fled to American shores in the last century to pursue that dream. They still come, though more likely from Haiti or Cuba than Italy, Germany, or Poland. Most gravitate to the same cities that offered hope and opportunity to nineteenth-century newcomers, but these have now become hopeless centers of pollution, noise, crime, drugs, and poverty.

The dream persists but takes new form with each generation. In September 1990, *Money* magazine asked the Gallup Organization to poll 300 of its subscribers to find out how they defined the American Dream. They listed these attributes:

1. Rewarding work
2. First-rate education for children
3. Competent, affordable health care
4. A house of one's own
5. A nest egg
6. Occasional indulgences
7. A comfortable retirement

Even though *Money*'s poll naturally reflected the magazine's financially astute readership, some traditional values were notably absent—career advancement, regular salary increases, and wealth. Another poll of 500 adults by *Time/CNN*[1] revealed the growing importance of whole-life concerns. More than two-thirds of the people surveyed said that they would like to slow down and lead a more relaxed life, and about the same number said that earning a living today takes so much effort that it's hard to find free time. Nine out of ten felt it was more important to spend time with their families, and just over half expressed a strong need for more time to spend pursuing hobbies and personal interests.

Polls such as these suggest a new definition of the American Dream; however, the corporate workplace is not where it is being forged. Though people want time to spend on family and personal activities, they come up short because of longer working hours and increased commuting time. In an article in *The Public Interest,* George Harris and Robert Trotter claim that the average worker's leisure time has shrunk by 40 percent over the past 15 years—down from 26.6 to 16.5 hours per week. Meanwhile, after decades of getting shorter, the average workweek is now 15 percent longer.[2]

So much for more leisure time.

What about the dream of owning one's own home? Mark's example illustrates the squeeze his generation faces. He and Diane have a house of their own—or, more accurately, theirs and the bank's. The three-bedroom ranch home they bought in 1984, with a small lawn separating it from its neighbors, was not grand by any standards yet comfortable enough for a family of three. And it was the best Mark and Diane could afford at a time when real estate prices were skyrocketing in the Boston metropolitan area. There's nothing wrong with this house, but there's nothing very remarkable about it, either.

Houses like Mark and Diane's were replicated by the millions in the 1940s and 1950s to satisfy the postwar demand. Suburbs grew in concentric rings around the larger cities—some even becoming entire new towns in themselves such as Levittown, Pennsylvania. And most middle-class families could afford a home of their own through a combination of their own savings and governmental loan assistance programs.

But by the mid-1980s the dream of "a home of one's own" had grown from an unpretentious dwelling such as Mark and Diane's into something more akin to a two-story, 5000-square-foot house on an acre or more of ground. Those who aspired to this version of the dream usually managed to attain it by incurring a level of personal debt unthinkable in the 1940s. And when the economy soured at the beginning of the 1990s, many found it impossible to keep up with the payments.

The other parts of the redefined American Dream—rewarding work, access to health care, and a nest egg for retirement—are also becoming more elusive as the world changes. This leaves Mark—and all of us—anxious about the future. Can we have more rewarding work *and* a high quality of life, or do we have to sacrifice one for the other?

I think both are possible. The economy at present harbors both peril and promise. The keys to a rewarding career in the world of the 1990s may lie in redefining our careers to integrate them into our lives, spotting areas of promise, understanding how the world is changing, and being ready to change along with it.

Finding Your Niche in the Economy of the Nineties

How many economists does it take to change a light bulb? None—the free market will take care of it. This joke circulated through my college economics class, lightening an otherwise turgid subject that I always had trouble regarding as a science. Years later, I've concluded that you really don't need to understand the theories of Adam Smith or John Maynard Keynes to prosper, but it does help to know which way the economic winds are blowing if you want to gain control of your career.

Take job security. Even if you are willing to hitch your wagon to a corporate star, there's no guarantee that the corporation will not cut the rope when it deems necessary. On July 16, 1990, the giant defense contractor McDonnell-Douglas broke the record for layoffs made in a single day when it cut some 17,000 jobs. Most of the victims were nonunion, white-collar employees. On the CBS nightly news of November 19, 1991, Dan Rather likened the plight of professionals to a movie: "America's White Collar Workers Sing the Blues . . . probably playing at an office near you." His report concluded that there is no such thing as job security anymore and that the biggest target for cost cutting is the white-collar work force. Saving yourself means not relying on the company.

By November 1990, the number of managers and professionals who had lost their jobs had reached 361,000, 8.6 percent of the total jobless population and more than twice the 3.6 percent they had made up at the end of the 1982 recession. And companies who let white-collar workers go in a downturn aren't as likely as before to rehire them, argue Joseph H. Boyett and Henry P. Conn in *Workplace 2000.*[3] The same technological advances that accelerate production and the flow of information will permanently eliminate layers of management, supervision, and support.

Much of the apparent shrinking of the white-collar work force comes from the basic shift away from a manufacturing-based to service-based economy. In *Innovation and Entrepreneurship,*[4] Peter Drucker describes this change in terms of models. The first model was the machine. This phase began around 1680, when the steam engine heralded the start of the industrial revolution. Machines produced goods, and the people who worked in the factories were regarded as extensions of those machines. Until the demand outstripped cheap and economical supply, energy derived from fossil fuels drove the mechanically based economy.

Today, a new model is emerging—the organism. This model is fueled not by energy, in the physical sense, but around information, as processed by the human brain and its electronic imitator, the computer. High-tech robots, telecommunication and office automation, biogenetics, and bioengineering are the fruits of this new model.

But Drucker doesn't think we can depend on advanced technology alone to rescue the American economy in the 1990s. High-tech jobs will account for only one-sixth of new jobs by 2000. Despite the explosive growth of computers, for instance, he predicts that data processing and information handling won't add as many jobs to the American economy as will be lost in the steel and automotive industries.

And maybe we put too much faith in high tech, anyway. Has it become not only the primary hope for rescuing our economy but also the controlling force of our lives? Neil Postman thinks so. According to his book, *Technopoly: The Surrender of Culture to Technology,* we have arrived at the third—and most destructive—stage of technological evolution. In the first stage, we used tools. During the second stage, the technocratic societies that appeared in Europe around 200 years ago stressed conformance to time rules and to the needs of the machines the workers operated. Now, we are in a stage he calls "technopoly," in which all forms of cultural life are subordinated to technology. Elderly people kept alive by machines against their will is a poignant example of where this can lead.[5]

So if our traditional economy is on the way out and high tech is questionable both in practical and societal terms, what kind of economy should we hope for and how will the changes necessary to bring it about affect our working lives? Here's what writers Marvin Cetron and Owen Davies have predicted in the magazine *The Futurist* for the next decade:

- Companies will continue to trim staff.
- Downsizing will mean most people will be laid off at least once.
- Most people in the emerging work force will have more than one career.
- More microbusinesses will be started by entrepreneurs. These will be common and highly specialized in the twenty-first century as entrepreneurs search for narrower niches.
- People will change jobs, residences, and careers more frequently, with a corresponding increase in occupational retraining.
- Multinational corporations will continue to grow, and many new ones will appear.[6]

If these predictions prove true, they portend both good and bad—bad, obviously, if your job is in danger of disappearing, and good if a trend opens a door for you. Opportunities exist, but you have to know how to spot them and turn them to your advantage. For example, when companies downsize, they often end up contracting out services formerly done in-house ("outsourcing"). Those who cut their teeth working inside corporations are in the best position to offer these services—but now as private consultants.

For example, IBM Corporation eliminated 60,000 positions in the past few years but created more than 300,000 off-site jobs, says Eugene Jennings, an emeritus management professor at Michigan State University. Jennings foresees opportunities for small businesses to expand in banking, automotive parts, environmental services, computer software and hardware, pharmaceuticals, chemicals, communications, telephone systems, office equipment, health care, medical supplies, capital goods, and research.

Although products and services both figure into Jennings's list of opportune areas, the Bureau of Labor Statistics expects most job growth to occur in the service sector, which in 1988, accounted for 92 percent of all new jobs.

But what's a service sector job anyway—driving a cab or becoming a corporate consultant? If you are a college-educated professional such as Mark, your challenge is to find a service sector niche that makes use of your education and talents while providing a livable income, rewarding work, and the opportunity to improve the overall quality of your life.

Improving life outside of work may mean moving away from a city or suburb to cleaner, greener, quieter place. We are freer to do this than ever before, because of the convergence of two trends—the economic trend toward downsizing and decentralizing the workplace and the technological trend of continued advances in telecommunications and transportation. Both trends are replacing the big corporate workplace located in or near a metropolis with many smaller businesses scattered throughout the new American landscape.

The New Landscape

> Linked by telephones, fax machines, Federal Express, and computers, a new breed of information worker is reorganizing the landscape of America. Free to live almost anywhere, more and more individuals are deciding to live in small cities and towns and rural areas. A new electronic heartland is spreading throughout developed countries around the globe, especially in the United States. Quality-of-life rural areas are as technologically linked to urban centers as are other cities. This megatrend of the *next* millennium is laying the groundwork for the decline of cities.
>
> John Naisbitt and Patricia Aburdene,
> *Megatrends 2000*[7]

People are coming to regard where they live as being as important as what they do. They are increasingly willing to trade earning power for quality of life. Americans have been fleeing the big cities for years—first to the suburbs, then to the exurbs. But we used to just live outside a city; we now work there, as well. The trouble is that many of the new environments have all the negative trappings of the old city centers—traffic, noise, pollution, ugliness—but none of the perks. For example, how far is it from the office park where you work to the nearest sports arena or theater that offers live performances?

The big, all-purpose city that we have grown to loathe, for all its sins, boasts an impressive concentration of cultural amenities. Try to imagine another place where you can find as many restaurants, theaters, sports arenas, libraries, art galleries, and museums packed so closely together as Manhattan.

But cities, like other organisms, change over time. "The cities were victims of forces beyond their control," writes John Herbers in *The New Heartland.*[8] "Always open to the uneducated and unwashed, they were overcome by economic and political changes that left them with an unprecedented social burden too large to bear without the kind of upheavals we have seen."

Before the middle classes fled to the suburbs, cities contained all levels of society. Today, the permanent residents—the elderly and very poor who cannot leave—live in inner-city slums or even on the street. The well-to-do may live near the city center, but they isolate themselves from its woes in gentrified row houses or well-guarded apartments. The city, no longer all-purpose, has become a specialized node for tourism, culture, entertainment, finance, and communication, says Herbers.

Meanwhile, the middle classes have migrated out of the suburbs in droves to what Herbers calls "The New Heartland." These places "can be seen on the outer fringes of metropolitan areas; around small towns far removed from large cities; along rivers, coastlines, and reservoirs; near recreation and retirement areas; on marginal farmland; along country roads; and on remote land that is barren except for its physical beauty."

Americans are also gravitating southward and westward. This probably won't surprise you. Growth has been occurring in the Sun Belt for years; California became the largest state in the 1980s. It will still be on top by 2010, when Texas will oust New York from the number two spot, forecasts demographer Judith E. Nichols. She predicts that Florida will stay in fourth place and that Illinois will replace Pennsylvania as fifth by 2000. The other farm belt states of the Midwest will continue to lose population. West Virginia, Vermont, and North Dakota will be the least populated.

For decades, cities attracted upward-bound achievers on career fast tracks. Though people have been steadily migrating to the outland for some time, the collapse of Wall Street in 1987 might have been the event that signaled the end of the big city as the only viable place to shape a career. When legions of investment brokers were turned out of their jobs with uncertain prospects for getting back in, they started to rethink their lives and careers. Some, such as ex-stockbrokers Mathew and Deborah Loving, quit their fast-lane, urban-based jobs to start new careers far outside the city. Today, the Lovings are happily raising ostriches in Central New Jersey, as we'll see in Chapter 6.

Unless you are chained to a specific business that has taproots in a big city—the big publishing houses in New York City, for example—you will have many more kinds of choices as to where to work, whether you continue to work for a company or opt for self-employment.

Here are some of the trends predicted by demographer Judith Nichols and various futurists. How can you use them to improve your work or lifestyle?

- **Age.** As a whole, society is growing old. The ranks of the middle-aged and elderly will swell; the percentage of young people will decline. The "baby boomers" born between 1946 and 1964 are now middle-aged. In the 1990s, the total number of people aged 45 to 54 will increase by 46 percent, compared to an overall population growth of 7 percent. Similarly, the elderly (anyone over 50, according to the American Association of Retired Persons) will constitute 28 percent of the total population by 2000.[9]

- **Families.** Single-parent and other nontraditional households will continue to increase in number, resulting in slower growth in the housing market and more flexibility in the workplace. Expect more female heads-of-household and people living alone.[10]

- **Health.** The AIDS epidemic will affect millions worldwide, especially in Africa. Medical technology will continue to extend life and make it more comfortable in the industrial world. Americans will continue to cast off unhealthy practices (smoking, drinking, bad diets) and adopt healthy habits.[11]

- **Ethnic mix.** The percentage of minorities will swell to around 30 percent by 2030, with Hispanics as the fastest-growing segment. This will affect schools, cities, courts, and political parties.[12]

- **Food.** Production will continue to exceed consumption in developed countries, but inefficient delivery systems will prevent it from reaching the hungry. Family farms will continue to wane, but part-time "hobby" farms will survive. Food supplies will become healthier and more wholesome.[13]

- **Technology.** Computer technology will continue to expand (surprise!) to incorporate "superhighways," information paths that travel over fiber-optic cable to link scientists, business people, educators, and students. By 2000, applications of artificial intelligence will affect

60 to 90 percent of the jobs in large organizations—displacing, down-grading, and eliminating workers.[14]

- **Women.** Women, traditionally shut out of the corporate power structure, have gained and will continue to gain footholds in the business world. Women start twice as many new businesses than men, and the Small Business Administration reports that 30 percent of small businesses are now owned by women.[15] Women who interrupt their careers for family reasons ("career gappers") may do better on their own than trying to pick up in the corporate world, where they are likely to encounter permanent handicaps regarding income and advancement.

- **Education.** Computers and related technologies will threaten educational institutions by opening ways for people to educate themselves outside the classroom.[16]

- **Home.** The home will become a center of American life, equipped with high-tech entertainment, appliances, computers, and security systems, as middle-aged consumers—short on leisure time and busy raising children—spend more time at home.[17]

- **On the way up.** Environmental cleanup, home entertainment, health and convenience foods, time- and cost-saving devices, catering, highway and air-traffic congestion, telecommunications (all sorts), information services, computer and office machine repair, low-energy sports, day care for children and elders, career counseling, flexible work hours, printing/copying, mailing, educational products and services.[18]

- **On the way down.** Vinyl LPs, college enrollment, real estate, network TV, birthrate (U.S.), convenience stores, high-energy sports, manufacturing jobs, pesticides, mainframe computers, divorce, job security.[18]

A decade ago, John Naisbitt's best seller, *Megatrends,*[19] told us why trends such as these are important. But he never suggested that determining which were hot and which were not was an exact science. The world moves too fast these days for anyone, regardless of expertise, to be able to call the shots with complete accuracy. Naisbitt's 1990 sequel, *Megatrends 2000,*[20] hinted of emerging nationalism and economic changes in the former Soviet Union. It didn't foresee the earth-shaking events of less than two years later, when communism collapsed and the USSR dissolved.

But trend watching's difficulty doesn't make it a waste. Gerald Celente, a pioneer trends analyst, describes how to spot, analyze, and profit from trends in his book, *Trend Tracking.*[21] It is a "must read" for people seeking opportunities in the economic and social ferment of the day. Celente explains how to develop a system to spot trends in news sources, set up files to track trends by category, and find relationships between trends that can lead to business opportunities. Here's how I might use Celente's method in my career as an architect/writer to capitalize on two trends:

1. People are living longer and staying longer in their houses.
2. There is a growing number of women who work outside the home.

Women, for better or worse, have traditionally been the caregivers for aged parents no longer able to cope by themselves. Direct care for a parent is impossible if you are working, but elderly people can care for themselves for a longer time if their home environments are specially adapted. Adaptations could include higher lighting levels for better safety, a home alarm system that would alert local emergency agencies in the event of an accident, and adjusting bath and kitchen facilities to accomodate the decreased reach and mobility that comes with aging.

As an architect, I might specialize in helping people prepare their homes for the special needs of the aged. As a writer, I might write articles or a book on the subject.

Or, to take an example from Celente's book, if you had been tracking the advances in video technology along with the trend of people fanning out from cities, you might have spotted the connection between these developments and the shift to home-based entertainment, for example, movies that can be shown at home.

The important thing is to see how seemingly unrelated trends are related and what kinds of opportunities these convergences may open. You can do this by spotting trends through reading and research and then using your imagination to find the connections that could affect your future.

Realizing the Dream

The economic and demographic trends discussed so far will, I hope, seed your imagination with possibilities for redirecting your career and enhancing your life. If present trends limit, threaten, or change your present occupation and lifestyle, they also open new opportunities—if you know how to recognize them. Just look at how trends in two areas, transportation and electronics, can affect how and where you live and work.

The same cities that have recently become so unlivable were shaped by the modes of transportation common during the latter decades of the nineteenth century and first half of the twentieth century. When railroads were the primary link between major cities, raw materials flowed in and finished goods flowed out from the factories by train. Merchants and workers alike had to live within walking distance of where they worked or sold their goods.

With the extension of rail lines into outlying areas and the rise of the automobile, people could live miles from where they worked. Those who could afford to move to the suburbs did so.

Air transport and trucking replaced the railroads after World War II. Airlines reduced the time required to get things and people from one place to another, whereas trucking increased the number of places that goods could be shipped. Both enabled businesses to decentralize their operations.

Solar Age, the magazine I worked for in Harrisville, New Hampshire, in the mid-1980s, was an excellent example of this new reality. Magazine publishing in the past had been concentrated in major cities such as New York or Chicago, in close proximity to service networks. By the 1970s, widespread and rapid transportation enabled magazines to set up shop almost anywhere and secure services from the most economical source, regardless of location.

Our headquarters was tucked away in a picturesque village similar to the one in the picture on Mark's calendar. A Farmingdale, New York, firm handled fulfillment (subscriptions). Typesetting and color separation were "subbed out" to the most economical provider, again regardless of location. The magazine was printed, bound, and mailed by another firm in Burlington, Vermont, 125 miles to the north.

Because magazines operate on tight production schedules, the proof sheets, galleys, and other material that circulate between the disparate parts of the operation were sent by parcel service or mail, reaching their destinations within 24 hours.

A score of administrative and editorial personnel worked in a restored brick mill building in a historic village overlooking a small brook that meandered down from a lake, within yards of the office. Because Harrisville was too small to provide much housing, most of us lived in other rural villages or small towns within a 30-mile radius. Although a 30-mile commute into Los Angeles or Philadelphia would have been enough to cause migraines, here it was a restful and scenic interlude between home and work.

This was how things were on the eve of the electronic revolution. *Solar Age* folded in 1986 with the demise of the many small solar industries that had provided its advertising base. If it were around today, there wouldn't even be a need to ship proofs back and forth physically; this could be done by computer modem or fax.

We take so many aspects of the electronic revolution for granted that it's hard to realize how truly recent some of these tools really are and how they might change the way we work. As a beginning editor in 1983, I tapped out my copy on a well-used IBM Selectric II typewriter—the state of the art at the time. Our editor-in-chief could be heard from some distance pecking away on his stone-age Smith-Corona. We computerized in 1984. The editors had to learn how to use satellite CRTs linked to a mainframe computer. As I write this on my own personal computer, I can't imagine writing a book or magazine article any other way.

As to my earlier statement that trends cut both ways, I admit that electronic word processing has undoubtedly taken a toll on workers in the typing pool and the manual typewriter industry. But at the same time it has opened the door to a host of new jobs that allow people to work out of their home offices, including desktop publishing, data base management, and specialized consulting.

And word processing is only the tip of the iceberg. Similar advances in other areas are happening so rapidly that it's hard to keep up. Look at what has happened to fax machines, copy machines, and cable TV in recent years. Each development has taken a toll on the status quo while opening new opportunities. VCRs undercut movie theaters while spawning a new industry—home videos. Movies, which are now the biggest-selling items in the home video market, may be eclipsed by other products, such as how-to videos. Almost anyone can get access to a videocamera to produce them.

Decentralization of the office could be the key to breaking loose from an urban-based corporate workplace and reinventing your work and personal life in a friendlier setting. Universal access to ever more powerful personal computers has made it possible to tackle projects that would have been unimaginable only a few years ago. The "side dishes"—modems, fax machines, electronic bulletin boards—make instantaneous communication to almost anywhere a reality.

You might not even need to leave your present employer in the city to move out to where the lifestyle is better. Growing numbers of white-collar workers now work where they live—and live where they want through telecommuting, as we'll see in the pages that follow.

Mark's dream of freeing himself to start over in the *outland,* (a term I'll use throughout the book to refer to any location away from a metropolitan area) requires courage, timing, and probably a healthy dose of good luck. Tradeoffs will be inevitable.

For starters, he'll probably earn less. If he launches a business, he will trade a steady income for a variable one. The success rate of new businesses after five years is only around 15 percent (or the failure rate is 85 percent, if you are a pessimist). With these odds, who but the foolhardy would venture forth? About 600,000 entrepreneurs do so each year, roughly seven times as many as made the attempt in each of the boom years of the fifties and sixties.

What else? In trading job stress, smog, heavy traffic, and the blandness of his suburban residence for clean air and the room to breathe it, Mark may find that life is decidedly duller in the outland. He may, in time, crave a restaurant that offers something other than steak and baked potato. Maybe he'll miss the live theater, spectator sports, or just the energy of the big city.

There's no denying it—the high school production of *Les Miserables* comes nowhere near the one Mark and Diane saw at the Schubert Theater. Only they can say how important these kinds of amenities are to their well-being.

It's possible to get the best of both worlds by relocating within reach (say 100 miles) of a major city. If Mark and Diane moved 85 miles northwest of Boston to my neck of the woods in southwest New Hampshire, they could still get to Boston three or four times a year to see the bright lights or drive down to the college towns of Northampton-Amherst, an hour away, where the academic ambience provides a constant selection of interesting things to see and do.

My aim throughout this book is to explore these and other major questions facing people like Mark and Diane. Along the way, we'll see how others—real people—have redirected their careers for more rewarding lives outside the metropolitan fray. In doing so, I do not condemn big cities nor mean to suggest that life in the outland is without stress. Rather, I offer a variety of views, my own and those of the many people I have interviewed, so that you will be in a better position to decide your best course.

In the next part of the book we'll look at the basic decisions that people face during career transition and how to make career decisions while still keeping goals you have for your life outside of work. We'll then go on to explore some of the kinds of opportunities that exist out there as we look into the experiences of several people who have consciously chosen to live and work away from large metropolitan areas. We'll also consider how you can select the location that best allows you to fulfill your career ambitions while enjoying your desired lifestyle.

In the final part of this book, we'll get down to the practical issues you may face in relocating to a small town or rural area and examine the quirks of starting a life and business out there.

Part Two

Decision Time

Chapter One

On the Edge of Change

You don't want to spend the rest of your days selling sugared water to kids, do you?
Steve Jobs, founder of Apple computer company,
to PepsiCo's John Sculley, to lure him
into the new company.

We left Mark recovering from the ordeals of his morning commute and building up enough steam to get into the day's work. As he drank his coffee, he pondered his growing dissatisfaction with his job, which left him with so little time and energy for his life outside of the office. A glance at the calendar picture triggered memories of his youth in a more relaxed setting.

Mark is a composite of millions of professionals who have invested years of commitment into jobs that pay well but offer too few other rewards. He knows that living in the suburbs and working in the city causes stress that affects both his mood at work and at home. Should Mark change jobs or even careers? If so, what are his alternatives? Would his life be improved by moving out to a place such as the village in the calendar picture? Maybe you are among the many urban-based professionals who are asking themselves some, if not all, of the same questions. But this process of deliberation can be overwhelming. Some system is needed to break the puzzle down into pieces that can be fit together one by one.

We'll build such a system in this chapter, starting with your present job. Your decision to stay or leave depends on your attitude toward work and how your job fits into the rest of your life. Next, you will be asked to question your living environment to help decide what kind of place you want to end up in and whether relocating would improve your life.

When the Bloom Is Off the Rose

Job burnout is common among middle-level managers such as Mark. It afflicts many whose jobs involve dealing with people. Experts have defined *burnout* as a syndrome in which emotional exhaustion, depersonalization, and reduced personal accomplishment occur due to unrealistic devotion to a cause, way of life, or unrewarding relationship. The symptoms of burnout are a loss of interest in co-workers, a blunting of the sense of humor, boredom, decreased creativity, inability to handle complex tasks, and procrastination. The exhaustion and fatigue you take home from a day at work survives a good night's sleep.

Although burnout can result from any job, the corporate workplace is an especially fertile spawning ground. Practices that promote burnout include limited input by employees into the decision-making process, disproportionate workloads, the inability of individuals to reach career goals, poor communication between administrators and employees, and dysfunctional support systems, says Doris B. Matthews of South Carolina State College.[1]

Commuting to work through the morning gridlock compounds Mark's stress at work and adds to his burnout. The return trip intensifies his stress and lessens the quality of the few evening hours he has with his family.

Is your situation in some ways like Mark's? If so, you are not alone. The pressures and frustrations of climbing the corporate fast track are causing professionals to rethink their values. In her book, *Downshifting*, Amy Saltzman cites a 1989 survey of 1,000 men and women conducted by Robert Half International, Inc., in which "82 percent of the women and 78 percent of the men said they would choose a career path with flexible full-time work hours and more family time, but slower career advancement, over one with inflexible work hours and faster career advancement."[2]

At first glance, the new mindset seems born out of the ashes of the high-rolling 1980s; that sense of euphoria came tumbling down when the stock market collapsed in the fall of 1987. But cracks in the corporate workplace were apparent as early as the 1960s to writers such as Charles Reich. In *The Greening of America*[3] he wrote, "The professional is able to afford many of the luxurious rewards of society, but he may be far too busy to enjoy them; he knows that when he retires he will be too old."[4] One of the biggest sacrifices was freedom: "The great selling point of America is 'freedom.' . . . to travel, ski, buy a house, eat frozen Chinese food, live like a member of the 'now generation'; freedom to buy anything and go anywhere. For work, on the other hand, there is no freedom at all."[5] Reich claimed that the majority of adults in this country actually hated their work. Their dissatisfaction was rooted in the debilitating effect of success, the loss of autonomy, the worker being out of sync with an oppressive hierarchy, and falling short of his or her potential.

An ad for men's leisure pants that includes the phrase "for a man's happiest hours" suggests that maybe men (and women) have given up altogether on finding happiness in our jobs.

To Stay or Leave?

Most of us spend around a quarter of our working lives on the job or in transit between work and home. To forsake any expectations of happiness during this time is a terrible waste. If this hits home with you, then it's time to take stock of the sources of your dissatisfaction. Through interviews for his book *Working Free*, John Applegath found that the number one source of workers' dissatisfaction was neither the amount of money they made nor the perceived degree of comfort and job security. It was the limits that employers put on workers' individual aspirations. Some major reasons that people gave for wanting to leave jobs were:

1. The nature of the work itself, which generated boredom and a sense of wasted talent.
2. Lack of opportunities for growth.
3. Lack of personal freedom.
4. Too little money.
5. Desire to change location out of the big city.[6]

Some may have a familiar ring to you, some not. Individual complaints are as numerous and varied as people themselves, but all gripes can be labeled either temporary or chronic. Temporary problems, such as a particular project you don't like, aren't reason enough to leave your job; fundamental problems that aren't likely to change (or may change for the worse) are. If you are not sure whether to stay or leave, answering the questions in Worksheet 1-1 might help you decide.

Even if you decide to quit your job, there may be reasons to hang on for a while, such as reduced prospects for generating an income in a recession. Perhaps you want to postpone taking the plunge until the end of the school year to smooth the transition for a child. If your decision affects others, as most do, make them part of the process of deciding. Consider seeking help from counselors if you and your family are not used to dealing objectively with such complex decisions. (We'll look at this more closely in the next chapter.)

Deciding to move on and move out requires a plan unless you are truly adventurous. The rest of this book is designed to help you make one.

In interviewing people for this book, I discovered that the ways people make basic decisions for changing their careers and locations were as

Worksheet 1-1   Should You Quit Your Job?

Check the statement of each the following that most closely describes your situation.

---

1.   A. _____   Commuting isn't a significant problem.
     B. _____   Commuting is a problem now, but there are ways to improve
                  things (mass transit, carpooling, telecommuting).
     C. _____   Commuting is a problem that can only get worse.

2.   A. _____   People I work with generally trust each other.
     B. _____   The level of trust varies with changes in personnel.
     C. _____   Distrust pervades the staff.

3.   A. _____   My organization generally welcomes new ideas.
     B. _____   The company is receptive to some change.
     C. _____   I have never felt that the firm would welcome new ideas.

4.   A. _____   I make about as much as I should, for my value to the
                  company.
     B. _____   I am overdue for a raise, but feel comfortable pressing my
                  case.
     C. _____   I am long overdue for a raise, and have no idea when I may
                  get one.

5.   A. _____   My collegues treat me without respect to my sex.
     B. _____   Occasionally, I feel my sex works against me in the firm.
     C. _____   Sexual discrimination is the rule here.

6.   A. _____   I like my work station.
     B. _____   There are things I don't like about my work station. I could
                  probably get modifications, if I tried.
     C. _____   There is no way the company would let me change my work
                  station.

7.   A. _____   People are treated pretty much the same at work, whatever
                  their age.
     B. _____   Some younger staffers don't give the older members the
                  respect they deserve.
     C. _____   Older staff members of my company are out out as a matter of
                  course.

(continued)

Worksheet 1-1   *Continued*

8. A. _____   I believe my company's product or service is a benefit to society.
    B. _____   I'm concerned primarily with my own job, not whether the company helps society.
    C. _____   I am increasingly uncomfortable with the company's product or service.

9. A. _____   I am content with my upward mobility in the company.
    B. _____   My next promotion will come, if I have the patience to wait, or when the company's profitability improves.
    C. _____   I haven't moved up as I should and don't see much prospect for change.

10. A. _____   I am interested in the work I do most of the time.
    B. _____   My interest comes and goes, depending on the project or task I am working on.
    C. _____   I am constantly bored and no longer find any challenge in my work.

How many A's did you check?   _____
How many B's did you check?   _____
How many C's did you check?   _____

If you scored more than 5 in "A" you are generally content. More than 5 for "B" means you are dissatisfied, but you can improve the situation without leaving. A high score under "C" indicates chronic dissatisfaction. Because you don't see the possibility for improvement, you might do well to consider leaving. Why haven't you left yet?

numerous as the people themselves. A rational plan is only one way people face change. Some bust loose with not much more than a hope. Others start with a plan but find that things often turn out differently than we intend. Such was the case of John Suter.

John left his Brooklyn apartment and a steady income as director of the Ethnic Folk Arts Center in New York City to migrate to the quieter and greener world of upstate New York, hoping to better the quality of life for his family of three. He dreamed of producing his own folk art videos there. But when he got down to setting the specifics in a formal business plan, he saw more promise in another direction: high-quality children's videos. Armed with the plan—and one-third-time income from continuing to work for his former employer—he took his family of three to a rural area near Ithaca and bought a house. But the closer John got to starting the business, the shakier it appeared. He saw no way he could compete with the low-priced children's videos that the big studios were producing.

Serendipitously, a statewide organization based in Ithaca that raises funds for agencies involved with folklore was expanding and needed a full-time director. John's background made him a natural for the job.

For every success story such as John Suter's, there is probably another without a happy ending. Many people leave jobs abruptly and don't come out so lucky. Leaving a job with a steady income is a step into the unknown even when you have another job to go to. Making a clean break with no idea where you might end up may mean trading short-term satisfaction for long-term woes. You can reduce the risk by objectively taking stock of your present situation and then setting goals that lead to a plan of action.

I have assumed up to this point that the decision to stay or leave your present job has been entirely up to you. But with the increasingly ruthless personnel cuts that companies have been making to stay competitive, your job may be eliminated overnight through no fault of your own. If this seems in any way imminent, the earlier you start planning, the better.

What Do You Really Want Out of Your Work?

Before you start formulating a plan, I suggest you do some heavy thinking about your attitudes towards your work as it relates to your life. With your partner (if you have one), question how you feel about power, control, and rewards. Then, by thinking through how your present work falls short in each area, you can begin to discern the common threads that you can use to set goals for the future.

Money, Wealth, and Financial Security

"Money, makes the world go around . . ." sings the emcee in the Broadway musical *Cabaret*. This song captures one common attitude toward money, as do a host of aphorisms: Money is the root of all evil (negative); money can buy anything (overconfidence); money is a good servant, but a lousy boss (control); the best things in life are free (outright lie).

How can you know if money is your primary driving force or just a means toward an end? Dr. Joyce Brothers would ask you the following questions:

1. Are you sure money is what you want more than anything else in the world?
2. When you make your fortune, will you change your lifestyle to indulge your desires for travel, jewels, a beautiful home, expensive automobiles, a fabulous wardrobe, the best of everything?[7]

If you answered any way but yes to the first question and no to the second, you are not seeking money as an end in itself, Dr. Brothers would conclude.

Regardless of the place money occupies in your value system, at some point you need to decide how much you really need and if your present income is adequate. After figuring what it costs just to keep up with the bills, you need an extra amount to cover those things that make it possible to enjoy life in a wider sense. For me, that can mean little things like splurging occasionally on a bottle of wine that has a cork rather than a screw-on cap or a meal at a special restaurant. I don't think of vacations in the category of life-enhancing extras but as necessities to keep body and soul together.

Financial security is harder to estimate. How much and what type you think you need depend a lot on how close to the edge you care to live. Knowing my family could be wiped out financially by any kind of major illness, I wouldn't think of forgoing health insurance, but I haven't carried life insurance for years, preferring to squirrel away whatever I can into investments, not insurance companies.

In recent years, financial security for retirement has also gotten more elusive in the private as well as public sectors. Because companies no longer offer the kind of long-term job security they once did, few will stay with the same employer until retirement even if they want to. At the same time, some companies' retirement programs have become jeopardized by shaky investments. The Social Security system appears solid at the moment, but talk of its instability surfaces with alarming regularity.

College costs are another thing to worry about if you have children. Unfortunately, they may hit you at a time when you are presumed to be in your peak earning years but have been set back by a major change in your career or location. As a parent, you can no longer expect your children to cover most of the costs of their college education. I paid my way by working in architectural offices in the summer and playing piano in small dance bands on weekends. I doubt if I could do it today. Few can get through four years without outside help, even though post-secondary education has passed from dream to necessity.

Regardless of how you think about money and wealth, any change you make in your residence or your career will have financial implications. Chapter 10 deals with the practical aspects of estimating the cost of a major career and location move.

Challenge and Fulfillment

Lack of challenge and its offspring, boredom, kill job fulfillment. Insufficient challenge accounted for 59 percent of the reasons one group of men in their thirties and forties gave for leaving their occupations. Challenge comes with having to deal regularly with the unknown. Ironically, many managers try to eliminate as many unknowns as possible to streamline the operation—just the opposite of what they should be doing, according to management expert Richard K. Irish. He advises employers to keep every job challenging by seeding them with "a little danger, excitement, and anxiety."[8]

Fulfillment has nothing to with the external rewards or compensation you receive from your employer. It is that warm feeling you get from doing your work well. In *Pulling Your Own Strings,* Dr. Wayne Dyer says you should measure fulfillment in terms of the little bits that litter the daily path rather than achievements that span long periods of time. "There is no way to happiness; happiness is the way," he concludes.

Rewards and Recognition

If you work for a big company and started at or near the bottom, you probably measure the upward ladder in years. You can expect small, incremental strokes here and there in the form of modest raises or increases in responsibility and status. But unless you are part of a truly enlightened organization, the company will mete out these rewards with great parsimony. Its goal is to keep you producing at your maximum rate and at minimum cost. Your employer may believe that to have the greatest effect, rewards should be used sparingly.

Maybe your contributions reach beyond the usual call of duty—an original idea that could lead to a new product or an innovative plan to streamline some part of the operation. It probably occurs to you from time to time that your chances of reaping rewards and recognition might be better outside than inside the firm. Not long after reaching this point, many entrepreneurs strike off on their own.

Commitment

Management professor Rosabeth Moss Kanter divides commitment in the workplace into two types: the emotional and value commitment between the company and its employees ("people feel that they 'belong' to a meaningful entity and can realize cherished values by their contributions") and the company's commitment to change. Innovative people are more likely to thrive in organizations with strong commitments in both these areas, she argues.[9]

How do you feel about committing yourself totally to your job? Probably ambivalent, if you are like most. Employers have long used total commitment as a yardstick to measure the value of employees. Remember how Scrooge regarded Bob Cratchit's request for Christmas Eve off as a lack of proper commitment to the firm. But total, absolute commitment has been linked to a plethora of physical ailments, including hypertension, heart disease, and ulcers as well as broken marriages, alcoholism, drug abuse, and poor communication with family. No wonder we are coming to value people for qualities other than blind commitment to their work.

Just like me, you are probably already struggling with the question of how much commitment you can devote to your job without eroding other parts of your life. As I see it, we have three choices:

1. Total commitment to a well-rounded life (to the detriment of work).
2. Total commitment to work (to the detriment of your outside life).
3. Some compromise of both.

No one size apparently fits all. Although most us in the end opt for the middle ground, you don't have to look far to find someone at one extreme or the other.

The real strivers devote their all to their work. Always reaching higher than before, these folks reap money, influence, power, and prestige through their total commitment.

With the decline of total commitment to work that has come from higher mobility in the workplace, another factor threatens total job commitment: the two-earner family. As the complete burden of supporting the family is removed from the shoulders of a single breadwinner, both partners have more security; the family is no longer dependent on a single employer. They can spread their commitment more evenly between their various jobs and family.

Power and Control

Power and control in the workplace are loaded concepts that make people fidget, but they are what most people want. You may resent a colleague's describing you as autocratic, yet you welcome more autonomy in your job—which is to say you strive to exercise power and control over your own domain. The amount of control you can tolerate, or even need, over your work situation depends on where you see the locus—or source—of control, according to Donald Sanzotta, a professor of psychology at Cayuga County Community College. Sanzotta cites the concept of *internals* and *externals* proposed by psychologist Julian Rotter.[10]

Externally dominated personalities see forces outside themselves responsible for their rewards and punishments: chance, luck, and people in power, for example. They often make loyal, dedicated employees who willingly follow instructions but aren't good bets for nonstructured activities.

Internally dominated personalities believe that rewards and punishments are controlled by their own actions. These people tend to be skill-oriented and perform poorly in tightly controlled job situations. Those at the extreme end of the internal locus of control would apparently be happiest in self-employment.

You probably know by now whether you are a "take charge" person or one who is more content acting on the instructions of others. If there is any doubt, think back over your prior jobs. How much of your satisfaction was due to the amount of power and control you had?

Status

We Americans define ourselves through externally confirmed status. If you tell people at a social gathering, "I am a physician," you attain immediate status. No one asks, "Are you a good physician?" The title itself bestows respect. If you are unlucky enough to have an occupation that can't be summarized in one word, you probably grasp the closest respectable description. Is that why companies have so many vice-presidents?

But in some cultures, you have to earn status. My Peace Corps colleagues were surprised to learn that in Somalia an externally confirmed title meant nothing. Instead, personal characteristics meant everything. If Somalis didn't like you as a person, it mattered not that you were a doctor, lawyer, or president.

If you have distinguished yourself in your field, you deserve the status that goes with it. One of my case studies for this book, Gil Gordon, is a pioneer in the telecommuting movement. I was comfortable granting him that title—and status—from other accounts I read before I interviewed him. Earned status follows you, wherever your career path leads you. A company title such as "operations manager" disappears when you leave the firm. When rethinking the next chapter of your career, you might gain direction by deciding how you have achieved status in the past. How much was a result of a job position or college degree? How much did you earn through your own efforts?

Advancement

Were you, like me, taught to see life as a kind of ladder? If so, you probably felt guilty if you stepped sideways. I ascended the first steps through public school in a straight line but veered between entering college in 1957 and finally getting my architecture degree in 1969. I took two years out for work and two more for a Peace Corps tour of duty in Somalia. Even so, I always had my eye on the next rung. After graduating and getting married, my goal was to earn my architect's license, which required a 30-month internship and passing the state architectural exam. Instead, I stepped off the ladder again and signed a 30-month contract to work in Liberia.

After returning and finally getting licensed in 1973, I looked forward to the day when I could spring loose and establish my own practice, mindful of a warning I had heard somewhere along the way to the effect that if you don't go out on your own by the time you reach 40, you probably won't. I beat this deadline by two years.

What I didn't realize was that the trail didn't end there. You have to constantly redefine your career path. In the years since starting my own office in 1976, I have worked as an editor for two national trade magazines, served a stint with another architectural firm, and then returned to self-employment as a writer/architect. The zigzag path my career has taken has been more interesting than a more conventional one, but not without costs. I probably sacrificed advancement in my original field—architecture. I know, at the age of 53, that I will never be an I.M. Pei or Frank Lloyd Wright. This doesn't bother me constantly, but I find myself wondering from time to time what might have been if I had stayed on the narrow track.

My zigzag career path has taught me two things about advancement. First, you can advance in other directions than straight up. Instead of a ladder, my path looks more like a series of concentric circles. Each ring builds on some part of the center, but in a different direction than the previous ring. Second, time presses more urgently—whatever shape the path—with age.

I realize how strongly my attitudes toward advancement are tied to my concept of time. The more urgency I sense, the more drive toward action I feel. In college, with my whole professional life before me, I had all the time in the world.

Psychologist Donald Sanzotta sees a relationship between our sense of urgency related to time and our evolving religious attitudes.[11] The more importance we assign to the here and now, the less we believe in a long-term future. Today's youth, disheartened by ecological and economic perils to their future, are hard pressed to envision a temporal future. Meanwhile, their elders have been losing faith in the eternal future of the afterlife.

So the perception of limited time drives many of us to work longer hours to advance our careers. Some of us achieve our advancement, but not without sacrifices in other areas of our lives.

Is It Time to Relocate?

How much of your current dissatisfaction is due to where you live? If you decide to change jobs or even careers, you may not necessarily want to leave the area where you live. Separating how you feel about your present job from how you feel about your residence will lead to a more objective plan for the future. Thinking through the factors that are meaningful to your desired lifestyle will not only help you decide whether to leave the area but also spark your thinking about the kind of place you want to end up in if you do move. Worksheet 1-2 lists a number of factors of possible importance. Cross out any that don't matter to you and add any additional factors that do matter.

This worksheet spans a number of areas of concern to many people. If your satisfaction index is less than, say, 50 percent, you are more unsatisfied than satisfied and might do well to consider relocating. Later on, we'll set criteria for relocating based on your business requirements and lifestyle.

How Much of a Change Could You Make?

Leaving a job gone sour and pulling up stakes to move on represents a major change for most people. Even so, 50 million people in the United States are in the midst of or are contemplating switching jobs, reports Carole Hyatt in *Shifting Gears.*[12]

Before striking out, you should ask the advice of people whom you know and trust. I've found that people like to be asked for their advice, and they usually offer much more than you ask for. And three different people will likely give you three different approaches. That's fine. Think of it as a buffet where you can take what you want and leave the rest.

Naturally, you should fully air the consequences of a major change with your family, but because they will be affected as much as or more than you, you can't pick and choose parts of their attitudes with the same abandon. And family members bring other questions into the equation—dual-career couples, children, and aging parents—which we'll explore in Chapter 3.

Trading the Known for the Unknown

You know what you will leave behind if you move on and move out; it's the future that's unknown—and frightening. Well, even after you have researched another place or career step to the nth degree, you still won't be able to predict with any certainty just how the story will play out. There will always be a wild card somewhere along the line.

Decision making is tougher for some than others and can usually be postponed indefinitely. Worse, the difficulty in deciding is not necessarily proportional to the gravity of the thing to be decided. A friend may brag

Worksheet 1-2 Location Satisfaction Index

In column "A," rate the importance of each statement (1 = unimportant, 2 = moderately important, 3 = very important). In column "B," rate how close the statement matches your locale (0 = poorly, 1 = somewhat, 2 = well, 3 = very well). Multiply "A" times "B" to get a figure for column "C."

A x B = C

The Natural Environment

___ x ___ = ___ I feel close enough to rivers, lakes, and oceans here.
___ x ___ = ___ This locale gets enough sunshine annually.
___ x ___ = ___ There are sufficient mountains close by.
___ x ___ = ___ I live close enough to rivers, lakes, and the ocean.
___ x ___ = ___ The air here is clean enough.
___ x ___ = ___ The water quality here is good.
___ x ___ = ___ I feel safe from hazardous waste.
___ x ___ = ___ The proximity of nuclear power plants isn't a concern.
___ x ___ = ___ Earthquake danger here does not worry me.
___ x ___ = ___ I am not threatened by floods here.
___ x ___ = ___ Fire danger is not great here.
___ x ___ = ___ High winds or heavy snows do not worry me here.
___ x ___ = ___ _____
___ x ___ = ___ _____

The Built Environment

___ x ___ = ___ The buildings here are pleasing to me.
___ x ___ = ___ I like to look at the human-made sights I drive by daily.
___ x ___ = ___ There are enough parks, walking and bicycling paths.
___ x ___ = ___ _____
___ x ___ = ___ _____

Transportation

___ x ___ = ___ The time I spend commuting is acceptable.
___ x ___ = ___ I can get to a major airport easily enough.
___ x ___ = ___ Transporting children doesn't eat up too much time.
___ x ___ = ___ Travel time required for household needs is acceptable.
___ x ___ = ___ _____
___ x ___ = ___ _____

(continued)

that she can shop for a new car with about the same amount of agonizing as when she shops for a new pair of shoes.

Because the human brain doesn't work in a linear pattern—proceeding from one point to the next in a logical, rational sequence—it helps

Worksheet 1-2 *Continued*

Housing

___ x ___ = ___   I am satisfied with my present housing.

___ x ___ = ___   If I moved nearby, I would have a good selection of housing.

___ x ___ = ___   _____

Access to Goods and Services

___ x ___ = ___   This area is well supplied with food, drugs, and household supplies.

___ x ___ = ___   Clothing and other personal necessities are widely available.

___ x ___ = ___   There are adequate repair services (auto, home).

___ x ___ = ___   _____

___ x ___ = ___   _____

Health and Personal Care

___ x ___ = ___   The variety and quality of doctors and dentists is good.

___ x ___ = ___   There are adequate hospitals or clinics nearby.

___ x ___ = ___   Ample facilities for health maintenance (fitness centers, health clubs) are available.

___ x ___ = ___   _____

___ x ___ = ___   _____

Public Safety

___ x ___ = ___   This area is adequately policed.

___ x ___ = ___   In an emergency, I could expect a fire truck at the house within a short time.

___ x ___ = ___   My area is adequately served by ambulances.

___ x ___ = ___   _____

___ x ___ = ___   _____

Educational Resources

___ x ___ = ___   The public schools here are adequate for my needs.

___ x ___ = ___   There are enough colleges or universities nearby.

___ x ___ = ___   _____

___ x ___ = ___   _____

Child Care/Elder Care

___ x ___ = ___   There are sufficient pre-schools or day care centers.

___ x ___ = ___   Baby sitters are easy to obtain here.

___ x ___ = ___   There is a sufficient variety of elder care facilities locally.

___ x ___ = ___   _____

(continued)

Worksheet 1-2 *Continued*

Cultural Amenities

___ x ___ = ___   I am satisfied with local museums and performing arts.
___ x ___ = ___   There are sufficient religious organizations.
___ x ___ = ___   There is a good variety of organizations (hobby, civic, arts, service).

___ x ___ = ___   _____
___ x ___ = ___   _____

Recreational Amenities

___ x ___ = ___   This area has enough sports outlets (bowling alleys, golf and tennis courses).
___ x ___ = ___   There are enough movie theaters here.
___ x ___ = ___   The variety of restaurants and clubs is adequate.
___ x ___ = ___   There is sufficient opportunity for outdoor recreation nearby (hiking, boating, camping, hunting, fishing).

___ x ___ = ___   _____
___ x ___ = ___   _____

_____   Total of Column "C"
_____   Total of Column "A"

Divide Total of Column "C" by total of column "A" to get your **Location Satisfaction Index (LSI):**

_____

If your LSI was 3, you are very content with your present locale. If your LSI was between 2 and 3, you are content with most of the attributes of your present area. Between 1 and 2, you are more unsatisfied than satisfied. You are unsatisfied with your locale if your LSI was between 0 and 1.

many people to make and analyze lists. I have included many worksheets in this book not because they are scientific but because they provide a system through which you can make your own decisions. My premise is that when you put your thoughts down in writing, you can isolate, organize, and prioritize them in ways that lead to the most rational conclusions.

At this point, for example, it might help you deal with your fear of an unknown future if you write down everything important to you that you will leave behind if you move and/or change jobs and then compare the list to things you think you can gain by making a change.

Your Capacity to Change

What physical or mental obstacles stand between you and a major change? Are they real or just imagined? I used to think that aging itself decreased the ability to change. But that was before I interviewed a number of folks who are happily blazing new trails in middle age and beyond. Consider the Bufflers.

Charles and Nancy Buffler met and married at Harvard in 1956 when Charles was winding up his work toward a Ph.D. in applied physics. Nancy was a fine arts student. Charles's career as a microwave physicist took them to eight different locations over the next 32 years, including a two-year stint in France. During this period, Nancy raised three children and sold real estate on the side. Each move meant uprooting the family and readjusting to a new city.

By 1987, the Bufflers, tired of bouncing around, were ready to settle in one place. Charles, at 53, was commuting between their Stamford, Connecticut, home and the General Foods branch in Tarrytown, New York. Nancy, at 52, got interested in sheep farming through a specialty shop in Stamford that sold everything from custom-cut lamb chops to wool hats. Nancy thought of moving to the rural area around Exeter, New Hampshire, where they had briefly lived, but rapid development in the eastern part of the state in the mid-1980s had caused the market value of the remaining farmland to skyrocket. A friend suggested they look in the quieter, southwestern part of the state.

They found Forest Hill Farm in Marlborough through a real estate ad. The prior owner had outgrown the farm, but the 15.5 acres overlooking a south-sloping hill was just right for the scale of sheep farming Nancy envisioned.

The move to Marlborough meant major adjustments in the couple's lifestyle. Charles, still working out of Tarrytown, began a weekly commute, with three days in New York and four days at the farm. The couple had to adjust to an even greater change when Charles was transferred to Chicago. As of this writing, they are still adjusting to the new arrangement, by which Charles flies to Chicago for ten days at a time and comes back for three-day weekends. (We'll look more closely at commuter marriages in the next chapter.)

The Bufflers are masters at adapting to change. Charles intends to stay employed as a microwave physicist while cultivating his own consulting foundation based in his home. Nancy wants to make the farm profitable and reinvigorate her real estate business, which specializes in farm properties.

How Much Risk Can You Accept?

Risk, always scary, extends beyond the financial uncertainty that first comes to mind with any change in employment. There are risks to your family, risk to your health, and risks to your career development. Risk tolerance varies greatly from person to person.

Risk means different things to different people. One night a mountain climber friend invited my wife, Lucie, and me to dinner and a slide show of his recent ascent of Yosemite Park's Half Dome. During dinner, the conversation somehow wandered into a discussion of our hobby of finding and eating wild mushrooms. Our friend asked how we dared to chance eating something like that. Later, Lucie and I had trouble keeping our dinners down as we gazed aghast at the slides he took from narrow ledges hundreds of feet above the valley floor.

What do you consider risky? You can get some idea by how you behave in routine matters. Take money, for example. Look back through the years and see how you have handled money. If you have invested heavily in stocks or futures, you show more willingness to live with risk than a person who stays mainly with certificates of deposit or money market accounts. How heavily insured you are is another indication. If you insist on full collision coverage on an aging car rather than just carrying liability insurance, you are opting for the safe end of the risk tolerance scale.

Your social behavior can offer other clues as to how much risk you readily accept. When planning a vacation trip to Europe, for example, would you more likely buy a plane ticket for, say, Paris, and make further arrangements as needed (high risk) or opt for a guided tour that took care of all contingencies including tipping (low risk)?

I'm not saying risk tolerance is either good or bad. Some people find risk exhilarating and constantly choose the unknown. They willingly leap from one change to the next with faith that they can solve the problems after the leap. Lucie, I suspect, is close to this model. I am at the other end of the scale with the folks who take six months to plan a 200-mile trip, willing to make the change only after pondering every single contingency to death. You probably fit somewhere in between. If you are the type who wants change with the least risk, go prepared. Know your career and mobility options thoroughly.

Setting Goals

Most companies don't set goals. They prepare "mission statements." That's fine, I guess, if the company's service or product is a positive benefit to society—something that ought to have a mission—but can you imagine being assigned to a team to come up with this mission statement for the tobacco company losing sales: "Addict 50,000 consumers within the next 18 months?" Still, the concept of a mission statement as a means of combining a set of goals is sound and can serve individuals as well as organizations.

Goal setting, a popular sport among management executives, peppers the pages of numerous business-oriented books. Individual goal setting, strangely enough, seems to come under the rubric of psychology. Of the techniques I have run across, the most appealing one is also the simplest. In her book *How to Get Whatever You Want Out of Life,* Dr. Joyce Brothers suggests the "Quick List Technique."[13] Start by writing down the three things you want more than anything else right now. Write them as quickly as possible without watering them down by pondering or analyzing. The idea is to draw out urges hidden in your subconscious.

Put the list away and repeat the exercise once a week for six to eight weeks. Then take all of the lists out and study them to see if a pattern emerges. If you discover common threads, you are on the track to establishing meaningful goals. To help give you deeper insight into your psyche, Dr. Brothers proposes two variations to the Quick List Technique. In the first, write the names of the people you admire most, the three people you would most like to be or be like, and the three nicest things anyone ever said about you. Then write down the happiest and most miserable days of your life, the person you feel closest to, and your proudest accomplishment.

Put the lists aside to age for a few weeks. Then get them out and see if they still apply and what they tell you about yourself.

You can set goals around any number of categories: achievement, sex, love, wealth, power, control, fame, success, friendship, marriage, family, fun, beauty, excitement, health, respect, autonomy—to name a few. Some of these relate directly to your work and some to your life outside of work.

Start with goals. Make a list of factors important in your work. Then list goals for your life outside of work. Try to weed out goals that are a means to an end, such as money. Though money may be an end in itself for some, it's only a way to get to the real goals—travel, freedom, a sports car. Of course, a sports car might also be a means to another end, such as attracting the opposite sex, which, in turn, could be a means to another end—marriage. Psychologists make human behavior sound so simple.

Start with short-term goals (say, those attainable within the next five years) and then list your goals for the longer term. Goals included in your list should be realistic. "Within five years, I will be president of the United States" probably isn't.

But how do you know if your goals are achievable and realistic? Can you be sure you will improve your life by moving on in the same career, moving sideways, or taking up a whole new career? You may know yourself well enough to answer these questions with confidence. If you don't, the next chapter describes some of the ways to find out about yourself—what you do best and what you should be doing.

Chapter Two

Rethinking Your Career

*Alice . . . went on, "Would you tell me, please, which way I
ought to go from here?"*
*"That depends a good deal on where you want to get to," said
the Cat.*

Lewis Carroll, *Alice in Wonderland*

Isn't there a better word than *career* to describe what we are rethinking
here? That term implies a life-long commitment to a certain type of work
or occupation that college students look forward to making: it doesn't
quite fit people in mid-life who are reconsidering their work in relation
to their lives. But other terms don't work any better—*business, employment, field, line, occupation, profession, vocation*—so we may be stuck.

A major rethinking of your career begets basic questions: What should
I be doing? How should I prepare to do it? Where should I go? The more
specific questions will vary for each person. Maybe you fit one of the
examples that follow, composites of people whom I know; you probably
know people like them, too.

Bill: How can I downshift without sacrificing my expertise?

Bill, a respected surgeon earning a six-figure income, realized as he approached 48 that he was simply tired of the stress of his occupation and
the limitations it placed on his personal life. He isn't ready to dump his
expertise as a surgeon to take up refinishing antiques. Last time I talked
to him, he was taking management courses at the local community college.
But he didn't know how he would use the training to redirect his career.

Sarah: How can I pick up a dormant career?
Charles: Should I start my own business?

Sarah was content at her job as a statistician in a large oil company based in Houston. After receiving her B.S. in statistics, she had been working for slightly less than two years when she married Charles, an ambitious young architect in the Houston branch office of a prestigious international consulting firm. When offered the chance to relocate to Algeria to coordinate a large university project, Charles accepted, taking Sarah and their 10-month-old twins with him for a three-year stint.

During their sojourn and the three years following their return to Texas, Sarah devoted all her time to being wife and mommy. Last year, with the twins in school, Sarah's life became empty. Now she wonders what she could do that would allow her to work, say, 30 hours per week, leaving time for her family.

Meanwhile, Charles has been languishing in his office since returning from overseas. Having lost the upward momentum he had built up prior to the Algerian hiatus, he finds himself the perpetual outsider. He would consider another overseas project, but none seems likely to appear. American companies now find it more economical to staff their foreign offices with local personnel.

At a recent professional conference, Charles met an old college classmate who glowingly described the small architectural practice he had built up in the ski resort town of Vail, Colorado. The seed was sown. Now Charles feels ever more the outsider at work as he dreams of doing something similar. But he wonders if he has what it takes to manage such an undertaking on his own.

Alvaro: What do I want to be when I grow up?

Alvaro, 42, *is* grown up. But he has never landed in a position where he completely felt at home over the course of his checkered, 20-year career. Since college, he has managed a fast-food franchise, owned a music store, written advertising copy, and sold insurance. He lost his most recent job as a sales representative for a Columbus, Ohio, biotechnical firm when the firm was bought out by a British conglomerate and consolidated with another U.S. company.

Alvaro and his wife went separate ways two years ago. Now, with his only child in college, he feels completely free to start fresh. But feeling the press of time, he wants to do something more than just land another job. The next step should be something he can truly get into—something that rewards him with more than a paycheck.

These examples point up some of the big questions people must examine at a career crossroad. You may face some of the same issues or others—the career of a spouse/partner, children, and finding a location that meets your goals for career as well as your lifestyle. Dealing with related issues such as these could easily overwhelm you at a time when you are already stressed out by having to make decisions that are directly related to having lost your job unintentionally or by choice.

Though marked by uncertainty and insecurity, switching careers is an opportunity unique to America. I can't imagine any other country in which I could continuously redefine myself as effectively. Yet, just like at a real crossroad, you do have to choose which way to take, and there are no road signs to steer you down the best career path.

I like the approach to problem solving that my father-in-law evolved over the course of his 30-year career as a United Nations expert in public administration. In dealing with bureaucracies in seven third-world countries, he learned to regard every quandary as a puzzle to be solved by identifying the pieces one by one and then fitting them together.

Does this approach sound too simplistic a way to rearrange your life? Why not try it? If you set goals, as suggested in the last chapter, they can become pieces of your puzzle. More free time, less commuting, or a greener living environment may also figure among your pieces. But if you, like Alvaro, are questioning the direction that your life is taking as a result of your career, your biggest goal should be to make a career move that will gain you personal fulfillment.

What Do You Want to Do?
What Can You Do?

Miles: Man, I get so tired of eating peanut-butter-and-jelly sandwiches day after day.

Rita: Why don't you ask your wife to make you a different kind?

Miles: I make them myself.

Most of us, like Miles, get stuck in routines that we ourselves have made. Even though we have the power to change, we don't. We have invested too much in getting to where we are. But are we where we want to be, or are we simply hanging on for fear of change? When you reach a point where you have strong doubts, it's time to reevaluate your assumptions.

You might start by asking yourself, Why am I spending a major portion of my life doing something unrewarding? Then ask, How did I get here? Go back to the beginning and work forward. Perhaps you never really wanted to be a sales manager in the first place. But that's not enough. It leaves a vacuum to be filled by what you wanted (or still want) to be. Do you know what this is?

For young people starting out, career questions are simpler: What do I want to do? What am I able to do? Counselors put the first question under the category of "interests" and the second under "aptitudes." Numerous tests have been devised to measure each. Tests of this type that I took in high school, for example, showed I had good manual dexterity and liked the outdoors. A quick match of occupations corresponding to this combination suggested I might become an outdoor cheese wrapper. What could be simpler?

People in their thirties and beyond take on extra baggage when considering a change of careers. The need to maintain a steady income is foremost. It's beside the point to ponder a more fulfilling career when you have to work like hell at your present occupation just to keep bread on the table or if your child is just starting college. But another part of the baggage that limits career choice for experienced workers is just that— experience. They see their experience as an investment and are understandably not eager to chuck it overboard at this time in their lives.

Experience equals knowledge—the key to success in any field, say career counselors. Without it, a person shy of natural talent for an occupation can't hope to succeed, and a talented person won't rise beyond an equally talented person who has more knowledge. If a young person facing career decisions is like the pilot of a speed boat who is able to cut figure eights without a second thought, you may be more akin to the pilot of a supertanker. You can change course, but not quickly.

Well and good. Ideally, you will steer your supertanker of a career in a direction that makes use of your knowledge and experience. But remember, you never lose the knowledge gained so far. It's yours to keep, whether or not you use it in your next career move. Maybe you will discover an exciting way to apply what you consider to be specialized knowledge in a new direction, one that you can really get caught up in. Which brings us back to the original questions: What do you want to do? What can you do?

What you want to do depends on your interests. But interests are fleeting. Think back to when you first thought about what you wanted to be when you grew up. Chances are, you began by picturing yourself as, say, a fireman or nurse; within a few years you decided to become a forest ranger, and your decision has changed several times since. Though your interests change, they are still an important part of career decisions because they fuel your drive to succeed. But career counselors maintain that interests are not in themselves enough for success. You also need capability, effort, and probably a good dose of luck.

You start to acquire knowledge at birth and continue throughout life. Every field requires some knowledge, and specialized fields such as law, engineering, or medicine require a great deal just to enter. And the information age has upped the entry-level requirements for many occupations.

Unlike knowledge, which is an acquired characteristic, your aptitudes—natural abilities and talents—are innate, say career counselors. The aptitudes you are born with never change. Without the appropriate aptitude for an endeavor, you might succeed through hard work and knowledge, but you will always be swimming upstream. The naturally inclined person with the same degree of knowledge will sail by you every time. And you won't succeed in some fields, regardless of how hard you work at it, without a minimum of aptitude. A tone-deaf person bent on becoming a professional singer is wasting time.

Self-Assessment through Tests

By this time in your life you probably have a fair idea of what you are good at and where you fall short, but the odds are that you know much more about your interests than your aptitudes. There are many tests in a variety of formats you can use to help you find out what your natural talents are. I tried out tests from these sources: books, computer-software, and testing agenices. The first two kinds of tests are cheap and easy but nowhere as deep and—to me—accurate as the tests administered by specialized organizations.

The most interesting (and, in my opinion, the most fun) of the aptitude tests found in books is the series of personal inventory devices in Richard Bolles' book, *What Color Is Your Parachute.*[1] First published in 1970, this book has been so popular with people considering changing the direction of their career that it has been reprinted and updated every year since. Bolles starts by asking you to evaluate how good you are at various skills. To find out how well you can write, for example, he asks you to rate yourself in writing ability rather than having you write something.

Another useful book for self-assessment is Barry and Linda Gale's *Discover What You're Best At.*[2] The first half of this 170-page book is almost entirely taken up by an aptitude test. The second half explains how to score the test and match your results to possible career choices. Aptitudes tested in the Gales' book cover six general areas of skill: business, clerical, logical, mechanical, numerical, and social.

After taking the test, areas in which you've gotten high scores are arranged in clusters designated by the first letters of those areas. If, for example, you scored high in business and relatively low in everything else, you end up with a "B" cluster. But if you had high scores in business, clerical, and social areas, you have a "BCS" cluster.

In the back of the book, 41 career clusters are matched against possible careers for three levels of educational background. A "B" cluster person with a high school diploma might consider becoming an appliance salesperson, club manager, or circulation manager; a person with the same aptitudes but with two years of college might do well as a broadcasting announcer, claims adjuster, or executive chef; and with four years of college, this person could try his or her hand as an advertising account executive, city manager, or literary agent. A "BCS" cluster makes use of business, clerical, and social skills. A person with a bachelor's degree might consider taking a position as an employment interviewer, head nurse, home extension agent, or secondary school teacher.

Having gotten high scores in all areas of the Gales' test, I suspected that I should either be feeling the effects of a shot of adrenaline to my ego or question the efficacy of the test. My highest scores were in business, clerical, numerical, and social aptitudes. But this was not necessarily useful later when it came to matching aptitudes with career opportunities. I couldn't chart a specific direction.

When I asked co-author Barry Gale about this, he conceded that too many choices can be as stifling as too few. "You're in the candy store with all the candy in front of you and you don't know how to choose." People good at many things might easily end up with unused aptitudes that eventually come back to haunt them. Gale advises finding outlets in your non-professional life—such as sports and hobbies—for talents you don't need in your work. The people at the testing agency I visited concurred with this advice, but after taking their test I had fewer high scores to choose between.

Computers were bound to enter the testing arena, and I have no doubt that a computer-given test could be designed in many ways. Unfortunately, the test I took at a local community college's counseling center seemed superficial and easy to see through (I distrust any test in which the questions are so obvious that I know exactly what their authors are looking for).

I completed the first two parts of the SIGI+ test battery, self-assessment and search, in about an hour and a half. I passed over the remaining four sections that deal with preparing for a career. They seemed better suited to beginning college students than middle-aged people in career transition.

The self-assessment section asks you direct questions about your work-related values, interests, and skills, and then prioritizes your responses. The search section that follows matches your responses to possible occupations. If you are attracted to an occupation that the computer doesn't suggest for you, you can query it as to why. When I asked the computer why I shouldn't be an architect or musician, it responded that my strong preferences for leisure time and independence didn't fit. Hmmmm.

If the computer and book tests lack depth, the personally administered tests excel in it, at least if the Johnson O'Connor test battery is a good representative.

Aptitude testing at Johnson O'Connor got its start back in 1922 when its founder tested workers at General Electric to increase productivity on the assembly line. When friends and families of employees requested the same testing, O'Connor started a foundation and incorporated it as a non-profit, independent scientific organization in 1939. The foundation has since tested over 300,000 people. Most candidates are young people looking for direction to help chart a course of study. The remainder are mostly people in mid-life who are switching careers or looking for a productive way to spend their retirement.

The testing, which takes place at one of the foundation's 13 branch offices, spreads over three 90-minute sessions. In a fourth session, a counselor interprets the results and explains how to use them in making career decisions—though the foundation does not provide employment counseling. Seven aptitude areas are tested along with motor skills, color acuity, and personality orientation.

The tests I took in Johnson O'Connor's Boston office began with one designed to measure my vocabulary. The Johnson O'Connor folks hold that vocabulary is an acquired skill rather than an aptitude. It is the single most reliable indicator of general knowledge—one that you can increase if necessary to make full use of your aptitudes. I scored in the 95th percentile, which meant I was making full use of my aptitudes. "If you scored low in vocabulary, we would have been after you with the whips and chains," noted the administrator, Robert Westmoreland.

Tests measuring color acuity (degree of color blindness), eye dominance, and hand preference follow. Then come tests to measure visual perception, divergent and convergent thinking, certain numerical abilities, spatial visualization, auditory perception, four types of memory, and two types of motor dexterity.

One test uses word association to classify personalities as either "objective" or "subjective." Three fourths of the testees (well, what would you call them?) fall into the objective slot. These folks are generalists who like to work through other people. Successful people in business and other high-contact fields tend to be objective.

The loner-individualist falls more naturally into the subjective category. These people define the world through their own personalities rather than through other people. If they work with others, they are more likely to be the star who calls the shots than the team member who considers all points of view. Look for them in the ranks of specialized fields such as science, medicine, or law.

Westmoreland illustrates each personality type by citing two famous artists: Pablo Picasso and Walt Disney. Picasso, a subjective type, could paint his masterpieces locked up in a room for weeks without need for other people. Disney, an objective type, started out drawing cartoons but attained success only after he was able to create vicariously through people in his organization. "Where would *Fantasia* be, if Disney had insisted on drawing it himself?" asks Westmoreland to drive the point home.

One of the pluses of a personally administered test is the interpretation of the results. In my last session, a counselor guided me through each section's findings and suggested how I might best make use of each result in my career and life.

How much should you rely on aptitude tests to steer your career choices? Barry Gale says aptitudes are but one among many other factors. Follow-up interviews with people he has tested have yielded various responses. "Some say, 'Thank God, you have saved my life.' Others say, 'You kiddin'? I married the boss's daughter.' " Interests, achievements, and what you want out of a career also enter into the mid-life career changer's mix of factors, says Gale.

My own interests, which were examined by a separate test at Johnson O'Connor, centered around technology, followed by written communication and the arts. I would do well to consider them in tandem with my aptitudes, but because interests change, they should be subordinated to aptitudes where necessary.

I recommend aptitude testing if you are unsure of your strengths and weaknesses. Patricia Cox, a middle-aged professional woman who took the Johnson O'Connor tests with me, agrees.

"I now clearly know why I find my current job so frustrating," she observed after her interpretation session. "What it needs that I don't have is the stick-to-itiveness ability to keep nagging people. . . . I'm just no good at that." Patricia's 25-year career in math and computer science has led her to her present position as customer satisfaction manager at Digital Equipment's Acton, Massachusetts, branch. Her job, implementing quality-control programs at the company's overseas branches, involves projects with long time lines. This and the lack of a direct line of communication in her network have frustrated her. The test revealed that the aptitude to maintain interest in a project over a long period of time is exactly what she lacks.

Before the tests, Patricia had planned to take early retirement in a few years and leave the stress-filled world of high tech to relocate to New Mexico and teach computer-related college courses. The test administrator suggested law, psychology, sociology, diplomacy, or consulting might make better use of her strength at inductive reasoning. Patricia is now looking for business possibilities along those lines when she relocates to New Mexico.

If you take more than one kind of test, you will discover striking differences in how each classifies and measures aptitudes. For example, I rated "superior" in clerical skills according to the Gales' test in *Discover What You're Best At* but low (20th percentile) on the equivalent section (graphoria) of the Johnson O'Connor test. Robert Westmoreland thinks the disparity lies in subtle differences in the testing. The book test rated the ability to spot differences in series of word groups, whereas Johnson O'Connor's used minor differences in columns of numbers. The difference between numbers and words is enough to cause such variations in test scores, according to Westmoreland. He suspects there are thousands of aptitudes. Those that appear on the test are selected because they have been shown over many years to correlate to success in certain fields.

When selecting a testing agency, you stand a better chance for an objective assessment if you choose one that doesn't have a vested interest in using the test to sell you another service. For example, I'd steer clear of testing done at an employment placement agency. A few testing agencies are listed in the Appendix; you could also check with the career counseling department of your nearest community college.

Career Counseling

Though aptitude tests can point you toward fields for which you show potential, they don't tell you if you should enter those fields. Other factors come into play, such as your personality, external limitations, and goals. Sorting these out is the murky domain of career counselors. High schools and colleges offer career guidance to their students, but advisors for adults facing a career crossroads are harder to find in spite of the growing number of adults who need their help.

Community colleges may be your best source for this kind of service, says Judy Perry, director of adult learner services for Keene State College, Keene, New Hampshire. "There are little offices tucked away that do things you may not realize," she adds. Perry's department aims primarily at helping the adult learner returning to school to retool for the next career step but also offers resources anyone can use, such as an extensive career library and the computer-administered aptitude test that I found unimpressive.

Job clinics can be a good source of occupational information, if not career counseling. Perry's department has begun offering one-day workshops for people in career transition that cover such issues as job dissatisfaction, employment search, and starting a business.

Many of the commercial employment agencies that abound in metropolitan areas offer career counseling in addition to their other services, but author Barry Gale doesn't think much of them. "They can teach you how to write a resume, interview, and dress properly, but they are not really in the decision making business." William J. Morin and James C. Cabrera concur. They note in their book, *Parting Company,*[3] that anyone can call him or herself a "career guidance counselor;" you're better off seeking viable career counselors through personal referrals, business schools, graduate schools of psychology or the human services director of your former employer. Their services may include interest or aptitude testing as well as counseling and cost between $75 and $200 per session.

Defining the Shape of Your Career

Three career models bobbed up frequently among the people I interviewed: adapting an urban career to an exurban setting, switching careers, and taking up more than one career. Here's a sketch of each model, as illustrated by some of the folks you will meet again later on.

Adapting Your Present Career to a New Setting

When she hung her shingle as a business consultant in the small Arizona town of Jerome, Barbara Blackburn had solid business credentials from her prior work in banking in San Francisco and graduate studies in business administration. She needed only to scale down from the big city to a low-density rural area.

Dave Cadwell had no restaurant experience when he and his wife, Alice, moved to rural northwest Connecticut. But five years of managing warehousing and purchasing for an Orlando coffee distributor taught him enough about food retailing to open a small restaurant.

For Montana cattle rancher Mike Lee, moving into llama breeding was a new and exciting prospect. Although llamas aren't cows, they are grazing animals. Lee's degree in animal husbandry and cattle ranching experience prepared him for the leap into unfamiliar territory.

None of these people have actually switched careers. Yet what they are doing now differs substantially from their prior occupations. Each has applied the knowledge, skills, and experience gained over several years to a new direction.

Some of you will find through aptitude testing or other means that the field you've been in for the last several years is in tune with your aptitudes or interests. It's your present job that's off the mark. You would be more or less content to carry on in this line of work but prefer to find another setting. By changing your job rather than your career, you build on a proven path. And even if you crave the adventure of a more radical shift, your age and health may preclude risking a major change at this point in you life. Economic hardship may also limit how far you stray from the field you are grounded in.

Your challenge boils down to finding a way to transfer your knowledge and skills into a more rewarding work situation. We'll look at some of the ways to do this in the next chapter.

Switching Careers

One in ten Americans changes occupations in an average year, but the likelihood of career switching in any given year decreases with age, from

29 percent (teenagers) to 3 percent (ages 55 to 64). Many middle-aged workers who do switch are middle or upper-middle managers who fall victims to the corporate downsizing frenzy, says James Cotham, author of *Career Shock*.[4]

You may be ripe for a complete career switch if your self-assessment leads you to conclude that your life won't be improved much by merely changing jobs. What are your chances of success if you switch? It depends on what you mean by "success." One study tracked 165 former managers and executives who switched careers at the average age of 44, driven for the most part by a desire to achieve more meaningful work and a stronger link between their values and their work. Of the 92 who stayed with their new career, 74 reported greater job satisfaction, and 3 reported less.

Not all experts paint such a rosy picture for career switchers. "People generally have to continue doing what they have been doing," says James E. Challenger, president of a Chicago outplacement firm. "They cannot change professions as they would a pair of shoes. A career change usually means a severe loss of income and few people want to work for smaller salaries," he adds.

What Challenger overlooks is that after examining their lives, many people are willing to accept smaller salaries to regain control of their careers. "I see a guy working 30 years for the government and he's got that little house in Florida. He retires on Monday, has a massive heart attack on Thursday and is dead on Friday," observes cardiologist Cleve Francis. His 13 years of daily contact with stressed-out patients caused him to see that his own profession was burning him out. At 46, he traded his stethoscope for a guitar to pursue a long-suppressed dream of becoming a country music star. Francis sees his new career as an extension of one of his motives for going into medicine: "People want to be loved, they want to be cared for," he notes. "It's the same with music."

Job dissatisfaction has caused many doctors such as Francis to switch or consider switching careers. A poll by CBS's "60 Minutes" reported that 40 percent of doctors polled said they wouldn't go into medicine if they had it to do over again, citing job pressure, frustration with paperwork, insurance, and bureaucracy as causes of despair. Even insufficient salary was an issue. One doctor complained that he took home only $18,000 a year after meeting costs and making payments on his college loans.

People in high burn-out careers such as medicine are the most likely to switch careers, says Susan Breen, executive director of a branch office of Gal Friday, a temporary employment firm. But there are other reasons why you might switch, such as the realization that your career doesn't fit your aptitudes, as was the case with Patricia Cox (the customer satisfaction manager at Digital Equipment).

If you suspect your dissatisfaction with work goes deeper than the problems of the moment, a complete switch may be for the best, though

Worksheet 2-1   Should You Switch Careers?

By Donald Double and Gale Grossman, Ph.D., first printed in *New Choices for Retirement Living,* February 1991. Used with permission.

Rate how you feel about each of the following statements, from 1 to 5 (1 = strongly disagree, 5 = strongly agree).

Your Work In General

_____	I look forward to work every day.
_____	My work assignments appeal to me.
_____	My relationship with my boss is satisfying.
_____	All other relationships I have at work are satisfying.
_____	I am satisfied with the financial rewards of my work.

Your Job

_____	I feel competent because I am able to use my skills.
_____	I am working at or near my maximum ability.
_____	I can help others (individually or in groups).
_____	I have the right amount of contact with people inside and outside the office.
_____	My boss gives me the right amount of feedback, recognition, and respect.
_____	I feel secure that my job will not be eliminated.
_____	I have the right amount of autonomy.
_____	I value friendships and relationships I have with my co-workers.
_____	I am empowered to make decisions.
_____	I have opportunities to grow, advance, and develop new skills.

Your Career

_____	I am satisfied so far.
_____	I have achieved success (by my definition).
_____	The demands match my personal/professional desires and expectations.
_____	I believe my career will enable me to achieve my future work and personal goals.
_____	My career is the best for me.

(continued)

this gets harder with age and experience. Don't do it lightly, warn career counselors. Undergo aptitude testing, career counseling, or whatever else it takes to completely assess your strengths and weaknesses. You may get

Worksheet 2-1 *Continued*

Your Family

_____	I am satisfied with my relationship with my significant other.
_____	I am satisfied with my relationships with my children.
_____	I am satisfied with my relationships with my parents.
_____	My family relationships probably won't change drastically in the next five years.

Your Social/Spiritual Life

_____	I have enough leisure time.
_____	I am able to spend time with friends.
_____	I am satisfied with my current social life.
_____	I have time to pursue personal interests and hobbies.
_____	My spiritual life is satisfying.

Your Mental and Physical Well–Being

_____	I am satisfied with the physical environment at work.
_____	I find myself actually smiling on my way to work.
_____	I seldom miss work because of illness--real or feigned.
_____	When I talk to others about my job, I spend more time emphasizing the positive aspects than the negative.
_____	I sleep well--even when I have a lot of work to do.
_____	My work does not exhaust me physically or emotionally.

_____	**Total**

To get your average, add your scores and divide by 35. If the result is 3 or below, you probably should explore a career change further. If your average is higher, great--you can think about how to improve any section or individual items that you scored at 3 or below.

an idea of your need to consider a change in direction from the questions in Worksheet 2-1.

Multiple Careers

In our culture, we are used to defining ourselves by our work rather than by personal traits such as interests or beliefs. When someone you meet asks, "What do you do?" they are really asking, "Who are you?" If you reply, "I'm a comptroller," you can almost hear the other party's mind clicking to come up with a file for "comptroller" as a springboard for further dialogue. If you had said something like "I'm in rubber," the other person might have been at a loss, not knowing whether you deal in prophylactics or fix flat tires, but because rubber is a familiar concept, it still provides a stepping-stone for further conversation.

In my experience, this pattern is more widespread in Manhattan than Rocky Flats. When I came to rural New Hampshire eight years ago, people confused me by sidestepping the question "What do you do?" In Salt Lake City people usually had only one occupation. I realized in time that life wasn't quite so pat in these parts. Instead of doing just one thing, folks patched together a livelihood out of several bits and pieces. One of my neighbors cuts trees and mows lawns in the summer (a major undertaking, because lawns here tend to be measured in acres). Comes fall, he sells firewood. He plows snow in the winter and probably has a few other odds and ends in his portfolio. Another combines a small horse-breeding farm with a bed-and-breakfast. Some who can't make a complete living, even with two or more occupations, depend on the contributions of a spouse, who, likewise, may have more than one source of income.

My neighbors are heirs to a long tradition in rural New England of an economy that depends on small farms and light manufacturing. Unlike the giant farms in the Midwest that were blessed with rich soil and specialized in one crop, such as wheat or corn, farms in these parts were cursed with a short growing season and poor, rocky soil. They adapted by diversifying—a little dairy, a little corn, maybe a few other crops. Many small farmers supplemented their income by working in one of the nearby mills.

The farms have been disappearing for years. Today, manufacturing is also disappearing. People have to scramble for a living. But the long-entrenched habit of staying flexible will be their key to survival. This pattern could well become the career model of the future in an economy that no longer guarantees upward mobility in traditional straight-line paths.

In her book, *Altered Ambitions,*[5] Betsy Jaffe classifies multiple careers into two types: parallel and concentric. Karen Ryan is an example of someone with parallel careers.

Karen's divorce left her with a new baby to care for and house payments to make. She needed a business she could manage out of her home to bring in an income and allow her to care for the baby. She discovered sprouts. Sprouting alfalfa and beans in her kitchen required very little capital, and the sprouts had a ready market in local restaurants. A short time later, Karen started a second business, a nanny referral service, that now serves a national client base. Karen has since married a rancher. The couple now derives their income from three businesses, all seemingly unrelated.

Steve and Lisa Carlson show how concentric careers develop. Both had written a book and had decided to self-publish. If writing was the center of their career circle, self-publishing their books became the first concentric ring. In time they published the works of other authors, adding a second ring. A third and fourth ring, mail order and specialized software, were later added, as we'll see in Chapter 5. Each ring originated from the center; the whole pattern is interrelated.

Like Karen Ryan and the Carlsons, many rural entrepreneurs believe they better their chance for economic success by spreading themselves over several endeavors, whether parallel or concentric. But there is a trade-off. It's harder to rise to the top in any one area. As John Applegath put it in *Working Free*: "I decided I never again wanted to be totally dependent on only one sort of work to earn income. My plan was to begin immediately developing at least three, and preferably four or five, different ways to earn money. It took some time . . . The great advantage of this strategy is that I am never locked into one 'career.' If one thing isn't working out well, or if I'm getting bored, I can choose to drop it and put more time into one of my other projects, without feeling that I'm making a major 'career change.' "[6]

This approach may also have positive benefits on your mental health. The aptitude-testing folks at Johnson O'Connor say that if you have several strengths but focus on only one, you may be in for frustration over the long haul.

Multiple careers can mean anything from entrepreneurs who provide more than one product or service to employed persons with more than one job. The latter group contains over seven million people—6 percent of the total work force. A trend is building that is even being acknowledged by the corporate world. Southern New England Telephone established a personnel planning group to assist their employees in multiple career planning.

Equipping Yourself for a Career Change

Even though his new career as country musician demands skills worlds apart from his cardiology practice, Cleve Francis was able to make the switch. He had sung and played guitar since childhood. But for most, a complete change will require some kind of training. After you know what your target enterprise requires in the way of knowledge, skills, and abilities, you can determine where you come up short. Then comes the question of how to acquire the necessary retooling.

Of the many ways to add to your expertise, from self-tutoring to being taught by others, here are the four approaches I think work best for people who already have a store of education and work experience.

Transferring Skills from a Prior Position

If your new career direction overlaps a past area of expertise, you are part of the way there. Architectural topics were the subjects of my first writing endeavors—and still are. Building on past strengths is a common thread among the people I interviewed for this book, such as Gil Gordon and Karen Ryan.

Karen Ryan's search for work she could run out of her new domicile in Montana led her to respond to a newspaper ad from a Canadian company looking for "a person with good interviewing and writing skills." The company turned out to be a national referral service, the ad sought a recruiter to screen potential nannies before placing them in homes. Karen worked for the company for two years on commission. She learned how to use state-of-the-art communications technology to operate a national referral service—skills she later used to start her own business.

While a human resources manager at Johnson & Johnson in the 1960s, Gil Gordon was intrigued by the concept of the "electronic cottage" in Alvin Toffler's book, *The Third Wave*.[7] Through the proper marriage of telecommunications to computers, Gordon saw how the idea of the electronic cottage could revolutionize the corporate workplace. To help corporations successfully implement telecommuting programs, Gordon would need two different kinds of expertise: personnel management skills and computer-telecommuting know-how. Years of experience in personnel management enabled him to hit the ground running when he struck out to establish his own telecommuting consultant firm.

Learning as You Go

The other kind of expertise Gordon needed, telecommuting applications of computers, was not as accessible. He acquired it the hard way—through individual research while he was getting his new enterprise running. Standard personnel consulting work provided him an income during this transitional phase.

Many people ease into their second career without a great deal of additional expertise. They learn by doing. Many of the folks I interviewed for this book took this tack, supporting their new enterprise from the steady income of the former.

Carol Conragen, a writer you'll meet in Chapter 6, is writing a major account of the struggle of ethnic minorities in Burma (now Myanmar) against the repressive government there. Carol's extensive experience as an ad copywriter won't help her write this book, but it will help keep bread on the table while she learns how to craft a nonfiction book.

Ron and Dorothy Weber (Chapter 6) are urban professionals who have learned how to farm by farming. For ten years they have lived a Jekyll-and-Hyde life, working at their professional jobs in Salt Lake City Monday through Friday and commuting 140 miles westward on weekends to work on the farm.

Going Back to School

Adults in mid-life transition are returning to college campuses in record numbers. Peter D. Syverson, director of information services at the Council of Graduate Schools, reported that graduate school applications were up about 10 percent in 1991, and the number of students over 30 is on the rise. The U.S. Department of Education says 43 percent of college students enrolled in 1990 were over 24—up 5.5 percent from 1980. The agency expects the trend to continue.

Going back to take classes is a bigger step than you may be ready for. You may need to continue earning an income to support other family members. Even if you don't, you may somehow feel guilty for leaving the income stream to retrain yourself. And if you have a family, you may have to divide your time and efforts between it and your studies.

Returning to the educational world itself can be daunting—your younger colleagues have known nothing but school for most of their lives. On the plus side, you return with a seriousness of purpose and sense of direction that many of your younger colleagues lack. Campus externalities—social struggles, sports—won't likely distract you from your studies.

As colleges adapt to a changing balance between younger and older students, you can expect them to focus more of their slant in your direction. And don't undervalue your years in the work force. They have probably taught you discipline, how to capitalize on your strengths, and how to compensate for your weaknesses.

Finally, you may receive liberal nonclassroom credit for learning acquired through your professional experience. Here are some of the ways suggested by Robert Woessner in *USA Today:*[8]

- Take the College Level Examination Program (CLEP) tests offered at 2,800 schools.
- Challenge a course by taking an equivalency exam.
- Compile a portfolio to document your expertise. Include work experience, previous college work, and courses taken on the job or in the military.
- Seek out an adult-friendly school—one that is geared toward the needs of the nontraditional student.

To smooth your reentry into academia, first make sure your school is accredited by checking with the Council on Postsecondary Accreditation at (202) 452-1433. Visit classes in your field of interest. Talk to recent graduates of the school to get their views. If the school is a community college, many of the graduates likely work in the same community. Talk to them and, if possible, their employers.

D.I.Y.

The fourth approach for acquiring additional knowledge or skills is "do it yourself." D.I.Y. might appeal to you if you are an independent, resourceful sort or are short of time or money for more formal preparation. You may have no other resource if you, like Gil Gordon, are blazing new trails for which there are no precedents.

I offer no preferred method for D.I.Y. except to open your eyes and ears to everything. What you need is undoubtedly out there waiting somewhere, and you need only know where to look.

Your local public or college library is probably the best place to start. Spend some time learning which databases your library has and how to use them. Learn the types of general reference sources for occupations, trade associations, business directories, and business books. From a directory of trade associations, for example, you can find out if there are publications that relate to your venture.

Libraries also contain phone directories of other cities that may help you develop a network of resources, persons and organizations.

Seek out people who have experience in the kind of occupation or enterprise that interests you and then be bold enough to call on them for advice. Most people with expertise, I've found, are anxious to share their advice.

Bill Hammond, a retired sheriff's deputy from San Diego whom you'll meet in Chapter 6, started a trout farm in Hamilton, Montana, after talking with other trout farmers and reading a book on the subject—combining two sources of D.I.Y.

In our rethinking of the meaning of *career,* we began with how to discover your proper career fit and then explored various shapes your career might take in the next phase of your life. We finished with how to equip yourself for your next vocational venture. In Chapter 3 we'll look at how you can blend a reshaped career with family concerns and a new physical setting.

Chapter Three

Work, Family, and Place: Making a New Fit

The Greeks regarded work as a curse.

Seymour Martin Lipset

It is the will of God that man must work.

John Calvin

Attitudes toward work have changed over the course of time. The Greeks' disdain for work prevailed in Western society until the sixteenth century, when Protestants made the work ethic a condition for salvation. We've had our noses to the grindstone ever since.

To quote George Harris and Robert Trotter: "Work has become our intoxicant and Americans are working harder than ever before. In the past 15 years, the typical adult's leisure time has shrunk by 40 percent—down from 26.6 to 16.6 hours a week. And the work week, after decades of getting shorter, is suddenly 15 percent longer."[1]

"Leisure time, not money, is the status symbol of the '90s," notes University of Maryland sociology professor John Robinson. In a study for Hilton Hotels, he reported that 70 percent of Americans making $30,000 a year or more would give up a day's pay each week for one or two days off. Another study concluded that more people are working to gain quality leisure time and achieve a healthy balance between life and work. Although they may want to excel in their careers, they want more time with their families, for themselves, and just to do nothing.[2]

So it's not a question of working hard—we seem bent on doing that. It's a question of what you get out of your work besides subsistence. Many of the entrepreneurs you will meet later in this book are working longer hours than they did in their former urban jobs. Steve Carlson left his 9-to-5 job as a legislative assistant in Washington, D.C., to start a small publishing firm in northern Vermont. He and his wife, Lisa, put in 80-hour weeks now.

Others have found ways to operate their businesses with far fewer work hours. Jim and Mary Alinder's art gallery in Gualala, California, which specializes in photographic art, is open to the public five days a week. Their work shifts overlap four out of five days, two of which are Saturdays and Sundays when as many as 200 people visit the gallery. Each partner takes one of the lighter days off for a three-day weekend, meeting one of Jim's original goals: "We promised ourselves not to get into the small business trap of spending your whole life running the business."

Major differences divide the other people in this book from people like Mark, my earlier example of the disenchanted corporate employee. Whether they put in an 80-hour workweek like Steve and Lisa Carlson or a much leaner one like Jim and Mary Alinder, all have found a meaning in their work that is so often lacking in the corporate workplace. By consciously choosing their work, they control their careers. Although some have incomes comparable to what they might be making in the corporate world, most have willingly traded their former level of affluence to realize other parts of the American Dream, and this decision is shared by a growing number. As stated by career counselor Betsy Jaffe, "In numbers that would have seemed incredible just a few years ago, women, and increasingly men too, are trading earning power for a better quality of life."

Those who do work long hours do so without sacrificing their family life. As with the mom-and-pop stores of the past, their families often become partners to the success of the business.

And all of these people who have moved to the outland report a richer lifestyle than they had in their former urban residence.

So in this chapter we'll turn our focus from the question of *what* you do in your career and work to *how* you can do it to achieve a better balance between work and life in a new setting.

Work Arrangements in the Outland

If you contemplate relocating to improve your quality of life but are content with your present work situation, you may take heart from the fact that moving out need not mean having to choose between keeping or leaving your present job. Your options are greater today than ever before, thanks to a growing awareness of the need for flexible work alternatives among corporate employers.

Contingent work, flex-time, independent contracting, and telecommuting are a few of the new buzzwords that define the new working relationships between employers and employees. Let's scan some of the ways you can stay with your employer but work wherever you want and then examine the ultimate key to mobility—self-employment.

Telecommuting

Nick Sullivan is a senior editor for a Manhattan magazine publisher. Donna Cunningham is a media relations manager for a New Jersey telephone company. Both work amid rustic serenity, miles beyond the congested metropolis of New York City where their corporate headquarters are based. They and more than five million other Americans "commute" to their work via electronics. A typical telecommuter, according to a recent survey by Link Resources, is married, 35 years old, part of a dual-career household, and works in an information-related field such as word processing, data entry, bookkeeping, sales, or marketing. Most work at home on a part-time arrangement.

Nick Sullivan works out of a loft in his home on the Atlantic Ocean in South Dartmouth, Massachusetts, about a four-hour drive from the Manhattan headquarters of *Home Office Computing*. After dropping his daughters off at school each weekday morning, he returns home to begin the day's work. At half past nine, he boots up his computer and reviews the electronic mail that may have arrived over any of the three electronic services he subscribes to. He also checks any faxes that may have come in overnight. Sullivan spends the morning writing, without family or other office workers around to distract him. At noon he goes downstairs to read the *Wall Street Journal* and have lunch. Then it's back to work until about three o'clock when his wife, Debbie, returns with the kids. With more bustle in the house, his late afternoon pace is less intense.

Sullivan maintains frequent contact with his New York boss through phone, fax, modem, and the mail. Two or three days each month he travels to New York to touch base.

Donna Cunningham works out of an office in her Huntington, Vermont, home—the only office in the company heated by a wood stove, she boasts. Donna's telecommuting arrangement came about when she followed her spouse to Vermont, as we'll see in Chapter 5. Rather than lose a valued employee, her employer chose to keep her on and foot the bill for her to work at a distance.

Telecommuting works better for people in fields like Nick Sullivan's and Donna Cunningham's than some others. Programmers, translators, engineers, sales representatives, computer systems analysts, newspaper reporters, public relations professionals, technical writers, stockbrokers, and data entry clerks are naturals, writes Brad Schept in *Home Office Computing*.[3]

Under the right circumstances, telecommuting benefits companies, employees, and even society. Companies can retain valuable employees and save on overhead (even with the cost of long-distance communications). Employees save time and avoid the hassle of traffic and parking. They work where and when they want in an environment free from distraction.

There are even gains for society: less traffic and cleaner air. This benefit is one of the forces propelling telecommuting in cities such as Los Angeles and Phoenix.

In response to the Clean Air Act of 1990, Phoenix passed an ordinance requiring companies that employ more than 100 people at any given site to reduce their commuter mileage by 5 percent each year. Because mass transit is not widely available in Phoenix and carpooling works better in denser cities, AT&T started a telecommuting program in 1990.

The program was a hit, according to spokesperson Sue Sears: "We found that our employees love it and their morale and productivity increased." Sears notes that between 100 and 150 employees in AT&T's Phoenix office telecommute—but not all to the same extent. Most work at home one or two days, though a few are away five days at a time. Some, who use the time at home to work on reports, plans, or employee reviews, telecommute by phone only; others need a home office equipped with a modem or fax.

Sue Sears believes that we have barely scratched the surface of telecommuting's potential; she cites the example of a hotel chain that has to answer a lot of customer calls for information and reservations. Rather than maintain an expensive centralized communications center, calls could be automatically routed to an employee's home office. Bringing the office to physically disabled workers is another untapped application.

But telecommuting isn't without pitfalls. Remote employees miss out on face-to-face meetings. "Out of sight" may end up meaning "out of the promotion track." And they still have to travel to the office periodically— an obstacle that increases with distance. Finally, employees not used to working outside a structured office environment may not be up to working alone out in the boonies.

The fear of poorer worker performance and loss of control has kept some employers from embracing telecommuting. "Telecommuting is the kind of thing that nobody wants to be the first to do; everybody wants to be second," explains Gil Gordon, a New Jersey consultant who helps companies set up telecommuting programs.

"Worries of poorer performance haven't proven true," observes Gordon. "Work I've seen indicates telecommuting workers are even in all respects—they are as productive and satisfied as beforehand, but in the majority of cases there are significant gains," he says.

Pacific Bell, Apple Computer, AT&T, and J.C. Penney now offer telecommuting as an option to certain employees. Some companies escape having to deal with employee benefits in the arrangement, notes Gil Gordon, ". . . but every company I deal with doing telecommuting treats their workers just as if they were in the office. The only difference in benefits is if someone happens to shift from full-time work in the office to part-time work at home, and therefore comes under a different benefit program, but that would have been the case if they had stayed in the office."

Before asking your boss to set up a telecommuting arrangement, you should understand what you are getting into. First, you'll need a workable office in your home (discussed in detail in Chapter 13). Second, you'll also need equipment that can "talk to" headquarters. It will help to know your way around the rapidly changing world of modems, electronic mail, and fax technology.

Finally, ask yourself some hard questions: Am I a self-starter? Can I work alone, away from daily face-to-face contact with my associates? Can I structure my work environment to allow me freedom from family distractions?

Half In, Half Out: Transitional Arrangements

Cutting the tie with your employer and forsaking a steady paycheck to start over in a new location may entail more risk than you want to (or can) assume. You may ease the financial shock by working out a transitional arrangement with your employer. By becoming an independent contractor, you do some of the work you had been doing, but from your new location. If you relocate far from your employer, you might be stuck with frequent travel to headquarters to keep in touch. Could you do contract work by telecommuting?

Because of the downsides of the half-in, half-out arrangement, it is probably better as a means to an end than as an end in itself. Be clear about your motives. "Separate the choice 'I want to work at home,' from 'I want to work for myself,' " advises Gil Gordon.

If the work you do for a former employer by contract is the only work you have, you will not only kiss the employer-paid benefits good-bye—a scary prospect in these days of astronomical health insurance costs—but you may also lose the tax advantages of a business owner, particularly if you work out of your home. The IRS would love to classify you as an employee or hobbyist. If your contracted work is simply a way to carry you over financially while looking for other employment, you may have to forego the temporary benefit and tax losses.

If the work is a step toward full independence as a proprietor, contracting out work from your former employer can provide you some income and time to work out the kinks of getting established with other clients.

To achieve legitimacy in the eyes of the IRS, heed the advice Robert Laurance offers in *Going Freelance*:[4]

- Tie down the terms of your services with a contract.
- Have a place of business identified on business cards and stationery.
- Legitimatize your business name by getting the appropriate license in your municipality or state.
- Solicit business from several sources.
- Make sure your clients fill out IRS Form 1099-B for fees paid you.

Part-Time Employment

Scaling down your hours could be an effective alternative to the half-in, half-out arrangement if you relocate close enough to your employer to commute. More likely, distance will cause you to sever the tie and work part-time for a new employer. Part-time employment has helped many bridge the gap from one full-time job to another or to self-employment, as it did for Steve and Lisa Carlson.

In 1987 Steve worked as a part-time editor for a builder's magazine in nearby Burlington while Lisa taught school. Their earnings enabled them to start a small publishing firm without an outside infusion of capital.

The business world is not only accepting part-timers more readily but also creating work arrangements especially to accommodate them. A recent study of 521 firms revealed that more than 93 percent offered some type of alternative work schedule. Almost half offered flexible work scheduling. Another 20 percent offered job sharing. Work-at-home options were offered by 7 percent. Unfortunately, as we saw earlier, what companies don't offer part-timers is benefits.

Steve Bergsman reported in *Personnel Administrator* that the lack of benefits is the most difficult adjustment to make, which is why many part-timers have a spouse who also works and receives full family benefits.[5]

Job sharing is when two persons split the responsibilities and income from one position. This is a part-time option that pleases both employer and employee. Employers gain higher productivity, fewer turnovers, reduced absenteeism, and reduced overtime expenses. Employees suffer less burnout and have more free time to pursue other interests—a boon to budding entrepreneurs.

Temporary Employment

Temporary employment, whether full- or part-time, is another way to bridge the gap between your former income and a new job or business enterprise. And finding a "temp" job may be easier than finding a part-time position. The trade journal *Office* says the demand for temps often exceeds supply.[6]

I know—you can't see yourself as a Gal Friday hired in a squeeze to do menial office work. Don't worry. Mid- and upper-level professionals today find respectable temporary employment through specialized agencies in hundreds of cities and towns.

TPI, one such agency in Keene, New Hampshire, places designers, engineers, technicians, nurses, machinists, and drafters. TPI's owner, Pat Ryan, explained to me how the service works. If you are moving to a new locale, you might locate a professional temp agency from the area's yellow pages or through the local Chamber of Commerce.

In your initial contact, you tell the agency about your qualifications, the kind of work you are looking for, the range of compensation you would accept, and when you will be available. After finding a position, the agency negotiates the terms of employment with the recipient employer, who pays the placement fee to the agency. Because the fee is a percentage of your compensation, the agency gets the best compensation it can. The agency—your actual employer—pays you and takes care of all taxes, workers' compensation, and liability insurance.

Temporary professional employees placed by TPI usually earn 30 percent to 40 percent more in basic wages than comparable salaried employees. The downside is (wouldn't you know it?) lack of benefits. TPI pays for major holidays after an employee has been on the payroll for more than a month and grants a week's paid vacation to those exceeding one year's stay. "The stickler is health insurance," says Pat Ryan. "The ideal candidate for us, typically, would be someone with an engineering degree whose wife happens to be a school teacher. She picks up their benefits."

If you or your spouse is a medical doctor, you may find a suitable temporary position at your new address through an agency such as CompHealth, Kron Medical Services, Staff Care, or another of the 30 or so firms that specialize in placing medical personnel. An estimated 10,000 doctors, representing all ages and specialties, are working as temps, reported *USA Today.*[7]

Full-Time Employment

Looking for a job in uncrowded locales is much the same as looking for a job anywhere, except that jobs are fewer and less diverse.

You should start with a plan that encompasses milestones, goals, actions, resources, and timetables, advises business writer Donald Pizzi.[8] After you narrow down your target destination (the subject of Chapters 8 and 9), your next step is to find job leads in that area. If you have a network, use it. One study says as many as 80 percent of new jobs are found through networking and suggests that you should not only rely on your network for leads but also ask the leads for additional leads.[9]

National publications such as trade journals and newsletters are fertile sources of job leads. If you have a specific location in mind—say Santa Fe, New Mexico—get hold of a Santa Fe telephone directory from a library (or order one through your phone company). The yellow pages will be a treasure trove of job leads (and much else related to relocating, as we'll see in Chapter 9). For current job openings in the area, you'll want a copy of the local newspaper. If you don't know anyone there, obtain the phone number of one or two local real estate brokers. Call them and say you are considering locating in the area and are interested in finding out what type of housing is available. Take note of anything useful they tell you and then up the ante a bit by asking if they would send you a Sunday newspaper to help you get a feel for the community.

Computers can save you time on your job search. Executive search firms store applicant résumés and openings in computer databases. A growing number of universities offer similar services to alumni. One employment agency, Snelling and Snelling, is pioneering its own database, Silent Search, that matches job applicants to openings in 100 national locations. As of this writing there is no software available to the public that maintains job openings databases, nor are they offered through online networks such as CompuServe, Genie, QuantumLink, and Prodigy, but keep your eyes peeled.

In the meantime, there is software that can help you manage other aspects of the job search. Here are some examples. (See the Appendix for addresses.)

- *The Perfect Career* asks you 180 questions to determine your interests and abilities and then matches the results to 650 occupations.
- *BetterWorking Resume Kit* helps you organize your skills, experience, and education into a concise résumé, with nine résumé formats to choose from.
- *ResumeMaker* is similar but comes with a glossary of action words (such as *managed, implemented, developed*) and a form to help you track your job search (activities, appointments, tips for prospecting, and interviewing).
- *The Career Management Partner* contains word-processing software to help you create, edit, print, and store letters, proposals, and résumés. A database of 100 executive recruiting firms is included. The software lets you use your modem to get company information from online databases and send résumés to companies that use computerized recruiting. Help for online prospecting is also included.

Another way to land a job in your new location is through a local employment agency. Every town of any size is likely to have one or more private employment agencies, and hub towns that serve wider areas usually have a state office of employment security. In their book, *Fifty and Fired*, Ed Brandt and Leonard Corwen say your chances of finding a job through an employment agency are good for lower-paying jobs, worse for middle-management and executive positions, and dismal if you are over 50, regardless of the level of employment.[10]

If you were fired (excuse me, "outplaced"), your previous employer may attempt to sweeten the memory you'll hold of him or her by steering you toward an outplacement firm—a fancy moniker for a private employment agency that provides career assessment, aptitude testing, help with interviewing techniques, and résumé preparation. Authors Brandt and Corwen say outplacement firms are great—if the company pays the tab. Otherwise, approach them with caution.

James E. Challenger, president of the Chicago outplacement firm, Challenger, Gray & Christmas, Inc., suggests you look for an outplacement firm whose main focus is finding you a similar position within a short time. Effective outplacement firms land 10 to 20 job interviews for their clients, he says, leading to a job offer within an average of 3.2 months.

Self-Employment

"How can you tell when it's the right time to strike out on your own?" I asked a friend back in 1976 when I was on the brink of making the leap. "When you can't stand to work for someone else any longer," he replied. His advice still rings true. I suspect that most people who start their own businesses have nurtured the dream for a long time. When they eventually break loose to become their own bosses, they cite the need for more autonomy, creativity, room to grow, and the like. But the real reason was freedom, pure and simple.

But to gain this freedom, you pit yourself against tremendous odds. Two out of three new firms close their doors within four years of their founding, says a report by the Advisory Committee on Industrial Innovation. Laundries, used car dealerships, gas stations, trucking firms, restaurants, infant clothing stores, bakeries, machine shops, food stores, and car washes are the most vulnerable, according to Mike McKeever in his book, *How to Write a Business Plan*.[11]

Warnings like these won't stop you, I suspect, if your dream has smoldered for long. It didn't stop me from barrelling ahead back in 1976. My initial one-person architectural practice didn't make me rich, but it did gain me the freedom to control my own career and kept us solvent for six years until I received a grant to do research overseas.

You, too, can succeed if you have a solid business opportunity and the skills and abilities required to give it life. Beyond an opportunity and knowledge, some folks are better suited to working for themselves than

Worksheet 3-1   Do You Have an Entrepreneurial Personality?

Check the answers to the following questions that best describe you.

1. At work one Friday, I finish the task I am working on one half hour before quitting time. The next task in the sequence will require at least an hour to complete. I will most likely:

A._____ Begin the new task and work late.
B._____ Begin the new task, leave on time, and finish at home over the weekend.
C._____ Leave the new task until Monday.

2. When I speak in a meeting,

A. _____ I get my meaning across with little difficulty.
B. _____ Most of the people understand what I mean.
C. _____ I know how to express myself, but others don't always understand what I mean.

3. If my computer locks up and I can't restart it by re–booting, I

A. _____ Get out the manuals and try to track down the problem.
B. _____ Try a few other remedies, then call in an expert.
C. _____ Call in an expert without messing with it.

4. If I go to town to see a movie and find that the film I came to see is playing next week, I

A. _____ Find a substitute diversion in town.
B. _____ See the movie that is playing.
C. _____ Go back home, planning to come back in a week.

5. If I could travel through time, I would most like to:

A. _____ Visit the world of 50 years into the future.
B. _____ Visit the world of 100 years ago.
C. _____ Not use the machine.

(continued)

others. Worksheet 3-1 incorporates some of the personality factors that business writers say you need to succeed on your own.

But even if you have the right stuff, you need the right business opportunity. If you are reading this book, you may already have definite ideas of what you want to do or at least what you want to avoid. But don't

Worksheet 3-1 *Continued*

6. If I have a major task to accomplish, I prefer to:

    A. ____ Head up a group of people to do it.
    B. ____ Work on it as a member of a group.
    C. ____ Do it myself, even though it might take longer.

7. If I begin a project around the house on a Saturday morning, I tend to:

    A. ____ Finish it, even if I have to spend most of the day to do it.
    B. ____ Quit when I get tired or bored and finish it later.
    C. ____ If I can't complete it over the weekend, I probably won't. Other, more important things will demand my attention.

8. At work, I

    A. ____ Often see things that should be done differently.
    B. ____ Occasionally see room for improvement but am content to leave those decisions to those in charge.
    C. ____ Don't worry about running the company. It's hard enough to do my own job as well as I can.

9. When I spot areas needing improvement, I believe that:

    A. ____ If it's my idea, it is up to me to implement the change.
    B. ____ If enough people see the need for the change, it will be implemented.
    C. ____ If people have good intentions and work hard, things will work out.

10. If I have a suggestion for changing a procedure, I am most likely to persuade people of its value through

    A. ____ Talking to people.
    B. ____ Writing a good report.
    C. ____ Writing an outline and letting a better writer draft the final report.

11. When things don't go according to plan, I

    A. ____ Try to make a new plan.
    B. ____ Get upset for awhile, then determine the best course of action.
    C. ____ Try to restore the original plan.

(continued)

Worksheet 3-1 *Continued*

12. **If a group I belong to makes a decision I feel is wrong, I**

   A. ____Listen to others to see if I might compromise or change my
        position.
   B. ____Make sure I have given each member their say, before I try to
        persuade them to my position.
   C. ____Try to persuade them to my point of view, even if it means
        alienating the whole group.

13. **If I believed in the cause, I could become**

   A. ____A monk or nun.
   B. ____A missionary for a few years.
   C. ____The chair of a committee to promote the cause.

14. **Vacuum cleaners would be better if they**

   A. ____Were available in kits you could assemble and repair yourself.
   B. ____Were as they are now, but without cords.
   C. ____Had a bit more suction.

How many A's did you check?	_____
How many B's did you check?	_____
How many C's did you check?	_____

If 7 or more checks were for A, you have some of the personality
characteristics business writers often link to success as an entrepreneur. If
7 or more were for B, you show some entrepreneurial qualities but might do
well to try your hand at a smaller project, such as heading up a group's
fundraising effort, to get a better appraisal of your overall strengths and
weaknesses. If the majority of your responses were in the C category, you
might be better off as an employee.

lock yourself into a decision before you have fully examined your
strengths, weaknesses, and experience. At the very least, get the opinion
of your spouse and close friends. If you have any doubts, I strongly recommend aptitude testing by a competent organization such as Johnson
O'Connor.

   Some business experts advise you to avoid the common mistake of
trying to turn a hobby into a money-making enterprise. "People who like
reading want to start bookstores. People who like animals want to start
pet shops," says Stephen Harper in *The McGraw-Hill Guide to Starting*

Your Own Business. His advice: Offer what people want, not what you want to sell.[12]

This advice seems tied to the business mentality of the past, the sole objective of which was to make money. It does not address the concerns of those who have invested themselves completely in the corporate workplace and come up empty. These people are taking another look at the profit motive and deciding that it isn't their greatest goal. Seeing growth for its own sake as no virtue, they want to measure business success in terms of a broader scale of values that includes leisure, family life, and making a positive contribution to society. Steve Carlson embodies this attitude.

When Steve left his job as chief legislative assistant to Congressman James Jeffords of Vermont in 1987, he had 12 years of expertise as a Washington insider. "I was suddenly in demand among politicians and interest groups who were willing to pay $50 per hour for political consultations," he says. Instead of sticking around Washington, D.C., to milk this asset, Steve quit cold to do what he really wanted to do—move to Vermont and start a small business.

Some mavericks have turned hobbies into business successes—even in monetary terms. Fourteen years ago, Amelia McCoy's hobby was making hair bows for her granddaughters and friends. Her designs attracted attention at pageants, dances, and other events around Lamar, Oklahoma. In the early 1980s Wal-Mart started ordering her bows for its stores in the area. By 1992, McCoy's company, Handmade Rainbows and Halos, produced 500 designs that grossed over $5 million. McCoy was named National Small Business Person of the Year by the Small Business Administration.

Many of the entrepreneurs in the following chapters knew and loved the objects of their work before they turned them into businesses. Walter Szykitka suggests in *How to Be Your Own Boss* that you should pick a field you know about. So in deciding on a business opportunity, don't give up your dream—instead, find a way to make your dream pay.[13]

If you are looking for a promising business opportunity, you might ask yourself, "What can I offer that people will pay for?" or turned around, "What do people want that I can I offer?" One way to come up with new business ideas is the "market gap" approach, where you spot an unmet need. In *Home Office Computing,* Ken Prigal suggests six ways to use this method to come up with ideas for a business:[14]

1. Record everything you wish you had thought of (Post-It™ pads and Velcro™ are two of my examples).
2. List the complaints you have about products or services to help you spot opportunities for improvement.
3. List your dreams.

4. Read voraciously, especially magazines that deal with small businesses and entrepreneurship.
5. Clip magazine articles, take notes on books, and make personal notes to create a library of ideas.
6. Brainstorm with other people in an open, nonjudgmental environment.

Keeping an eye open for new trends is another way to use the market gap approach. In his book, *Trend Tracking*, Gerald Celente created a system to spot trends and relate them to new business opportunities. The key is to separate trends from fads. Coleco's Cabbage Patch™ dolls and Reagan-era conservatism were short-lived fads. Dual-income households, an aging population, and "buying American" are solid trends.[15]

Using Celente's approach, you can see the connection between the shortage of time that dual-career couples have and the trend toward caring for elderly parents in their own home. Because homes and appliances are geared to "average" (able-bodied) persons, a whole world of specialized products and housing concepts awaits exploitation by the right entrepreneur.

Some entrepreneurs even stumble onto market gaps that grow into businesses. Barbara Oakley was driving with her young daughter past a field of grazing cows one day when she thought, "Gee, my daughter will never know the names of these cows." Barbara left her $50,000-a-year job as an audio systems engineer for Ford to make educational flashcards that show not only different breeds of cattle but also other animals as well.

What ideas lie fallow in the back of your mind that could turn into potential businesses?

Family Ties

Unless you are a single person without children, success in the next chapter of your working life will depend as much on satisfying the concerns and needs of your family as it does on your personal ambitions. Your biggest hurdle may well be your spouse's work if relocation is an option.

Four out of five marriages will be dual-career partnerships by 1995, predicts the U.S. Department of Labor.[16] The trend requires rethinking the division of responsibilities that supported the traditional "Dick and Jane" family, especially those relating to finances, household duties, and child care.

Who follows whom in a career move heads the list because it affects both partners so deeply. Yet how many couples have you known who have moved without compromising one partner's career? Does it come down to whose career is the most important, or is it possible to relocate and meet the career aspirations of both?

Whither Thou Goest . . . I'll Stay

"Commuter marriages" are the way out of this impasse for many couples. Charles and Nancy Buffler serve as an example of one of the many possible variations of this arrangement.

Finding themselves to be empty nesters after years of moving in response to Charles's career as a microwave physicist, the couple settled on a sheep farm in Marlborough, New Hampshire. But Charles still worked in Tarrytown, near the New York metropolitan area. A four-hour commute was too much every day but acceptable once a week. He left the farm at five o'clock on Tuesday morning and returned Thursday night in time for a late dinner. Charles spent one day of his long weekend on office work. When in New York, he initially overnighted at bed-and-breakfasts and later with his son and daughter-in-law.

The arrangement, although not ideal, worked. Nancy could manage the farm alone for three days of the week. But this was not to continue long. When Charles's employer, General Foods, merged with Kraft Foods, it got out of the microwave business and transferred Charles to Kraft's microwave division in Chicago.

The Bufflers decided to press the limits of their commuter marriage rather than move to Chicago. Charles now flies out of Manchester, New Hampshire, at half past seven on Monday morning and is in his office near Chicago's O'Hare International Airport two hours later. He stays at bed-and-breakfasts while in Chicago. Ten days later he returns to spend ten days on the farm, some of which he spends doing company work on his computer via a modem hookup.

Though the company pays for air travel, the new arrangement is clearly straining the Bufflers' lives. An arrangement that worked reasonably well when Charles was away four days and home the next three works less well for ten days in and ten days out.

How much time do couples need together to keep a relationship healthy? The answer varies from couple to couple. In *Commuter Marriage*, authors Naomi Gerstel and Harriet Gross cite a number of studies made since the 1950s suggesting that "a geographic distance between two people doesn't destroy their relationship or their ability to help each other in practical ways," which include long-distance telephone communications, rapid reunions by air travel, and fast transfer of financial assets.[17]

Commuter marriages, argue Gerstel and Gross, are necessary and natural responses to the conflicting demands, values, and expectations couples face in trying to forge the best fit between family and career. They may even liberate the partners from the limits to personal and career achievement that traditional relationships impose.

But commuter marriages engender other problems. Social relationships are the first to suffer. A spouse living without a mate has a hard time maintaining or developing relationships with other couples. Couples enter an in-between land where they are singles in a social sense but remain couples legally and emotionally. As such, many have trouble developing friendships with "true" singles and couples. Meanwhile, their relationships with members of their extended family may become strained as well. The older generation sometimes suspects that the new arrangement signals the beginning of the end of their marriage. And perhaps the worst hardship is loneliness.

And loneliness while living apart brings the threat of (or opportunity for) extramarital affairs. One study put the number of commuter marriages in which one or both partners were having an extramarital affair at nearly one-third. This may seem to be a high percentage, but the figures aren't really much different for noncommuter marriages. Gerstel and Gross conclude that setting up separate households doesn't necessarily lead to infidelity.

The costs of maintaining separate lives is another practical drawback. Charles Buffler's company values him enough to pay for his commute by air. Most couples with commuter marriages pay more for travel, telephone, and maintaining separate households. Some face the additional burdens of individually paying for household help, boarding schools, or day care.

Still, a commuter marriage may be worth the minuses if you are considering it as a temporary arrangement when you relocate to start a new business. Not having to resettle your family while trying to cope with the many problems of getting established will allow you to narrow your focus (and maybe keep your peace of mind).

The Trailing Spouse

Absolutely equal treatment of both partners' career ambitions is next to impossible to achieve when relocating. One career inevitably dominates, leaving the other as the "trailing spouse" (sounds like some kind of vine, but I couldn't find a better term). Although the result is seldom ideal, things don't always turn out the way they were planned. Let's look at what kinds of surprises were in store for two of the couples I interviewed.

"I thought he was taking me to the end of the world" was how Karen Ryan described her move to Missoula, Montana, in 1973. Karen, who grew up in the Los Angeles area, graduated from the University of California at Santa Barbara and went on to become a teacher and Pan Am flight attendant. Then she married her college sweetheart, who planned to do graduate work in environmental studies at the University of Montana. The newlyweds said good-bye to southern California and hello to a new life in the quiet college town of Missoula.

The marriage later dissolved, but Karen, now a new mother, decided to stay on. She bought a small house for $12,000, which is "not even a down payment in Southern California," she notes. Still, payments had to be met even on such a low-priced house. Within a few years, Karen had successfully launched two home-based businesses—a sprout farm and a nanny referral service. Each enterprise was sparked by her desire to remain in a small rural town. Karen found a market for her sprouts in the local restaurants. The nanny referral service is an example of a growing number of home-based businesses that can be located anywhere through state-of-the-art telecommunications equipment.

Karen saw her move to Montana as a short-term relocation driven by her husband's career. Through unforeseen events, she was forced to rely on her own resources. She used them creatively to carve a career of her own.

Wayne Carter's move from southern California took him even farther out—to rural New England. In 1969, Wayne's career as an aeronautical engineer in the defense industry took him and his wife, Marji, an interior designer, to the bustling Newport Beach area south of Los Angeles. Marji worked hard and eventually became senior designer in the prestigious design firm, Cannell & Chaffin, and five years later struck off on her own. Her client base expanded geographically as well as numerically.

The couple prospered over the next decade but grew increasingly unhappy with their lives in southern California. Newport Beach, a planned community with a gorgeous harbor, had everything going for it—but it reeked of artifice, smog, and traffic, noted Marji. "It's a never-never land, where all of the beautiful people are, but the buildings are artificial and the climate is deadly dull. We were small town people with small town values. . . . but in my practice I had to tell the guy who had just shown up with $10 million in his hand and wanted instant gratification that he had to stand behind other people before him with $40 million," she adds. "It was a case of success not being very wonderful."

While Marji's career careened between high-flying clients, cutbacks in the defense industry made Wayne's uncertain. Marji described how things came to a head: "We decided one Christmas night that we did not like the way we were living our lives. Wayne was 55 and I was 47. We were working very hard. We never had time for our friends or each other. . . . all we did was work. . . . We thought it would be nice not to for a while, or maybe forever."

Wayne took early retirement. Within two days of listing their home, they sold it for a tidy profit, bought a motor home, and embarked on a two-and-a-half-month tour eastward, finally settling in Dublin, New Hampshire.

Realizing that full retirement wasn't economically possible, Wayne and Marji discussed which one of them would resume working. If it were to be Wayne, they would have to move near a corporate employer. Marji, on the other hand, could resume her design business almost anywhere, and with longtime clients still asking for her services, she decided to give it a try, using telephone, fax, mail, and occasional travel to reach her far-flung clients.

Wayne, now officially retired but robust at 55, was far from ready for the rocking chair. He soon found a way to apply the business skills he had acquired through years in the corporate world while Marji began to relinquish the parts of her practice that she was neither interested in nor had time for. Today, Wayne manages Marji's design business, leaving ample time for her to focus on being creative. The partnership works for both of them; similar arrangements work for many others, as we'll see in the next section.

Karen Ryan and Wayne Carter, both "trailing spouses," ended up with satisfying career moves that were quite unexpected at the outset. Their stories represent but a few of the possible outcomes. Corporations have long realized that transferring employees often causes a trailing-spouse problem, but, as yet, they haven't done much more than offer counseling and help with job placement, for the transferred employee's spouse.

Uma Sekaran suggests in *Dual Career Families* that couples who thoroughly air the question of who will follow whom in a career move—before getting married—are more successful in dealing with this situation when it occurs.[18]

Spouses as Business Partners

Wayne and Marji's design partnership builds on a time-worn model—the mom-and-pop stores of the past. This arrangement is well suited to a growing number of professionals reinventing their careers. Further on, we'll see how several entrepreneurs vary this theme in the American out-land.

Janis Atkins, a former teacher, and her husband, Robert, a civil engineer, left their jobs in Houston to manage a natural foods restaurant in a college town, Bryan, Texas. Dave Cadwell, a former coffee distributor in Orlando, and his wife, Alice, a dance therapist, became restaurateurs in a rural corner of Connecticut. Professional photographer Jim Alinder and his freelance writer wife, Mary, left San Francisco to establish a photographic art gallery in the coastal hamlet of Gualala, CA. Former Washington legislative aide Steve Carlson moved to Northern Vermont where he and his teacher wife, Lisa, are starting up a small publishing firm.

These are examples of the estimated 1.5 million husband-and-wife business teams in the United States as cited by Kevin Thompson in *Black*

Enterprise. The "copreneur" movement is fueled by a shift from corporate to entrepreneurial values, growing acceptance of home-based businesses, new concern for quality family life, and the copreneurs' need to regain economic control.[19]

Thompson considers the constant togetherness and interaction to be both a pro and con of copreneuring. He advises couples contemplating the arrangement to establish clearly defined roles, communicate, and draw up a legal document that specifies what will happen to the firm in case of divorce or death. Finally, they must continually assess the status of both the firm and the marriage. Dyan Machan added one more caveat in an article in *Forbes:* Define different areas of expertise to avoid becoming competitors.[20]

Defining your turf in a business partnership with your spouse can only happen when both of you can clearly separate the business relationship from the marriage. This is never an easy task, and it's harder still if your marriage is shaky. "If you don't have a good marriage, you shouldn't go into business together," warns psychotherapist Trudy Schwartz.

One way to test your business compatibility is to test your success in some other venture before going into business together. It could be as simple as wallpapering a room or planning a trip (which is not simple in my house) or as complex as undertaking a fundraising effort for a community cause. If you can bring these off with relative harmony, you may be good as business partners.

Family Members Above and Below

Your spouse's career may be the thorniest, but not the only, part of your puzzle when you consider relocating. If you are in your forties or fifties, you are like the ham in a sandwich, pressed from above and below. You not only have to think of your children, who may be entering the difficult teen years, but also the needs of your own parents as well. Like children, old people also have social networks. Current thinking among gerontologists favors keeping people in their own homes as long as feasible. Doing so may be in the best interest of your parents, but it may also limit your relocation options.

I haven't found an easy way out of this dilemma from my research for this book. Books on caring for aging parents suggest sharing the responsibilities with your siblings. This might allow you to relocate at considerable distance and stay in touch through phone calls and only occasional visits. But even if transportation and communication are faster today, they can still be expensive if many trips are needed.

If you are the sole caregiver, you may have to choose between staying within driving distance or moving your parents.

What about the kids? You may have to balance the effect of uprooting them against the gains you foresee for them in the move. Moving away will mean severed friendships and, if your destination is very rural, a more difficult time making new friends. You can find out before moving what kinds of school and daycare facilities exist in the target area, but the psychological effects of a career and location change won't appear until after the fact.

On the other hand, the move may harbor some pleasant surprises. As a member of the local 4-H club, my nine-year-old daughter saw a calf being born, an experience she would never have had in Salt Lake City.

One certainty: your move and possible occupational change will affect the family dynamics, for better or worse. If you embark on a home-based business, your children may find it hard having you around so much. Just as easily, the demands of your new business can put you out of reach of your children. Both problems were reported in one study of career changers, but the most critical problem for the children was adapting to a new community.

Children develop social networks that become a factor in your decision to move on. Fortunately, they are born with minds open to new experience and new people. Later on we'll explore some of the ways transplanted urbanites can adjust to a rural community.

In part three, the focus shifts away from the individual pieces of the career-location puzzle to how real people are fitting the pieces together in small towns, in-between places, and truly rural destinations. I hope that you will find a part of yourself in their stories and that they will help you shape your own future for the better.

Part Three

Outland Opportunities

Chapter Four

Small-Town Prospects

They went and built a skyscraper seven stories high, about as high as a buildin' ort-a grow.

Richard Rogers and
Oscar Hammerstein, *Oklahoma*

This line from the song *Everything's up to Date in Kansas City* described the public's reaction to that city's bustling growth around the turn of the century, a time when cities were growing upward and outward. Chicago's skyscrapers reached unheard-of heights in the 1880s, astounding the world, but by the 1920s they were second-rate in comparison to Manhattan's exploding skyline.

Yet most Americans never warmed to cities of that scale—certainly not to the incumbent population density. The ideals embodied in the word *town* lived on in their collective consciousness. Small towns were clean places where people knew and cared for each other. Unlike suburbs, they had variety and individuality. They had identifiable centers—a town square, fountain, park, or gazebo where you could take your family on a summer Sunday afternoon to eat ice cream cones while a brass band was playing.

Today, with the big cities sliding into decay and the suburbs taking on many of their problems but offering few of their amenities, people are looking once again to small towns as the communities of choice. As David Heenan puts it in *The New Corporate Frontier: The Big Move to Small Town USA*, "They believe that small, low-density cities and towns offer the best potential for making a difference."[1]

In this chapter, we'll look into the lives of seven entrepreneurs based in towns ranging from Bryan, Texas, to Fairmont, West Virginia. Some of these folks operate scaled-down versions of businesses you might find in larger cities. Others, such as Barbara Blackburn's consulting firm in

Jerome, Arizona, have evolved to fit the demands and opportunities unique to very small towns. Some are successful by any yardstick; others mostly by their own measure. All of those who started out working in the big city share one attitude: they wouldn't willingly return.

Small-Town Entrepreneurs

Fundraising for Profit

Everybody loves to get two for the price of one. So it's no surprise that entrepreneurs exploit the "twofer" concept. The benefits split three ways. Sponsor companies advertise and promote their product or service while building a positive image as a supporter of worthwhile causes. Nonprofit organizations who sell the coupons get contributions (the fundraising aspect). Finally, the broker makes a profit through acting as a go-between.

Charles Moreau got into the fundraising business in Bryan, Texas, in 1985. His firm, Community Card Co., designs a discount dining program containing many two-for-one coupons that the buyer can apply toward area businesses. The businesses pay a fee for being listed in the book of coupons. Local organizations such as schools, churches, and civic groups market the coupon books to the public and receive a portion of the sales, ranging between 30 and 60 percent. The broker keeps the rest as profit.

Everything stays in the community with this program, says Charles, and "you don't feel guilty for selling people a bag of candy for five dollars that costs you maybe fifty cents."

A former geological engineer, Charles started fundraising after a brief fling as a direct mail executive proved too stressful. With his wife and two other employees, he serves approximately 100 clients in the Bryan area from a leased office. Branch offices staffed by one or two people have since been added to serve the Corpus Christi and Denton areas. The biggest office yet is planned for San Diego.

Charles says success in the fundraising business starts with identifying a market area that contains the right number of entertainment-oriented businesses and then making sure there is enough local demographic data to determine how many are likely to purchase coupon books.

Finding recipient charities isn't difficult—they abound in most any community. Charles rates fundraising as a risky venture requiring at least $40,000 to $50,000 plus a year's living expenses to start. Having seen several similar start-ups go under, he recommends a solid knowledge of management, sales, and marketing. In the beginning, Charles spent around $12,000 on radio commercials and newspaper ads and an additional $10,000 on direct mail to promote Community Card Co. Now, he relies on newspaper ads alone.

After seven years of hard work and long hours, the business is prospering. The Moreaus live comfortably and are building a 3000-square-foot lakeside home three miles outside Bryan. Now thinking of franchising on a nationwide level, Charles may be backing into the kind of stressful environment he sidestepped with direct mail. But he says he can handle the stress. "At some point in the future, I think I'm going to bow out, buy a place on the lake and take it easy the rest of my life."

Growing a Community Theater in Central Florida

Shots in the night followed by shrieks and sudden blackouts, part of the fun of murder mystery parties, are the stock in trade of Triangle Productions, Inc., a two-year-old community theater corporation in Sanford, Florida. The actors, all amateur, arrive in costume to foment the dastardly deeds that are solved with the help of the audience over the course of the weekend.

The company stages one or two mystery weekends a month at resort hotels between Sanford and Orlando, 18 miles to the south, and occasional performances on cruise ships in Tampa Bay. Musicals and plays, meanwhile, entertain local audiences at the company's home theater in nearby Winter Park, a leased building with a stage, cast room, and theater on the ground floor and space for props and wardrobes upstairs.

Rod Layer, a 60-year-old businessman, conceived the theater to provide a performing outlet for his 50-year-old wife, Diana, who had been part of a local amateur theater group until it dissolved. Diana, now a partner in Triangle Productions, oversees continuity and complaints. John Olbert, 38, a third partner with a background in music and theater, devotes full time to selling and directing shows and managing day-to-day operations. The rest of the company consists of amateur actors, plentiful in the area. "When we put out the first audition notice, we got about 500 applicants," says Rod Layer. "Everybody has a little ham in them." The actors share in a percentage of profits of each show.

There are community theater groups in cities and towns all over the United States, but the climate and demographics of Central Florida account for steady, year-round audiences. Always warm, the region contains a high percentage of retirees with discretionary money to spend on this kind of entertainment. And though the Orlando area attracts hordes of tourists who come to visit nearby Disney World and Epcot Center, tourists don't make up the main audiences. They are too pooped out after a day of "Disneying" to drive another 30 miles for evening entertainment. It's the people who work in the entertainment businesses, notes John Olbert. Disney World alone employs around 15,000 people, many of whom identify with live theater and look for something to do other than barhop in Orlando.

Rod Layer defines the demographic requirements for success in economic terms: 500 to 1000 well-heeled patrons to whom you can send flyers advertising future shows and know that many of them will attend.

Weekend mystery shows at local resorts gross between $500 and $1000. Shows staged in the company's own facility bring in about $2,000. So far, profits have gone toward buying costumes and sets. The Layers live off of Rod's printing and accounting businesses, whereas John Olbert depends on his savings; none of them has relied on the company for income. Rod Layer aims for an eventual return on the couple of thousand dollars he put up initially but doesn't foresee the company doing much more than covering its costs.

John Olbert commits all of his time to making the company succeed. He believes the operation is ready to emerge from the start-up mode and could be profitable enough to generate an income for himself of $30,000 to $40,000—a good salary, given Florida's low cost of living. The key to profitability, he says, will be investing enough time and energy into promotion and sales to generate more shows than the company now produces. He cites a recent monthlong push he made that booked 12 shows, a dramatic jump from the past two years when one or two shows per month were the average. John would also like the company to branch into more lucrative work in TV, radio, and travel promotion.

In its second year, Triangle Productions is still testing the waters, a process made more difficult than usual by the recent recession. But, if community theater can succeed anywhere, it should in Central Florida. Triangle Productions has the two main ingredients: actors and a paying audience.

Bulk Mailing in Fairmont, West Virginia

Jerry Ragen's Presort Plus, Inc., processes around 70,000 pieces of mail each day for large and small businesses in the northwestern corner of West Virginia. Now the largest mailer in the state, Presort Plus handles any mailing service that its clients request, including copying, layout, folding, labeling, obtaining mailing lists, and bar coding.

Presort Plus typifies one way small businesses capitalize on opportunities spawned by the information revolution. Caught between mounting costs and work volume in the latter 1970s, the U.S. Postal Service offered bulk mailing patrons a two-cent discount on postage as an incentive to get them to use zip codes. As mailing became more complicated, entrepreneurs began to spot opportunities to fill niches in the link between companies and the mailbox.

Jerry Ragen, 53, worked previously as a comptroller and operations manager with FMC Corp. in Philadelphia. The company transferred him to its division in Fairmont. When it sold the division two years later, Jerry was without a job. By this time, he had put down roots in the area and had no desire to return to the big city. The mailing business became available when the previous owner was convicted for tax evasion and had to sell.

Beginning in 1987 with the 4000-square-foot building in Fairmont and a leased building of 1600 square feet in Wheeling, 45 miles to the north, Jerry built up his client base from 107 to 500 over the first four years and later established a third branch in Parkersburg, 70 miles to the west. He thinks the location of the three sites provide the right fit for his market area. Fairmont is a small town of 24,000 people; another 75,000 live within a 50-mile radius.

The area contains several clients who regularly depend on bulk mailing, such as hospitals, schools, colleges, banking, and insurance businesses not served by a competing mail service.

To keep the mail flowing, Presort Plus employs 15 people at the Fairmont site (including Jerry's wife and a son), 10 in Wheeling, and 5 in Parkersburg.

Bulk mailing is in transition from being a labor- to equipment-intensive service, according to Jerry. It's also subject to the whims of the federal postal system, which encourages streamlining of mail handling through automation. The U.S. Postal Service rewards those who send barcoded mail with postage discounts and projects that all mail will be bar coded by 1995.

With the trend toward automation, just how future technology will affect bulk mailing is unknown. Will electronic mail erode the business? Jerry thinks it might—the rise in popularity of FAX machines is unquestionably affecting demand—but, he says, "companies aren't going to start faxing invoices."

Replacing manpower with more sophisticated equipment can mean a huge investment unless an owner leases. Jerry, who just shelled out $275,000 for a piece of equipment, estimates the lowest amount needed to start a mailing service would be around $50,000 and a year's living expenses.

In his case, the investment has paid off. The three branches gross over a million dollars annually, netting the Ragens a comfortable life in this small town nestled among the Appalachians.

Arkansas Antiques

A given market area can support only so many bulk mailing services such as Jerry Ragen's. Additional businesses can only compete for smaller slices of the same pie. Some businesses seem to benefit when several of the same sort cluster together to form a critical mass. One of these, antique shops, do especially well in areas that draw a lot of tourists.

The green mountains and lakes of the Ozark Plateau of northwest Arkansas attract enough tourists each year to support several antique shops. The owner of one of these, Bill Stiles, was convinced enough of the critical mass approach to open two other branch stores of his Long Ago Antiques in Fayetteville.

All of these branch stores are family enterprises. Bill's wife minds the show room and oversees promotion: a regular ad in a shoppers' weekly and a listing in a brochure alongside 60 other regional antique shops and flea markets. A daughter runs the second store; a daughter-in-law, the third.

The rear of the main store, a 2000-square-foot brick building, contains a well-equipped shop where Bill and one of his sons use their woodworking savvy to turn junk into gems. The team focuses on minor repairs and refinishing, avoiding the "basket cases." Both acquired their skills by doing. If they require expertise beyond their capabilities, they "sub it out" to local craftspeople who specialize in caning, basket weaving, and brass casting.

Long Ago Antiques specializes in period furniture dating from 1900 to the 1930s. Antiques are bought through estate sales, private buyers, and individuals for about 20 percent of the sale price. A carved wood hall tree with a mirror priced at $1,800 is the most expensive item on the floor at the moment. Most of the Stiles' merchandise sells for $300 to $350.

The Stiles started 20 years ago on a shoestring budget. The first shop had only three electric saws. Today, Bill values his shop equipment at around $35,000. The three stores provide a good middle-class lifestyle for three households, thanks to the untiring commitment each family member brings to the business. Bill says that the focus on furniture helps insulate the business from economic downturns.

Instead of buying new furniture, customers bring in old but damaged items and pay to have them repaired. Other dealers in the area who just sell manage to eke out only a meager income when times are hard. But Bill believes most of them are retirees or people with other jobs who deal in antiques as a sideline. Antiques have been Bill's life for the past 20 years.

A Natural Foods Store in a Texas College Town

Natural (or "health") food stores seem to come in two flavors. The first is typified by efficient-looking shops jammed with shelves full of vitamin bottles where middle-aged women in white uniforms sell alfalfa concentrated in tablets too big to get down. The second type sells alfalfa in the form of sprouts as well as other foods. This type had its roots in the back-to-nature 1960s. The demand for healthy foods is even greater today as one food after another is associated with a health hazard resulting from the chemical pesticides and the other short-cuts that drive agribusiness.

Brazos Natural Foods is unmistakably of the second type. Located in the Brazos River Valley, from which it takes its name, the store meets the local demand for natural foods in the twin towns of Bryan and College Station, Texas. Many of the customers are students or faculty at Texas A. & M. University.

In addition to fresh produce, the store offers herbs, spices, teas, nut seeds, bulk flour, and—yes—vitamins, as well as videocassettes dealing with holistic health topics. Customers are encouraged to record their comments in a small notebook at the check-out counter, which provides the owners, Janis and Robert Atkins, with a simple and direct form of market research.

Before coming to Bryan, Janis, 48, was a school teacher and stockbroker in Houston, 80 miles southeast, where her husband, Robert, also 48, worked as a civil engineer. Houston was exciting, compared to the small towns they grew up in. But the excitement wore off in time. "For peace of mind, quality of life, and sanity, I'd definitely choose a smaller town."

Janis Atkins's interest in natural foods started when she worked at a food co-op. When the co-op folded, it owed Janis money, which she took in the form of store equipment. The equipment, plus $2,000 and two distributors willing to delay billings, constituted her start-up capital. She says a figure closer to $85,000 would have been much more realistic (the National Nutritional Foods Association of Costa Mesa, California, suggests $85,000 to $150,000).

Janis and Robert co-manage the store, located in a leased building on Bryan's Main Street, assisted by two part-time employees. From the annual gross income of around $300,000, the Atkinses draw around $40,000. Janis sees increased competition down the road as more supermarkets pick up on the idea of natural foods departments, but she thinks the demand for natural foods will continue to grow for the foreseeable future.

To spread the word, the Atkinses rely on a mix of newspaper ads, local shoppers' weeklies, and a listing in the yellow pages. The college crowd, which provides much of the store's business, hears about Brazos Natural Foods on the local public radio station, where the store sponsors a program.

Natural Foods and More in a Utah College Town

College students and faculty also make up a big share of another natural foods store in Logan, Utah, but natural foods are only part of a business that now boasts a cafe, a coffee-roasting operation, and consulting service.

After completing a hitch as a draftee in Vietnam, Randy Wirth came to Logan, Utah, to study demography at Utah State University. He met Sally

Sears at a protest against the war. After they married, they decided they liked the Cache Valley enough to put down roots there.

Randy went to work for the local plant of Presto Products, Inc., the world's largest maker of plastic bags, eventually becoming production supervisor. Sally also worked for a time at Presto but kept an eye open for a career opportunity more in line with her long-standing interest: food. As a freelance food expert, Sally had taught classes throughout Cache Valley in ethnic foods, special diets, and how to use herbs and spices.

The Wirths considered launching a natural food business in the late 1970s. The logical location would have been the north end of Logan, where new stores were sprouting like weeds. But Randy identified with the center of the small college town that clustered around the Mormon tabernacle on Main Street—a section he didn't want to see die for the sake of random, commercial-strip development at the other end of town.

When the Straw Ibis Market, a natural food store just a stone's throw from Main Street, came up for sale in 1978, Randy and Sally naturally decided to buy it. With their home as collateral, they made installment payments to the seller, who carried the contract.

The couple reopened the Straw Ibis Market and expanded the prior offerings—whole grains and organic produce—to include dried flowers and wine- and beer-making supplies. Initially Sally ran the business, while Randy kept his job at Presto, partly to provide a steady income until the store could stand on its own. After five years, rather than renew the lease under higher rent, they bought the building through a loan for the down payment from their parents and a sales contract carried by the owner.

As the business grew, Randy's enthusiasm for his corporate job waned. "I didn't feel my career was leading anywhere," he notes. "The next promotion would have been to where people were having heart attacks." If he took this promotion, it would mean giving his all to the company and probably moving to another plant in Wisconsin or South Boston. Besides, the couple felt they would have to get in with both feet to make their business succeed or else get out.

The "both feet" approach won out. Randy said good-bye to 14 years with Presto to help Sally with the store. In time, several factors contributed to their decision to go beyond mere retailing. First, they realized that the local market for natural foods was too limited for much growth but that growth was necessary if the business was to provide a decent income. Next, they knew that Logan, Utah, even though the hub of an agrarian region, contained enough urban types to support a natural foods cafe, thanks to the university, hospital, and several other businesses. Finally, Sally had long hankered for an outlet for her culinary expertise, whereas Randy had been nursing the idea of an espresso bar.

To finance the expansion, they applied for an SBA "women in business" loan and put down deposits on new equipment. The loan application fizzled when the Reagan administration denied funding to the program. Undaunted, the couple took out a second mortgage on their home, and Randy did most of the remodeling work himself.

Today, the Straw Ibis Market, Cafe, and Roasting Company seats 26 inside and another 14 on fold-up wooden seating built onto an outside wall under a colorful awning.

The fare is simple, wholesome, and delicious. Offerings are made fresh daily and include soup, pasta, bean salad, New York paté plate, and dolmas (stuffed grape leaves) hand-wrapped by a Greek supplier in Oakland. Deli food, such as cream cheese and lox, is always on hand. For dessert, there is home-made Italian ice cream, frozen yogurt, and a choice of espresso and specialty coffees.

But there is coffee and then there is *coffee*. Randy noticed that coffees grown at high altitudes were healthier than low-altitude varieties. High-altitude coffee is around 30 percent lower in caffeine and free of pesticides—not because higher altitudes have fewer insect pests but because the farmers are too poor to afford pesticides and the topography makes application difficult. Randy saw an opportunity in importing raw beans, roasting them, and reselling the product to other retailers.

The result surprised him: "The aroma really pulls people in off the street. I was a little concerned, even though it's a small roaster, whether having coffee wafting through the air would be a problem. With a north wind, it goes right across the tabernacle." Randy's qualms trace to the Mormon disdain for coffee. But no one has complained yet, and the aroma of roasting coffee entices customers into the store as well as the cafe. The packaged product, currently sold to retailers in Salt Lake City, Ogden, and Park City, is finding new markets.

Randy's interest in coffee spurred another offshoot for the business. While touring Zion National Park in southern Utah, he asked a local restaurant owner if he had considered serving a better-quality coffee. Rather than taking the question as an insult, the owner brought his partners in for an impromptu meeting with Randy and Sally the same afternoon. They were impressed enough to recommend the Wirths to an associate in Salt Lake City, which led to their first consulting contract. They have since helped others in the state deal with start-up issues such as layout, equipment selection, supply sources, and getting the right kind of water.

As the Straw Ibis grows outward in concentric rings, it has now turned the profit corner. Randy carried the red ink for the first eight years with his corporate job. "It was very scary to drop that chunk [$40,000+] off of your bottom line with the hope that you're going to make it," he explains. "The cafe is what did it for us." Though the cafe occupies the smaller portion of the building, it accounted for 30 percent of receipts in its first year and 50 percent in the second. This year, Randy and Sally will take a hard look at the store to see if they can gain more space for the cafe by eliminating unprofitable merchandise.

The couple also holds high hopes for the coffee-roasting and consulting branches. Randy notes that as the market share for standard coffee declines, the demand for specialty coffees increases. The next venture could even be a franchising operation. As Randy puts it: "I think we have a formula, if it can work in Logan, Utah. It's a competitive market, but we are well positioned for it, because we have a lot of experience and know the industry."

When Randy talks about the struggle to make the Straw Ibis succeed, he comes across with the same upbeat tone I have noticed from other entrepreneurs. In describing a recent consulting contract, he said: "Even if it weren't for the money, it's so neat working with people who are so enthusiastic and excited and motivated and then you get to share in that. . . . We did some *pro bono* work at the end just to help them get the doors open. We got to know the people, we liked them and we wanted to see them succeed. That comes back to us, as well, because after all, they are selling our coffee."

Business Consulting in the Verde Valley: From City by the Bay to Ghost Town

Barbara Blackburn, 48, is also upbeat about helping minibusinesses succeed. A registered public accountant, she serves some 70 clients in the small Arizona towns clustered along the Verde River, some 25 miles south of Flagstaff and 80 miles north of Phoenix. A small town in the arid Southwest is a radical change from Barbara's previous locale, San Francisco.

As big cities go, San Francisco ranks among the most preferred, along with maybe Boston, New Orleans, Seattle, and Portland, Oregon. But working 12 hours a day, seven days a week for 17 months straight can dull the charms of any city, notes Barbara. In 1977, she fled an upward-bound career in banking to start anew in the old copper-mining town of Jerome.

When Barbara started her own business consulting firm, her second client was trying to launch a high-tech scientific instrument–manufacturing enterprise. Impressed with Barbara's abilities, he invited her to join his firm as general manager. She rose in the ranks to become president and part-owner in short time and managed the company until it was bought out in 1987. She left with enough capital to set out on her own for the second time.

Hoping to specialize in small business issues and long-range planning, Barbara found a more predictable demand for the less-exciting tax and accounting services, which today make up about 55 percent of her present work load.

Helping existing businesses deal with growth or improve operation comprises the bulk of her consulting work. A smaller portion involves counseling people buying existing businesses or starting new ones.

The region's laid-back lifestyle has attracted an influx of urban refugees in recent years—artists and craftspeople who thrive on the money flowing from the abundant crop of tourists who stream through the area in winter as well as summer.

Barbara lives with her husband in a former bakery he converted to a home. An office in one room was her business base until she concluded that it was conflicting with her private life. She now rents space in an old high school for herself, one full-time accountant, and a half-time administrative assistant.

The economics of Barbara's business, when seen on paper, might not cause too many people to quit their jobs and rush westward. She spent $40,000 to start the business and grosses around $85,000 annually, out of which she draws approximately $15,000 in personal income—a dramatic drop from the $50,000 salary she was earning in San Francisco. As is the case with many other such entrepreneurs, she considers the improved lifestyle and opportunity to be her own boss worth the tradeoffs.

And living costs are cheap in the Verde Valley (rents average $300 per month). Barbara stays debt-free. She takes off ten weeks each year to go backpacking and river running. One could do worse.

Finding Your Niche in a Small Town

Barbara Blackburn and the other entrepreneurs profiled in this chapter are all self-employed professionals who have found niches for their small businesses in small towns. I selected these folks because of the variety of their vocations and locales. My hope is that this wide sampling will expose something in the experience of small-town entrepreneurs that you can identify with—something that will help you understand some of the struggles and rewards that come with starting anew in a small-town environment.

The dozens of books that have been written on starting your own business agree on one thing: the need to spot an unmet need and find a way to fill it profitably. This is easier said than done. Some books offer additional help in gap spotting, but many market gaps aren't likely to hold steady because society and technology are constantly changing. This dilemma leaves you, the prospective entrepreneur, with a choice between focusing on needs that never change or becoming aware of trends.

If small-town life is your cup of tea, here are a few trends to keep your eye on that seem to fit a small-town market.

Food

Like bigger cities, small towns depend on big businesses such as supermarkets or fast food chains for most of their food. But being so big hinders the ability to spot or exploit sudden market opportunities. This creates a niche for small specialty retailers such as Brazos Natural Foods and the Straw Ibis, who have their ear much closer to the ground. Brazos Natural Foods, for example, keeps a comments/suggestions sheet on the checkout counter. Have you ever seen this in a supermarket?

The trend toward healthier diets and purer foods that began in the 1960s has steadily gained strength, so much so that the fast-food giants have responded with items lower in fat, sugar, and cholesterol. Kentucky Fried Chicken even changed its name to KFC, presumably because it foresaw the stigma soon to surround the word *fried*.

In addition to health, Americans have come to expect greater variety in foods, especially when they dine out. Mexican, Chinese, Korean, Afghani, Salvadoran, Caribbean, and Native American foods are all on the rise as of this writing. Overall restaurant traffic rose 10 percent between 1982 and 1986, while Asian restaurants saw 54 percent growth, according to *Megatrends 2000.*

Gerald Celente, the author of *Trend Tracking*, expects growing demand for take-out food, high- and low-end restaurants, and restaurants that offer live entertainment. Middle-range restaurants with mainstream fare will suffer.

Restaurants are among the most risky of businesses, and food-related ventures are not a quick and easy path to riches. As Randy Wirth of the Straw Ibis puts it, "It's the toughest market there is . . . You have to be real clear that you don't mind long hours." Randy and his spouse enjoyed at most four or five free days a month when he quit his regular job to add a cafe to the natural foods store.

Randy's success is due, in part, to his ability to capitalize on areas that have not been explored in Logan, Utah, such as coffee roasting and espresso bars. What other alternative food enterprises lie waiting to be developed in small towns—catering exotic meals? Restaurants operated as clubs that people subscribe to? Non–junk food fast-food joints?

Garbage

What is garbage? Stuff you want to get rid of. But the value judgment attached to that definition is constantly changing. Yesterday's cast-offs can become today's valued goods—the operative premise for thousands of businesses such as the antique and used furniture stores that provide a livelihood for Bill Stiles' family in Fayetteville, Arkansas.

People buy his merchandise for different reasons. Nostalgia and appreciation of a level of skill that can no longer be matched probably account for the appeal of antiques. More value for the dollar attracts buyers of used furniture. It is more economical to repair and recycle than to manufacture anew.

But used furniture and used cars aren't the only second-hand items that could make you money. Recycled waste, now a nuisance, will become a valuable resource by the year 2000, predict futurists Marvin Cetron and Owen Davies[2]. As ways are found to match the waste stream with facilities for recycling, savings will accrue both from material reuse and the energy required to remanufacture. Because successful collection of recycled paper, metal, glass, and plastic requires a concentration of people, towns are a natural location in which to base recycling services.

In his book, *Ecopreneuring* (John Wiley & Sons, 1991), Steven J. Bennett describes the gamut of small-business opportunities waiting in the areas of ecology and resource recovery—everything from transporting recyclable materials to retailing recycled products. "The environment is a vast field," he notes, "and so are the problems plaguing it. By keeping a watchful eye on the news, and paying close attention to your immediate environmental needs, you, too, can redefine profitable new market niches."[3]

Legal Services

No, garbage was not intentionally listed after food, and legal services was not intentionally listed after garbage. But whether or not society appreciates lawyers, the need for their services is expected to grow, and towns are a natural base of operations. Futurists Cetron and Davies see increased regulation of airlines, financial services, electric utilities and chemical companies. Environmental legislation, a growth area for the 1990s, will also create demand for specialized legal expertise.

The need for legal services won't be limited to attorneys. For example, paralegals will increase in number during the 1990s by 75 percent, according to a prediction by *The Futurist.*[4]

Hands-On Services

An expected labor shortage in the 1990s will create a demand for people who make and repair things, according to Gerald Celente in *Trend Tracking*. Celente lumps surgeons in with mechanics, masons, plumbers, and carpenters. Small towns are natural sites for service businesses of this type.

Arts and Entertainment

"We are on the brink of a renaissance in the arts," wrote John Naisbitt and Patricia Aburdene in *Megatrends 2000*. The movement traces to the increasing number of affluent baby boomers who make up the educated, professional, and increasingly female work force. Visual arts—poetry, dance, theater and music—will ascend in importance over the symbols of the industrial era just past: sports and the military. The renaissance won't be confined to the traditional centers of large cities, but will also flourish in towns, suburbs, and rural areas.

John Suter's position with the New York Folklore Society in Ithaca, New York, (discussed in Chapter 1) may be indicative of the kinds of opportunities that this wave of art appreciation will open to urban professionals who long to redirect their talents in small towns. Rod Layer's community theater, though struggling, demonstrates the hunger for live performances in an age saturated by high-tech entertainment. A report on regional theater in *Town & Country* cited in *Megatrends 2000* claimed that 90 percent of American theater is outside New York City in 155 cities and towns ranging in size from Minneapolis to Ashland, Oregon.[5]

Specialty Retailing

Town-based retail outlets should profit from the following types of markets in the 1990s:

- **Books**. Though threatened by high-tech alternatives, books should continue to sell because of their low cost and portability. Two growing sectors of the population will provide the markets: baby boomers entering middle age and the elderly.

- **Hobby supplies**. Manufacturing, distribution, and retailing of crafts and hobby materials have exploded into a $6.8 billion industry, according to a study by the Hobby Industries of America.[6] The group found that in 77 percent of U.S. homes, at least one person was involved in crafts. Factors that may propel the trend might be people's frustration with their lives and work, the growing number of elderly, people who live alone, and people seeking a closer relationship between product and user in an age dominated by high-tech consumer products. Look for steady or increasing demand for supplies related to arts and crafts, picture framing, photography, and beer brewing.

- **Sports and outdoor recreation supplies**. As baby boomers move into later middle age, they will favor low-energy activities such as walking, bowling, golf, and swimming over high-energy activities such as jogging, bicycling, and windsurfing, predicts Gerald Celente in *Trend Tracking*. Other growth areas of outdoor activity will be hiking and camping. Stores offering outdoor clothing and camping equipment should benefit.

- **Products for the elderly**. A trend toward more older people living alone, combined with the high cost of institutional or alternative living arrangements, is fueling a movement towards "aging in place." People can stay in their own homes much longer if their homes are modified to accommodate the changes that come with age. Special healthcare products, cabinets with special heights, and magnifying devices for TV screens are just a few of the products waiting to be exploited by small-town retailers.

Child Care and Elder Care Services

Women, traditionally the main caregivers to family members both younger and older than them, will continue to join the work force. Whether self-employed or employed by a company, a growing number of women will depend on outside caregivers for their children and aging parents. Corporations, in order to keep employees, are starting to offer on-site day care. Whether offered on- or off-site in private facilities, the market for daycare services seems assured.

Health and Personal Care

Healthcare trends will be driven by costs, technology, and the age of the population, and all of these are growing. Look for town-based business opportunities spawned by the following trends:

- **Health facilities**. Clinics are supplanting hospitals, with outpatient care displacing hospital stays. More, smaller facilities are replacing fewer, larger ones.
- **Practitioners.** Look for a growing demand for alternatives to traditional medical professionals in the areas of holistic medicine, acupuncture, herbal remedies, physical therapy, and nutrition. Nurses will continue to be in short supply. Midwives will be more popular, as well as mental health and counseling services.
- **Eyes**. Environmental pollution and increasing use of computer terminals will strain the eyesight of the young and middle-aged. Meanwhile, the percentage of the population over 65 continues to grow. Both trends augur well for growth among purveyors of eye-care products and services.
- **Teeth**. The need for traditional dental care has dropped off in recent years, largely because of fluoride toothpaste. The decline will be offset in the future by the special needs of the elderly for gum treatment, crowns, dentures, and other reconstructive procedures.
- **Skin**. Aging baby-boomers will seek the fountain of youth both in cosmetic surgery and cosmetic products that hide signs of aging.

Skin-care products may also benefit from the increased risk of skin cancer due to ozone depletion of the atmosphere.

- **Hair**. Periodic hair care is an affordable luxury. My barber assures me that his business increased, if anything, during the recent recession. The aging population should guarantee a large market for hair-care products and services.

Security

Alas—even in small towns, the need for property protection will rise, as Gerald Celente reports in *Trend Tracking*. An increase in unemployment will result in more crime and create a need for security guards and electronic protection equipment.

These are but a few of the trends that affect businesses in small towns. I hope they will seed your imagination with ideas for opportunities. In Chapter 5 we'll meet several people whose enterprises serve regional or national markets, leaving them free to live and work where they want to.

Chapter Five

Out, But Never Far Away

Towns are not your only choice these days if you are looking for a non-metropolitan locale for yourself and your work. In addition to strictly urban or rural areas, you could move to what I'll call *in-between land* for want of a better term. It contains the hard-to-define places John Herbers chronicles so well in *The New Heartland*—places neither truly rural nor urban that "can be seen on the outer fringes of metropolitan areas; around small towns far removed from the large cities; along rivers; coastlines, and reservoirs; near recreation and retirement areas; on marginal farmland; along country roads; and on remote land that is barren except for its physical beauty," in Herbers's words.[1]

In-between land is where you can operate a small business without worrying about the local market, as you would with the enterprises mentioned in the last chapter. Nor would you need a rural location as a condition of the business, as do agricultural and outdoor recreation businesses discussed in the next chapter. People choose in-between land because of the quality of life there.

The examples that follow represent but a few of the many ways that recent advances in communication and transportation have enabled people to work where they want to. Because they serve either a regional or national market, these folks enjoy great freedom of location.

That is not to say that their freedom is complete. Many of the current wave of small business books claim that you can locate an office almost anywhere. This is accurate for some—such as writers like Don Best, who needs only to be close enough to a post office to send off his manuscripts—but inaccurate for most others. Most businesses require some special proximity, be it to clients, suppliers, or services. Gil Gordon serves corporate clients all over the United States from his home office in Monmouth Junction, New Jersey, because he is within an hour's drive of a major airport.

The success of Jim Alinder's art gallery in Gualala, California, relies in part on the heavy tourist traffic plying the California coastal highway and visiting the adjacent Sea Ranch resort.

The people we'll meet in this chapter vary as to the type of work and degree of success they have achieved. But all have one thing in common: the ability to forge a career in in-between land.

The Folks Who Work In-Between

Selling Art Photography at Sea Ranch

Jim and Mary Alinder have turned a lifelong love of photography into a rewarding venture in the small seacoast community where they have long yearned to settle down. Their gallery in Gualala, 90 miles north of San Francisco, sells enough photo art each year to net them a six-figure income yet leaves them ample time for tennis, biking, and walking along the rugged shore.

The Alinders take work on consignment from a variety of both unknown and very well-known artists and sell it for a commission ranging from 20 to 50 percent. Specializing in the works of Ansel Adams, the gallery also features shows built around social or political themes such as "War and Peace" or "Shoot the Earth" (with a camera). The proprietors are even flirting with the idea of expanding into nonphotographic art by showing the work of a sculptor.

Jim Alinder's background puts him in good stead to manage a photo art gallery. After receiving his Master of Fine Arts degree in photography, he taught photography and oversaw the photography museum at the University of Nebraska for ten years. A 1967 meeting with Ansel Adams began an association that eventually landed Jim a position as director of the Friends of Photography, an organization Adams had founded to promote American photographers.

Jim went to Carmel in 1978 to take on the new challenge, moving with his wife, Mary, and their three children to a house in Pebble Beach. Over the next four years, he built up the membership from 11,000 to 15,000. When Adams died in 1984, the organization's trustees decided to build a memorial to his life in San Francisco and appointed Jim to lead the effort. He spent the next year hustling public and private contributions to fund the museum, which was built in a downtown area undergoing urban renewal.

While working out of San Francisco, the Alinders made vacation junkets to the unspoiled coastal area up north around Sea Ranch. They liked the area enough to buy a small vacation house there.

Jim and Mary had been dreaming of having their own gallery ever since their Carmel days and had even made concrete plans to establish one there. Meanwhile, three other galleries had opened in Carmel, so they adapted the plan for Gualala and set out to look for a site. A former video rental shop with 1,200 square feet became available in 1988. The Alinders leased the building for five years and invested $40,000 from the sale of their Pebble Beach house into improvements. To collect enough work for the 1990 opening, they called artists they liked and arranged for loans from other galleries.

The Alinders promote the gallery through a quarterly newsletter mailed to past clients and through notices of coming shows mailed to all past and prospective clients. Items are priced up to $25,000, attracting a middle- or upper-income market. The location helps attract clients who are both open to photo art and capable of buying it.

Gualala, a road stop of 500 inhabitants, is the service town to Sea Ranch, an ecology-friendly development started in the 1960s. The 1200 houses are about evenly split among full-time residents, seasonal occupants (those who own second homes there), and owners who rent their homes out to vacationers for part of the year.

Vacationing executives who don't have the time to visit more impressive galleries in their own cities end up spending their free time visiting the gallery and buying art (it doesn't hurt that the nearest competition is 90 miles south in San Francisco).

The gallery is open 11 A.M. to 5:30 P.M., Thursday through Monday. Jim and Mary schedule their work hours to leave time for leisure and family, placing them among the fortunate group who have achieved a healthy balance between work they love and their lives.

Audiovisual Production in Central Texas

Unlike Jim Alinder, Jim Jones's focus is not image as art but image as business communication. Jones's one-man company, A/V Productions Communications & Marketing, Inc., produces audiovisual media dealing with marketing, employee training, and medical research for corporate clients.

Because Jim works out of an office in his home in Bryan, his business might fit more aptly in the previous chapter, which treated town-based businesses. But his office is in Bryan because it's where he wants to live. Jim has clients all across Central Texas. He travels to their turf for initial meetings to shape the product concept and then returns home to complete the project. After writing the script, he subcontracts the actual filming and sound recording to local specialty studios.

Jim's background in communications serves him well for his audiovisual production business. After earning a degree in journalism in 1967, he worked for and later became director of communications for the National Association of Evangelicals in Chicago. Not wanting to raise his children in Chicago, he moved back to his native Texas in 1972 to work in mass media communications at Texas A&M University. By 1983 he was ready to turn his broad background in print journalism, radio, and television to his advantage in forming a business of his own.

After trying his luck at a variety of business start-ups, Jim noticed opportunities opening in the quickly developing field of electronic communications media, in particular slide shows and video films. Having made some training films on plant safety for Alcoa Aluminum planted a seed that grew into his present business. Alcoa, he realized, was one of several corporations in the region that saw the potential of audiovisual media but had no means of producing films in-house.

Three other a/v firms, all one-person operations, are located in the Bryan–College Station area. Jim's approach to competitors is somewhat unorthodox. "We don't try to compete down here," he explains. "We find out who is in the business, then try to work together so each is working in a special niche." Two specialize in weddings; one does specialty video.

Jim started the business in 1983 with $20,000, which bought a computer system and off-line VCR editing equipment. He estimates that equipping an operation to handle the production work he subcontracts would cost at least $200,000 today. Because demand for his services fluctuates, he keeps his financial risk to a minimum by investing only in equipment necessary for operations.

Jim reaps some promotion value from attaching his name to the credits that appear on each of his films. Most of his promotion, though, is by word of mouth. The best way to hook industrial clients, he says, is to find a friend on the inside who can introduce you to them.

His yearly earnings have ranged between "poverty level" to well into the six-figure bracket; the overall trend is positive. Video technology changes constantly—witness the move from analog-based production systems to digital systems and the merging of personal computer technology with video for interactive learning. But Jim is quick to concede that his market hinges on how his corporate clients opt to handle their communications in the future.

Fearing that the region contains too few industries to support an audiovisual production business on the level he aspires to, Jim is looking to extend his services to more distant clients. Though this will mean more travel, he believes that with the aid of a laptop computer he'll be able to adapt.

Nannies and Sprouts in Southwest Montana

"If you told me ten years ago that I would be placing nannies when I was 48, I would have said you were crazy!" But that is exactly what Karen Ryan has been doing since 1984. Being a new mother, she needed a business she could manage from her home in southwest Montana, one that didn't depend on the depressed local economy. A nanny referral service met both requirements.

Karen's Heartland Nannies recruits candidates through ads placed in local newspapers and those of the neighboring states of Idaho, Washington, North Dakota, and South Dakota. Successful candidates—women 18 or older who know how to care for young children and want the experience of living away from home—wind up serving families in cities on the East Coast.

In or near each town where ads are placed, an associate interviews candidates and sees to contractual and logistical arrangements. Each candidate receives a 75-page "nanny handbook" that spells out the details of the one-year minimum contract.

The client family, meanwhile, applies for a nanny by filling out an application and paying a deposit. The application helps weed out high-risk clients and ensure the best fit between client and nanny. After screening their applications, Karen mails clients their nanny's biographical data. Clients sign and send Karen the finding fee and air fare for the nanny.

If the nanny doesn't work out, she may leave and return home. If she can't return home for some reason, she can take temporary refuge in one of four designated safe houses.

Until recently, clients heard about Heartland Nannies through word of mouth. But the business is now listed in an annual directory published by the International Nanny Association of Arlington, Texas, which Karen recently joined. As a member of this trade association, Karen can also even out the peaks and valleys inherent in the business. If, for example, she has 20 nannies chomping at the bit and only five client families waiting, she can fax the files of nannies to another agency, which places them and kicks back half of the placement fee.

A referral service with a potentially nationwide market exploits the current state of electronic communications to the limit but requires little in the way of start-up capital. Karen has invested around $35,000 so far, but not all at one time. Nanny franchises, now available in the United States, provide an alternate route into the business.

Karen operates her service from an office in her home in Missoula, Montana. Low overhead and well-heeled East Coast clients help insulate the business from ups and downs in the economy. She hopes to increase her yearly net income from around $20,000 to more than $30,000. "After going through my mid-life crisis," she explains, "I decided this is what I will do until I retire. . . . I like working for myself so much I have to make it work."

By the time Karen discovered nannies, she had already started another home-based business—this one centering around sprouts. She grew them in glass jars in the kitchen and sold them to area restaurants. What started small eventually became too much for Karen to manage. Her second husband, a rancher, took over and expanded the business. He started by moving the sprouts out of the kitchen into the dairy cooler section of a semi-trailer that he bought and converted into a sprout farm. After cutting one corner out for a window and adding grow lights and a heater, the conditions were just right for the sprouts to germinate.

Sprouting itself requires little effort. The tedious, labor-intensive part is packaging and distribution. The Ryans sell to several local customers, which include restaurants, warehouses, and grocery stores in southwest Montana, but they would prefer to simplify by selling to one or two wholesalers.

The sprout enterprise that started with little more than a few bottles in the kitchen now nets around $12,000 a year, with potential for further growth. Karen reports that area restaurants are replacing iceberg lettuce with sprouts in sandwiches and salads. "Even your basic redneck gets more aware of his health [when] he goes to the doctor and finds out his cholesterol is sky high," she observes.

Corporate Consulting among the Blue Jays

"I'm looking out my window right now at a family of blue jays . . ." interjected Gil Gordon at one point in my first interview. This comment underscored the possibilities opened by telecommuting, the field Gordon has helped pioneer.

Telecommuting as a concept dates from the 1960s but remained obscure until Alvin Toffler attracted attention to "the electronic cottage" in his book, *The Third Wave*.[2] It wasn't until the 1980s that companies started to put telecommuting into practice.

Gil Gordon spotted the potential while employed as a human resources manager at Johnson & Johnson, the healthcare products giant. As he became more fascinated with telecommuting, he grew increasingly disenchanted with his corporate career track. He itched to spring loose and do something with this new concept, but former colleagues advised him not to put all of his eggs in one basket—particularly in one so fragile.

Gil heeded their advice when he began his consulting business in 1982. To keep start-up costs and overhead down, he worked out of an office in his home. To generate a steady income, he spent about half of his time consulting for companies on standard personnel matters such as management training. The rest of his time was devoted to learning all he could about telecommuting.

Because advances in computer technology were what enabled telecommuting to beome a reality, its first experts were naturally technocrats. This was not right, as Gil saw it. People aren't machines; the human element was missing. The ideal telecommuting expert would be someone who understood both the technical and behavioral aspects. Gil's years spent working for Johnson & Johnson as a human resources manager gave him plenty of experience in dealing with people. After tooling up in computer technology, he put the two skills together to create a niche for his consulting service.

Today, Gil Gordon Associates has a respectable list of clients for its telecommuting and personnel consulting, which includes corporations such as Sears, Monsanto, AT&T; the states of California and Washington; and companies in New Zealand, Belgium, Japan, and Finland. Gil travels to each new client at the project's outset and then handles subsequent dealings via phone or fax from his headquarters in central New Jersey.

When he bought his present home in 1976, Gil expected to be transferred within a few years. He wasn't and grew to like the area. "The irony is that I can drive ten minutes in one direction to be in beautiful farmland and ten minutes in another direction to be in a Route 128 [Boston] setting." The last undeveloped area in New Jersey between Philadelphia and New York City, the site is one hour away from either city. Gil flies out of Newark airport to meet with the 80 percent of his clients out of reach by automobile. He does not envy his many neighbors who have to commute daily to New York, which takes at least an hour each way by bus or train.

Gil works about 45 to 50 hours per week. He spends his time off "wrapped up in typical suburban things like soccer practice for the kids, household chores and an occasional game of golf." Gil and his wife, a part-time teacher, have a ten-year-old girl and a thirteen-year-old boy.

In addition to helping corporate clients with telecommuting, he also promotes the concept in a monthly newsletter, *Telecommuting Review*, which he publishes for 150 subscribers for an annual subscription price of $157. Although the newsletter brings in some business, a larger portion comes from word of mouth and his presenting conferences and seminars on telecommuting.

Two years ago, the business turned profitable as measured by his standard, which for Gil means making as much money as he would have as a corporate employee. Like many self-employed people, he values the benefits of running his own enterprise from where he chooses as much as the monetary rewards.

Telecommuting from the Green Mountains

Telecommuting was an untried idea at AT&T's Bell Laboratories in 1989 when Donna Cunningham, a media relations manager, faced leaving her job near Newark to join her new husband, Bruce, in northern Vermont. Bruce, an engineer at the IBM facility in Essex Junction, was willing to leave his position of 17 years, but Donna didn't feel she could ask him to. At first she looked into working out of a branch of the company closer to her new home. The nearest office was in Andover, Massachusetts, which would still mean a five-hour commute. Resigned to the prospect of leaving, Donna explained to her boss, "Bell Labs is the best place I have ever worked, but Bruce is more important." Her supervisor showed understanding by saying, "Well, you certainly have your priorities straight, but we don't want to lose you," and then surprised Donna by suggesting a third choice: "We are going to have to find a way that you can take your job with you."

Bell Labs's history of flexible work arrangements had paved the way for telecommuting. Employees who wanted to work part-time "off site" and whose jobs allowed it could arrange to work part of the week out of their homes. Even before she left her home in New Jersey, Donna would frequently fire off a memo to the office via her home computer modem before or after work hours. Her move to a site more than 250 miles to the north required little more in the way of equipment.

Donna's employer had state-of-the-art communications equipment installed in an office in the new home the couple built. Perched on a site near the edge of a cliff, the house overlooked 11 acres of wooded property. Ever since her childhood in a Detroit suburb, Donna had always lived in or near a city. She still likes to visit cities but gets her fill once or twice a month when she travels to headquarters to attend conferences or show reporters around the labs.

After three years of telecommuting, Donna is upbeat about the arrangement. "One of the things I discovered is that it really makes me more productive. I'm a hard-working person . . . and I was spending time going to and coming from [work] that I now spend getting some work done."

Her occasional trips to headquarters often come on short notice. On the Friday I spoke with her, she said, "I may get a call today from the *Wall Street Journal.* I'll say, 'Okay, how about Monday?' " If that happens, on Monday she will make the 20-minute trip to Burlington International Airport and board an hour-long direct flight to Newark.

The new work arrangement was not without tradeoffs, however. Although telecommuting didn't affect Donna's salary negatively, it did stem her upward mobility. "I'm a third-level manager now—a nonsupervisory supervisor." But on the whole, the move was worth its drawbacks. Her work is now undisturbed by the usual interruptions of a busy office.

The rural Vermont lifestyle brings its own perks, such as the time she and Bruce were seated on a meadow hillside watching an open-air Mozart festival when a cow sauntered across in front of the set. As Donna sums up her new lifestyle: "It is so quiet and peaceful, you can sleep like a baby. . . . I also like being able to look up beyond the treetops and see more stars than I have ever seen in my life."

Small Press Spin-Offs on Lake Iroquois

Not too far from Donna Cunningham's Vermont paradise, Steve and Lisa Carlson also live life close to nature in the house they built in a converted summer camp. Their business, Upper Access, Inc., derives from their address on the Upper Access Road to Lake Iroquois, southeast of Burlington, Vermont. But the name also clues what the business is about—access.

Steve and Lisa had both written books in 1987 and were seeking access to a publisher, an obstacle for any first-time author. Rather than pay a subsidy press to publish their work, they became publishers themselves, with Lisa's book as the pilot effort. "We figured that if we entered the field of publishing, let's make our mistakes with one of our books," says Steve.

Caring for Your Own Dead,[3] explains how to handle funeral arrangements without the help of a funeral director. It has sold around 9,000 copies to date, which is not bad by small press standards. Steve's book, *Your Low-Tax Dream House*,[4] their second venture, also did well, selling 8,000 copies by the time of its second printing. Then it caught the attention of a major New York publisher, Avon Books, who bought the rights to publish it as *The Best Home for Less*.[5]

Four other books, all by outside authors, have been published since 1987. Their titles bespeak the New Age thread that runs through each: *Herbs of the Earth*,[6] *Letters from the Other Side*[7] (about channeling), *Cheap Eating*,[8] and *Death Notification*.[9]

After Lisa's book about death, Steve was reluctant to publish another book on the same topic, but he now thinks it could turn into a best-seller and become a basic reference for professionals who have to notify families of death.

Just as lack of access to a publisher attracted Steve and Lisa to publishing, lack of another kind of access was the seed that grew into a mail-order catalog business. Lisa's book won her guest appearances on "Donahue," "CBS This Morning," and "Good Morning America" as well as a write-up in the *New York Times*. The nationwide publicity would have been a godsend except for one thing: customers couldn't buy the book in their local book stores. Steve and Lisa, surmising (correctly) that they weren't the only small press publisher in this bind, established Upper Access, Inc., a mail-order fulfillment service for small presses.

When their clients advertise a new title through press releases or broadcast media, the Upper Access's 800 number is included in the information. Steve says he is addressing a genuine need of the thousands of small press publishers. Books stocked are listed in an annual catalog, *Big Books from Small Presses*, currently sent to 32,000 recipients.

Yet another business got its start through an unmet need for access. "When we started expanding, we needed a good computer program and found that the only good one on the market was $9000," explained Steve. "So we designed a $500 off-the-shelf program called *The Publisher's Invoice and Information Generating System (PIIGS)*." Out just over a year, the software has attracted 130 users.

Keeping up with a growing business requires Steve, 47, and Lisa, 52, to work long hours. But Steve says the rewards are greater than any he ever reaped working for others. In his prior job as chief legislative assistant to Vermont's congressional representative Jim Jeffords (now a U.S. senator), he earned a good salary but still got into a financial crunch. The long commute between his home in suburban Herndon, Virginia, and Washington—1-½ hours at rush hour—added to his discontent. Each time he came back to Vermont in the course of his work, he felt he was coming home. "It was very clear to me that this was a better place to raise a family and keep sanity in the household," he explains.

Steve and Lisa have built their business on a pay-as-you-go basis through earnings from remodeling houses and part-time outside editing and teaching. Their rural location is ideal for keeping overhead low. Their business began in the house and then moved into one of the former summer camp's cottages. When warehousing needs overtook their garage, they built a new one for $13 per square foot, about what they would pay for rent alone in a city, says Steve.

The low-tech trappings often seem to visitors out of sync with the high-tech underpinnings of the business. Because the office has no plumbing, the first person there each morning carries in jugs of water. After grabbing the faxes that have come in during the night, he takes them to the outhouse to read.

Books are not the best choice for a new business if your main goal is an easy path to wealth, says Steve. "The CEO at Simon and Schuster makes a magnificent salary by my standards," he notes, "but a paltry one compared to the pay for comparable positions in other fields. People get into the book business because they love books."

Steve hopes the business will net enough this year to support his family of four without having to work part-time outside. He expects the mail-order branch to provide the biggest area of growth in the near future but wants to press forward with publishing as well. If they hit on a best seller—the dream of every publisher—their financial worries will be over. In the meantime, his advice is "Create a product you know there's a demand for, and if you do it right, you know you can make money off of it."

Freelance Writing in the Shadow of Mt. Monadnock

Rural areas have long been the location of choice for many writers. But in the past, only novelists and essayists—writers who didn't need to be close to their sources or markets—could get away with it. Today, with sources as close as a computer or telephone and markets as close as the nearest overnight shipping service, many other kinds of writers can live where they choose.

Many writers, among them Ken Burns, P.J. O'Rourke, and Joyce Maynard, choose my neck of the woods, the part of southwest New Hampshire known as the Monadnock Region after its focal point, the 3165-foot-high mountain of the same name.

Though unquestionably rural in character, the region conceals unexpected types of business activity, such as magazine publishing. The village of Dublin is the home of *Yankee* magazine. Five miles down the road in Peterborough several special-interest magazines are based. This concentration of magazine publishing and the region's proximity to Boston, 85 miles to the southeast, likely explains the number of writers who live and work there. I'd like to describe three who are carving out niches for themselves as freelancers, each in a different mode.

Carol Conragen fled the Boston area for the peace and quiet of the Monadnock Region, hoping to pick up enough freelance work doing posters, ad copywriting, proofreading, and editing, to support her real interest: writing a book about her sojourn among the warring factions of southern Myanmar, formerly Burma.

Carol got intrigued by the strife in Myanmar while working as a freelance writer in Osaka, Japan, where she had gone in 1987 to write English advertising copy for a local company. Two and a half years as a copywriter, first as an employee and later as freelancer, snuffed out her zeal for writing to promote consumerism among the Japanese.

While on vacation in Bangkok, Thailand, she heard about the plight of Myanmar's ethnic minorities in their struggle against an oppressive regime. The chance to be one of the few Westerners—maybe the only one— to witness and chronicle this struggle firsthand was too enticing to pass up. Carol returned to Bangkok the following February to get the story and spent the next six months among the soldiers fighting for the oppressed Karen people, recording what she saw and sending periodic reports out to UPI.

When she returned to the United States, Carol planned to turn her journal into a book while studying law at Boston's Suffolk University. Two weeks before school started, she had a change of heart. While walking in Boston, she was verbally assaulted by a stranger. It rekindled a dread of big city life that had intensified while she was living like a sardine in Osaka. "I just loathed being in the city. I would have to commute every day on train from Somerville [to Boston] . . . the thought of a daily train ride, after every day in Japan, was debilitating."

Instead, she took the advice of a friend who lives in Keene, New Hampshire, and came to the Monadnock Region to write her book. Today she is establishing a network of clients for her freelance writing, hoping in this way to support the project. "I'm happier than I have been in years," she says, "and I don't even know how I will pay rent, month to month, but I'll find a way."

Bruce Hammond, 17 miles down the road from Carol in Peterborough, has found his way: cartooning. This is an offbeat form of freelance writing that pays handsomely for the few at the top, such as Charles Schulz (*Peanuts*) and Jim Davis (*Garfield*), who earn millions, according to Bruce. His own strip, *Duffy*, plus a regular stream of business editorial cartoons, net him far less but still within six figures.

Bruce Hammond concocts his daily episode of *Duffy* and his editorial cartoons in a studio in his home. *Duffy* is syndicated in more than 100 newspapers, whereas the editorial cartoons appear in business supplements published by the *Boston Globe*. It takes Bruce about an hour and a half on Monday morning to script a week's worth of the strip. After another 12 hours or so doing the art, he packs it off to the syndicate by express mail.

Bruce got into cartooning through the back door. A native New Yorker, he expected to be drafted to Vietnam when he graduated from college with a degree in Classical Greek in 1968. He then came to the Monadnock Region, where his parents had recently bought a home, to await the inevitable call. When it came, he was rejected. He started working in the area, first as a machine operator in a ball bearing plant and then selling greeting card designs, which led to a position in the art department at a small ad agency in Keene. When that company folded, he bluffed his way into a position as book designer for *Yankee* magazine's book publishing division. One day the editor asked him whether he knew anything about book design. Bruce replied, "Of course." He now confesses that "the only thing I knew about books is that they had pages in them."

When the publisher added a regional business magazine to its portfolio, Bruce became its art director and quickly rose in the ranks to become managing editor. He persuaded the publisher to move the operation to Boston in 1978 to have a better chance for success than in rural Dublin. After becoming general manager, he improved cash flow over the next two years.

But as the magazine was succeeding, Bruce's satisfaction declined. He sensed he was doing something for which he had no interest and felt out of character marching off to work in a three-piece suit. With both job and marriage getting sour in 1980, he left Boston and returned to the Monadnock Region—without employment.

Cartooning had always fascinated Bruce, but he could never imagine it as a serious career: "I felt that when you are grown up, you should have a grown-up job." But with his props kicked loose, he was ready to explore a new direction. He decided to try freelance cartooning for one year. It was a lean year, but he managed to sell some editorial cartoons to business magazines, including *Barron's.*

Through editorial cartooning, Bruce developed a cordial relationship with an editor at Universal Press Syndicate, who hinted that the syndicate might be interested in a comic strip about the office workplace and asked Bruce if he would consider such a project. Bruce jumped at the chance. Launched as *White Collars,* the strip charted the daily travails of an over-weight, middle-aged executive, Arthur Duffy, as he bumbled his way among characters familiar to anyone who has ever worked in an office. Every white-collar worker has had to deal with people like Miles, the in-house bootlicker and backstabber, forever begging the approval of his colleagues for his latest sleazy scheme.

Now in its tenth year, *Duffy* is already well past the usual three- or four-year life span of cartoon strips and a proper candidate for retirement, suspects Bruce.

The market for cartoons, never great, has dwindled even more in recent years with the demise of many of the nation's local newspapers and trends away from cartoons in magazines and books. But Bruce thinks that cartoons are here to stay; if you are good, you will always find a market. "Humor has been around since humankind," he observes. "When a cave man got stepped on by a wooly mammoth, there was some guy laughing his ass off saying, 'Did you see what just happened to Og?' "

Another writer, Don Best, plies his craft in the small village of Surry, which would look quite at home in a Curier and Ives print. Articles for home magazines have supported him and his family since he struck off on his own in 1986, enabling him to spend a good part of four years writing a novel. Do-it-yourself articles he wrote also led to a book contract on home plumbing and heating systems.

Don, 42, has been writing since obtaining a B.A. in journalism from the University of Oklahoma in 1971. Following a tour of duty as a Peace Corps Volunteer in Paraguay, he joined the editorial department of a newspaper in Brazil and later spun off a weekly tabloid on data processing. A succession of newspaper jobs after returning to the United States led to employment in 1981 at SolarVision, Inc., a small publishing company situated in the renovated mill buildings of the historic village, Harrisville. Don was business editor of *Solar Age* and editor of an industry newsletter, the *Solar Industry Bulletin.*

But the renewable-energy fervor that propelled these publications had already started to recede by 1981, when Ronald Reagan began sys-tematically gutting the energy policies of the Carter administration. Sensing the winds of change, Don left to establish himself as a freelancer.

He left with a solid reputation as a writer on building energy topics and a network of contacts. With savings sufficient for a year's worth of living expenses set aside, his only debt was the mortgage on the home he bought at an advantageous price during the 1981 recession.

A low cost of living, not high income, has been the key to Don Best's survival as a freelance writer since 1985. Savings come from sources many people don't often think about. With commuting distance pared down to 60 feet, car expenses drop. Similar savings accrue from a simple working wardrobe—jeans and sweatshirt.

Don, his wife, and two sons, live in a modest (but by no means impoverished) life in their picturesque Monadnock Region homestead. "Let's face it," he observes, "writing isn't on a level with brain surgery, in terms of income. It's the intangible rewards that make it worthwhile. What is fresh air, clean water, six acres of living trees, and not having to lock your house worth?" Other nonfinancial perks include the freedom to work at his own schedule and take the two boys for spontaneous swims in the nearby Surry reservoir in the summer.

Don Best looks back on his writing career as a succession of forward steps, each of which led to the next. His goals for the future relate more to work than money. His present nonfiction work, he hopes, will allow him to move into fiction writing. His first novel, recently submitted to a publisher for review, will mark his entry into that world. Don admits that freelance writing is a risky business; "After March, I have no idea where my next job is coming from, but it's been that way for five years. My brother, who works for Occidental Petroleum, lives under the axe all of the time too."

Breaking or Lengthening the Chain

The people profiled in this chapter show that it's possible to live where you want while operating a business that doesn't depend on the local market. Achieving this enviable state isn't without struggles and trade-offs, though. Every business is chained to something or another, be it to its inputs (supplies, resources, and services) or outputs (markets and clients).

With imagination, you can stretch those chains. Through telecommuting, Donna Cunningham stretched her chain all the way from her corporate workplace near Newark to her home in northern Vermont. Gil Gordon's corporate consulting and Jim Jones's audiovisual production businesses feel the tug of similar chains when they occasionally have to travel to reach clients on their own turf. They rely on state-of-the-art communications technology to stretch the chain the rest of the time.

A Place for You in In-Between Land

Each of the people in this chapter have found ways to use the fruits of modern technology to enable them to live and work where they choose.

From her home in Missoula, Montana, Karen Ryan was able to find nannies in one part of the country and match them with clients in another part, thanks to instant communications and rapid transportation. Jim Alinder's art gallery depends on the large number of businesspeople traveling to or from San Francisco on business trips who may lack the time to visit galleries back home.

Americans are expected to continue moving out and away from urban settings in the foreseeable future. Change creates opportunity, if you know where to look. Here are some areas to keep an eye on in the future when looking for business opportunities in the in-between regions.

The Workplace

The corporate scramble caused by the recession that began in 1990 took a heavy toll on mid-level white-collar professionals, a trend that the authors of *Workplace 2000*[10] believe will continue. Companies of the future will be flatter and leaner, with fewer layers of management, supervision, and support. Downsizing will displace professionals who will start specialized microbusinesses of their own.

Without the in-house capabilities of the past, corporations will fill needs for many kinds of specialized services as they arise by hiring outside contractors. Who are these contractors? People like Gil Gordon, freelance consultants who cultivate expertise in specialized areas that corporations need, such as sales promotion, marketing, advertising, and direct mail. As an outside provider, you will have to make some personal contact, but you'll also enjoy great freedom to live and work where you want.

High-Tech Information Services

The information revolution of the 1980s is becoming an information over-load in the 1990s. To deal with the glut, more systems will be required to assimilate, store, and manage the ever-increasing flow. The U.S. De-partment of Commerce expects this trend to continue, underpinned by continued development of high-tech equipment. Demand for electronic information services is expected to increase at a high rate through the mid-1990s. Data processing and computer services will grow to become necessities rather than luxuries.

The DOC expects growth in the following sectors: telecommunica-tions and information gateway services, code and protocol processing and conversion, electronic mail services, electronic data interchange, voice mail services, audiotex services, enhanced fax, alarm/security services, utility and environmental monitoring, transaction and credit validation services, electronic funds transfer, on-line database access, information retrieval servicers, videotex, telecommunication network management, remote computer monitoring services, and electronic software distribution.

How many of the above enterprises could you manage out of a suitably equipped home office somewhere in the boonies? Most, probably.

Writing

As mavens argue whether high-tech, electronically transmitted information will eventually displace hard-copy media, people continue to buy books and magazines in record numbers. Will they ever produce an electronic alternative you can buy as cheaply as a paperback? one that you can stuff in your back pocket without fear of impairing the information output? one that you can read on the toilet? throw away, or keep indefinitely?

Between 1977 and 1988, new book titles and editions published in the United States increased 26 percent, whereas the population grew but 9 percent. Forget the scare stories you hear about the death of reading. One in five American adults buys at least one book a week, according to *Megatrends 2000*.[11] As the number of middle-aged and elderly people grows, so will the natural market for books and magazines.

Future demand will be for fiction and nonfiction alike. The rise of English as the undisputed international language is sure to open other doors (how many people do you know who speak Esperanto?). Texts from hundreds of other languages will need to be rendered into English. Native speakers/writers of English with a knowledge of other languages are the best candidates for this work. Technology itself begets a need for writing, and the ablest communicators won't be likely to come from the ranks of the technocrats. How many times have you wanted to strangle the writer who composed the instruction manual for your computer?

Finding a profitable niche in freelance writing is not easy, as shown by the experiences of the writers profiled in this chapter, but it is possible. And, like a book, the occupation is portable. Freelance writers are an opinionated lot as a rule; it comes with the craft. But all agree on one thing: The freedom to work for yourself where and when you want to is as important as the actual money earned.

Desktop Publishing

Desktop publishing is what happens after a document is conceived but before it is printed. The effort usually includes writing and editing the document and then compositing (typesetting) page layout, artwork, and tables in a camera-ready form for the printer. Almost any entrepreneur can afford the equipment: a personal computer with specialized software and a laser printer.

Specialized newsletters are the main product of independent desktop publishers. They bring subscriptions of around $100 to $300 a year. There are at least 60 newsletters that track mutual funds alone. One of these, *Mutual Fund Forecaster*, has a circulation of around 200,000.

To succeed at desktop publishing, you'll need to spot an unmet need by a large group for a specialized type of information and then produce a newsletter or report that regularly delivers the information. This sounds easier than it is in an age saturated with information, much of which ends up in the wastebasket. After spotting the need you aim to fill, you will have to collect information through databases, governmental sources, journalistic media, seminars and workshops, libraries, and whatever other sources you can discover. Then comes customizing the raw data for the specific market, producing the masters, getting your product printed, and mailing it out.

As corporations shrink their in-house capabilities, a growing market for information delivered by desktop publishers has formed. To target this market, however, you should know your way around marketing, advertising, and promotion. Other skills you or your collaborators should have, whatever your market, are graphic design, writing and editing, and the ability to coordinate the production of documents through the printing phase.

Telecommunications

As electronic communication equipment grows in diversity and network access expands, so will opportunities for commercially exploiting them. Today you can access information networks anywhere with a computer and a phone. Tomorrow you may not even need a phone. Satellite technology is making it possible to send a message worldwide with nothing more than a minitransceiver.

Software writers and engineers, stock-and-bond brokers, transcribers, translators, artists, composers, and writers are some of the city-bound professionals who will be increasingly free to work wherever they choose to live by exploiting state-of-the-art telecommunications advances.

Minibreweries

The vocabulary spawned by the information age boggles the mind. Telecommunications and information gateway services, code and protocol processing and conversion, electronic data interchange, audiotex and videotex—such words can swiftly induce a headache. The thought of a tall, foamy mug of beer is a pleasant contrast.

Author Gerald Celente forecasts flat demand for the brewing industry overall but holds high hopes for small breweries that make premium beers for regional markets. The number of small breweries should grow to around 200 by the mid-1990s. Celente expects the market for light beer to shrink because the product is neither a beer nor a health drink.[12]

Education and Training

Expanding technology and the rapidly changing national economy have combined to create a need for massive retraining, thus spawning a market for audiovisual materials produced by entrepreneurs such as Jim Jones. Both public and corporate clients will require training/educational materials, presentation media, presenters/teachers, and seminar and workshop development. Many of the products and services in this field can be managed away from an urban location.

Howard L. Shenson, in *How to Develop & Promote Successful Seminars & Workshops*, states that the adult education business—seminars, workshops, classes, and conferences—is one of the fastest-growing industries in the country.[13] Although a third of today's adults have enrolled in a seminar of some sort, 80 percent of the nation's adults will have done so by 2010.

Mail Order

Catalog shopping started early in the twentieth century to provide rural people access to the consumer goods made in the cities. Sears Roebuck and Montgomery Ward sold everything from shoes to refrigerators—all by mail. Though many outlanders found a worthy secondary use for the soft pages therein, they bought enough products to keep the catalogs coming.

Present-day mail-order successes such as L.L. Bean and Lands' End have found niches by offering trendy clothing to baby boomers who don't have enough time to shop the malls. Mail-order trade, a natural for high-tech communications and well-developed delivery networks, now includes thousands of smaller, lesser known entrepreneurs, many of which don't even stock the goods they sell. The $35 billion industry is growing at the rate of 8 to 10 percent each year (double that of retail stores) according to David Heenan in *The New Corporate Frontier* and now includes over 10,000 catalogers.[14]

Mail-order catalogs are perfectly suited to production in ex-urban locations, as witnessed by Steve and Lisa Carlson's *Big Books from Small Presses*.

Environment

Even if the United States suddenly halted the operations of polluting industries—which is hardly likely—the legacy of past sins remains to be dealt with. As baby boomers become senior citizens, their sensitivity to the health effects of airborne particulates will skyrocket, creating a demand for solutions to the problem and opportunities for those qualified and ready to take up the challenge. Expect to see steady demand for environmental consultants, compliance experts, and testing services.

There are, of course, many other fertile areas in in-between land awaiting people with the right combination of vision and ability. The few mentioned here were not intended as a complete rundown, but some I hope will spark your imagination. In Chapter 6 we'll visit some of the folks blazing trails in the real outland.

Chapter Six

Way Out

For the first time in 200 years, more people are moving to rural than to urban areas, lured by lower crime rates and housing costs, better recreational opportunities, and a return to community values, according to the authors of *Megatrends 2000.*[1] Because of this migration, unspoiled rural land is disappearing. It still exists, but you have to go farther out to find it. The good news for people looking for a way to work and live "out there" is that relocating to even the most remote places does not always mean breaking connection with the outside world, as it once did.

Maintaining necessary links to the urban world does not keep the rural entrepreneurs whom you'll meet in the following pages from finding the right fit between their occupation, desired lifestyle, and location of choice.

For some, the fit is as much one of spirit as practicality. When Ron and Dorothy Weber set out to farm in a remote western valley, they were driven as much by the peace and beauty of the setting as the need for a locale suitable for agriculture. Jim and Pat Lee's Vermont country inn and Dave and Alice Cadwell's restaurant near a covered bridge in Connecticut depend on a healthy number of tourists coming through their regions. But having met that condition, the owners get to live in the kind of place they would choose, tourists or not.

Cadwell's Corner

"We knew, innately, that we would succeed," said Alice Cadwell, recalling the quest she and her husband, Dave, had embarked upon in 1986: to turn a faded greasy spoon cafe in West Cornwall, Connecticut, into a tourist wayside. In spite of the rate of failure of new restaurants, Alice's optimism was not misplaced. Customers drive three or four hours to get to the restaurant, and it's not uncommon to see celebrities like Paul Newman wander in.

Alice, 38, and Dave, 41, originally aimed to open a gourmet specialty food store when they bought the place in 1986. But this would have meant enslaving Alice to the stove well into the wee hours of the morning to ensure that each day's offerings were ready. Also, they wondered whether there would be a demand for unusual food in the area. So during the months spent readying the building for the grand opening, they backed away from the original idea and chose to begin with a more standard restaurant that offered quality, if not elaborate, fare. "Let's not offer 5,000 things on the menu, but only a few things we know we can do well," said Alice.

Cadwell's Corner opened for breakfast and lunch with usual fare that transcended the ordinary through the addition of homemade breads, freshly ground gourmet coffee, and occasional Armenian specialties that Alice learned from her mother (her family fled from Armenia to Iran and immigrated to the United States when Alice was five). The 12-table restaurant serves a special Sunday brunch to a mix of local steadies and tourists during summer and fall, New England's leaf-peeping season.

The recipe works. The only other competition in West Cornwall is a more upscale dinner restaurant across the street. It complements, rather than competes, with Cadwell's Corner.

West Cornwall is situated on the Housatonic River in the picturesque northwest corner of Connecticut. Just yards from Cadwell's Corner is a 130-year-old covered bridge, which draws enough tourists to swell the town to around 1,400 in summer. After the last red leaf has fallen in October, the population shrinks back to 1,000 or so permanent residents, a mix of artists, craftspeople, and hippies.

The Cadwells started out together in southern California, and then moved to Orlando, Florida, where Dave joined the expanding coffee-retailing chain of a former college chum. The number of outlets in the chain grew from three to thirty-three during Dave's five-year stint as vice-president by siting new outlets in shopping malls.

After five years of helping build up someone else's business, Dave was eager for a change. "He never really cared for the suit and tie behind the desk," explained Alice. And Orlando was growing too rapidly for the kind of lifestyle Dave and Alice wanted for themselves and their new set of twins.

On a trip to upstate New York to check out an offer to work with a coffee retail business, Dave decided against the offer (it would have been too much like the job he had at the time) but fell in love with the region, particularly the area he had driven through surrounding Kent, Connecticut. He began to check out businesses for sale and eventually took Alice up for a look. A friend who taught in the school at West Cornwall, Connecticut, invited them to stop by. They did, and Alice was sold on the school—and the location.

Alice and the kids returned to Florida, and Dave went on to New York City for business—but via Cornwall, Connecticut. When Alice next saw Dave, he had two inches of materials from a real estate broker describing a restaurant property. Included with the deal were restaurant equipment and a 1600-square-feet apartment above the restaurant-to-be.

The apartment became their home, as befits the mom-and-pop model of the Cadwells's enterprise. Alice cooks; Dave serves and manages. One or two part-time employees lessen the load on weekends and during peak tourist season. This may change if Alice, who has a background in dance, lands a position teaching dance; this would open access to group health insurance, a substantial savings over the insurance currently available to them as a small partnership.

Insurance costs aside, the Cadwells have seen profits grow steadily, enough to put a little away for their retirement and college for the twins. To do so, they live frugally and get by with one car.

Where they don't cut corners is the quality of the restaurant, even at the risk of less profit. But as Alice points out, "I'm from a family where large portions were served and so I serve large portions so people will feel they have gotten their money's worth, and I haven't failed yet."

A Vermont Country Inn with a Side of Beefaloes

About 100 miles north of Cadwell's Corner lies a rural valley amid Vermont's Green Mountains. There Jim and Pat Lee operate a different kind of roadside attraction—a country inn. The enterprise is the embodiment of the hopes and dreams of a couple who sought a quieter, more fulfilling life after abandoning a long career tied to an urban-based corporate workplace.

Twenty-seven years with the same job was enough for Jim Lee. He yearned for more contact with people than he had as a manager for Monroe Calculators in Worcester, Massachusetts. When the Lees became empty nesters in 1980, they sensed the time was right for a change. The Vermont home and 250-acre farm that had belonged to Pat's recently deceased father went up for sale but failed to find a buyer. Jim and Pat bought nine acres (including the house) and set about to convert the two-story Colonial built in 1790 into an inn.

After a complete renovation, the interior contained five rentable rooms (six in summer) as well as living quarters for the owners. Open every month except April and May, the inn offers its guests relaxation and scenery in a postcard setting. The main building perches on a knoll overlooking a farm valley, with the Green Mountains in the distance. In summer, guests breathe in the fresh country air as they walk about on the network of trails, fish in a pond stocked with brook trout, or swim in the spring-fed pool. Wintertime guests can ski any of the several area resorts—Stratton Mountain, Bromley, Stowe, or Killington—or cross-country ski over the network of trails on the grounds surrounding the inn.

Breakfast is included in the price of the room. Dinners are extra and are offered on Tuesdays, Fridays, and Saturdays to guests only. Pat, who cooks the evening meal, keeps menus simple. One entree—usually grilled and occasionally beefalo from the inn's farm—provides the centerpiece, accompanied with salad, dessert, and wine. During the rest of the week, guests are on their own, with several quality local restaurants to choose from in the area.

Jim and Pat run the inn with help of two employees: one who cleans and one who serves as a grounds keeper. Workdays start around 6 A.M. and don't end until 10 P.M. during the ten months when they are open.

The Lees knew nothing about managing a country inn when they started out. They have had to learn by experience how to deal with the contingencies that beset all hospitality enterprises, such as the couple who shows up with a dog or baby in the car (neither are allowed) or guests who don't like their rooms.

Big city guests often arrive totally stressed out on Friday night. Jim begins decompressing them when he welcomes them at their car. On the way to their room, he talks about the beauty of the area and offers to show them around the place after they settle in. It works.

More than half of the Lees' guests are 45- to 60-year old residents of New York, New Jersey, and Massachusetts who have read about the inn in one of 20 books about country inns. The rest are repeat customers or referrals.

The Lees report a decent living, but they are not getting rich from the inn. The time and effort, although demanding when they are open for business, yields two and a half months of complete freedom each year, a perk enjoyed by few. During off hours, they ski on the cross-country trails or play tennis.

The inn might easily get lost among several other quality hostelries in Vermont's ski country were it not for the beefaloes roaming the grounds.

Cattle had roamed the property in times past. Jim had been eyeing ways to make full use of the lush pastures and hay fields when he was approached in 1981 by Joe Miles, who wanted to raise beefaloes, a cross between buffaloes and domestic cattle. Joe needed land, a place to live, and investors. Lee had the land and an unused farmhouse. Together they formed a corporation, bought ten head of breeding stock, and got into the beefalo business. The herd, now grown to 45, has been joined by 132 "feeders"—calves bought from other breeders to fatten and sell at market.

Jim Lee spends about two hours of his workday on administrative chores for Miles Beefalo, Inc., leaving the care of the livestock to his partner, Joe. The corporation sells all of its slaughter-weight livestock to a supermarket chain that retails the meat as a higher-protein, lower-fat alternative to beef. Although the chain buys all that the farm can produce, the money generated by beefalo sales hasn't yet reached a level exceeding the fixed costs of running the operation. Jim Lee expects that by continuing to acquire feeders, they will soon build a herd of a size capable of turning a profit. Meanwhile, the animals impart a certain interest and relaxed air to the inn.

Hatching Big Birds in New Jersey

Mathew and Deborah Loving already lived in the country before they started their business two years ago. But like many other baby boomers, their urban-based jobs prevented them from enjoying rural life to the fullest. The Lovings were Wall Street stockbrokers who spent an hour and 20 minutes each way commuting between work in Manhattan and their rural New Jersey home. Entertaining clients often meant arriving home only a few hours before starting the next day's cycle. Their schedule left little time for their two young children.

Then the Lovings heard about ostriches. Deborah first learned that ostrich breeding was a hot trend from overhearing investors' conversations. Impressed by the profit potential, she attended a seminar, and the couple decided to go for it in partnership with a friend and former realtor, Robert Cimarosa. The trio built pens and bought a breeding pair of ostriches from a Kansas City breeder for $37,500.

Deborah's seminar and a week that Cimarosa had spent watching ostriches being hatched in Oklahoma were the only knowledge the trio had of ostrich breeding. It wasn't enough. The first season was a disaster. Of 12 chicks hatched from 16 eggs, all died of bacterial infection.

Things improved in the second year, 1991. Seventeen pairs of chicks were sold, and orders were placed for the next spring's hatchings. The Lovings expect their net income soon to reach their former level of income as stockbrokers and to surpass it when they add a second breeding hen.

The Long Neck Ostrich Farm, now their primary business (they have some real estate investments), requires constant—but not full-time—attention. Birds have to be fed and watered daily; stalls have to be cleaned out. They have to take periodic cultures from the stools of hatchlings to monitor bacteria so that the appropriate antibiotic can be administered if necessary.

Why ostriches? Well, remember those garish women's hats of the 1900s? Producing them drove the demand for ostrich feathers high enough to almost wipe out the indigenous ostrich population in Africa. Today ostrich feathers find other uses, such as in the auto industry. They work well as a means of dusting cars off before the paint is applied. There's also

a steady commercial market for ostrich hide for boots, briefcases, and handbags because of its durability.

Then there's ostrich meat. Not eaten by the people indigenous to ostrich habitats, the meat is eaten in Scandinavia and catching on in Japan. The Lovings don't eat their own ostriches, but they have sampled several different ostrich recipes at a conference. Mathew describes the flavor as like beefsteak and the texture like poultry. High in protein and low in fat and cholesterol, ostrich meat seems destined to fill gaps in the U.S. market that are left as diet-conscious Americans continue to abandon beef, lamb, and pork. Mathew Loving believes it's just a matter of time—seven or eight years—until a domestic market develops for ostrich meat. Domestic ostrich breeders, now numbering 2000, are building up their stock for that day.

The ostrich industry began in 1986, when Texas cattle ranchers recognized that sanctions against South Africa would stem its ostrich exports and thus lead to an unfilled worldwide demand. The American Ostrich Association expects the country's present stock of 10,000 birds to multiply tenfold in the next decade.

Mathew Loving says you can start an ostrich farm with a breeding pair of birds and a fenced area of 70 feet by 200 feet (one for each adult pair to mate). With the onset of warm weather around March in New Jersey, mating begins and lasts throughout the warm months. Each pair produces 40 to 80 eggs within that time. Eggs are mechanically incubated. Adult birds tolerate the New Jersey winter, but enclosed pens are necessary to keep hatchlings warm and protect them from predators. The Lovings use heat lamps and heating pads.

The ostriches require the most attention during the first six months after hatching. After that, adult birds pretty well take care of themselves. Chores at the Long Neck Ostrich Farm are split among the three partners. With commuting to the city a thing of the past, the Lovings now live where they work and usually wear jeans. Always near their children, they now enjoy living on their three-and-a-half-acre farm in a part of New Jersey where the main signs of human enterprise are the white rail fences that surround the several horse farms.

Llama Breeding in Montana

Not all people warm up to 8-foot-tall birds that can't fly. That's fine. Ostriches are but one of several exotic animals that can be raised on a small scale that are attracting breeders in the United States. Llamas are another.

Back in 1926, media magnate William Randolph Hearst installed a bunch of llamas on his palatial seaside spread, San Simeon, presumably because he had everything else. But llamas otherwise escaped notice in the United States until the latter 1970s, when Oregon cattle ranchers Richard and Kay Paterson started breeding them and selling the offspring.

Recent laws that restrict llama importation have spurred domestic llama breeding. And these cousins of the camel are very easy to breed, according to Mike Lee, the owner of Storm King Ranch in Hamilton, Montana.

A former real estate developer of high-rise buildings in Houston, Mike fled the city 25 years ago, urged on by the thought of "three million people, six million cars and a lot of humidity." After two decades of ranching in Colorado, he settled on a ranch nestled among the foothills of Montana's Bitterroot Mountains.

About 11 years ago, Mike Lee bought a male llama and three pregnant females for pets. When the females bore young, he bought a few more and was in the llama business. Today some 180 llamas live on his 1,500-acre ranch.

Llamas, like camels, are all-purpose creatures. Dependable pack animals for Andes Indians, they also provide meat and wool. The llama count in the United States has grown from 3,200 in 1982 to 22,000 in 1991. Sold as pets and for their wool, llamas are also increasingly valued as pack animals. Mike observes that the U.S. Forest Service prefers them on trails in fragile areas because their soft feet do far less damage than horses' hooves.

Llamas even guard sheep on the Texas plains. A few mixed in with a flock of sheep keep coyotes at bay, claims Mike. As pets, he adds, llamas are intelligent, easy to train, calm, dignified and clean—so clean that some people actually bring them into their houses. Their maintenance requires only a backyard with a shady spot; cold is no problem, but heat and humidity are.

Domestic markets for llamas are growing. There is an increasing demand for gelded males for pack animals, guard animals, pets, and llama wool. Not as fine as wool from alpacas or vicuñas, llama wool is cleaner than sheep wool, which comes coated with lanolin. Mike Lee has even supplied llama wool to local fishermen, who use it to tie flies.

Mike finds buyers for his animals through ads in trade magazines and at national sales meets sponsored by the 1,596-member International Llama Association, based in Denver. Llama sales at Storm King Ranch gross around $500,000. Prices vary greatly for individual animals, usually ranging from $500 to $800 for a pet and $1,500 for a pack animal. Llamas of outstanding breeding stock fetch as high as $190,000. Mike ships his llamas to buyers all over the U.S.

Cattle are no longer raised on the Storm King Ranch, yet Mike's ranching experience and his degree in animal husbandry gave him a leg up when he branched into llama breeding. His advice to others contemplating the move is to ease into the business. Spend the first year or two as a passive investor with an established breeder to gain experience. Then start your own operation with a couple of acres of fenced land (most llama

ranches contain less than 100 acres) and some way to shelter the animals from the sun and strong wind.

Llamas, like cows, are ungulates with four stomachs. They graze except in winter, when they require a low-protein hay (grass). Daily upkeep requires little other than providing a fresh water source and food during the winter. A bale of hay lasts one animal three weeks. The annual cost for keeping each animal ranges between $150 and $300.

Mike manages Storm King Ranch with three ranch hands and two clerical helpers who also oversee the daily operations of Mike's other business, investment brokering.

Mike left an urban career for the more satisfying life of a cattle rancher. But where cattle were a means to an end—a commodity—llamas have attracted him in ways beyond their monetary value. As he puts it, "They are actually therapeutic; when you spend time around them, they make you feel good."

Retiring to a Fish Farm

Bill Hammond is another urban refugee who raises animals. Bill's quest for a postretirement enterprise in a rural setting led him to purchase a trout farm in the valleys of Montana's Bitteroot Range.

Bill was looking for a productive way to keep busy when he retired from his position as deputy sheriff in San Diego. After several pleasant summer vacations fishing in southwest Montana, he and his wife decided it was the right place for them. The trout farm that came with the house he bought in Hamilton seemed to fit the bill.

The Hammonds bought the three-bedroom house and 12.5-acre farm for $122,500. The trout farm consists of five 10,000-gallon metal tanks, which are 20 feet in diameter, and three ponds. A stream supplies a constant flow of fresh water to the tanks. Bill stocks the tanks with young fish he buys from a hatchery. The tanks presently contain 11,000 rainbow trout.

Mature trout are sold mostly to private landowners in the region who buy them to stock their ponds for fishing. The previous owner had declined offers from food stores to supply them with live fish (most commercially grown trout sold in the United States come from large trout farms in Idaho).

Trout farming requires relatively little in the way of facilities and effort, claims Bill, who learned everything he knows about raising fish out of a book and from talking to hatchery owners. Bill says ideal pond temperatures are between 70 degrees and freezing, though a layer of ice at the top won't harm the fish. A source of fresh water is needed for the tanks. Bill's daily care, for the most part, consists of distributing the prepared fish food four times a day.

In Montana, a commercial pond permit is required to ensure that the fish don't migrate into a stream or river. If you import eggs from out of state, a health department permit is also needed. Sales to food wholesalers may entail additional requirements, which may have discouraged the prior owner from entering this market.

Except for a customer list inherited from the prior owner and a listing in the local phone book's yellow pages, Bill foresees no other promotion for the time being. He prefers to keep the business low-key enough to allow him to hunt the deer, elk, ducks, and pheasant that abound in the area—and to fish in the Bitterroot River.

Weekend Farmers Building a Dream on the Western Plain

"Farming, like mountaineering, is a series of long huffing, puffing episodes rewarded with brief moments of euphoria." This is how Ron Weber sums up the struggle he shares with his wife, Dorothy, to breathe new life into an aging homestead in Ibapah, a tiny outpost in the Great Basin country of western Utah. The Webers knew farming wouldn't make them rich when they bought the 295-acre spread in 1980. The economics of farming, Ron says, put it in a different category from other start-up businesses. The cost of the land and equipment is so high, compared to the returns, that the only way to show a profit within a few years is to inherit the facilities, as is traditional with family farms. The Webers financed their farm through their own devices. They have since invested another $100,000 in improvements. Ron estimated the farm's 1991 value at $250,000.

Dog-eared in appearance, the "old Kemp place" was a diamond in the rough to the Webers. Surrounding the log house built in 1913 was a wash house, shop, bunkhouse, root cellar, small barn, and an assortment of used farm implements. The carcasses of 15 junked cars filled a nearby gully. The previous owner, a part-time miner, raised alfalfa and grain, horses, and 600 sheep—half of which lived on the front porch when the Webers bought the property, Ron speculates.

The farm perches on the eastern rim of a valley 20 miles wide and 30 miles long carpeted with desert sage and drought-tolerant native grasses. Snug against the backside of the farm are the Deep Creek Mountains, whose peaks reach 12,000 feet. The range's fragile ecosystem supports grazing of several thousand cattle. Grazing rights to the land are administered by the U.S. Bureau of Land Management (BLM). The Webers' share can support 28 cows with calves for a two-month period each year. They also hold water rights to two streams that flow from the heights of Deep Creek Range.

Besides the 100 or so members of the Goshutes tribe who live on the reservation in the south of the valley, Ibapah is home to another half-dozen ranches, each of which has 200 to 800 head of cattle. A general store, an elementary school, and a Mormon church mark the community's center.

Urban professionals turned farmers, Ron and Dorothy set about with fervor to resurrect the farm, but on a part-time basis. For a decade, the thought of spending the weekend at the farm carried Ron and Dorothy through each workweek at their professional jobs in Salt Lake City. Ron managed his own structural engineering firm; Dorothy was a healthcare administrator.

Like clockwork, the couple shed their pin-striped suits and donned jeans every Friday afternoon before trekking 90 miles across the Great Salt Lake Desert to the border gambling stop of Wendover, Nevada. Then they drove another 60 miles on a secondary road to reach the farm.

Because grain prices were favorable in the early 1980s, they made improvements necessary to raise wheat and a secondary crop of hay. After endless repairs to the existing above-ground steel irrigation system that brought water down out of the mountains, the Webers decided to take advantage of a grant assistance program offered by the U.S. Soil Conservation Service to install a new system. They buried a mile of plastic piping with takeoffs to feed a mobile irrigation system—a fieldwide pipe that snakes through the hub of spoked wheels at intervals. Sprinkler heads along the length of the pipe spray water on the soil. The ground was leveled to ensure its smooth passage along the length of the field.

The new irrigation system enabled expanding the land under cultivation from the initial 30 acres to 180 by 1985. To allow time to wrestle with the irrigation system and make other improvements, the Webers arranged with a neighbor farmer to provide the tilling, seeding, irrigating, harvesting, and trucking.

Crop yields have varied with the amount of land seeded each year. The gross sales from 30 acres of hard red wheat in the first year, 1981, amounted to $10,000. Twenty acres of alfalfa, already in place, were sold to neighboring ranchers for hay. By 1985, 180 acres of barley grossed around $32,000. With grain prices sagging in the last two years of the 1990s, the Webers did not put in a crop, opting instead to put the entire acreage into a federal set-aside program.

Ron estimates the farm's potential net earnings from grain and cattle at around $20,000 and says his first profit forecasts were too optimistic.

But assessing the farm's value to the couple solely on the basis of money misses the point. The real motivations for ten years of hard work and personal devotion are rooted in a shared dream that combines independent living with a love of the outdoors and the rural lifestyle.

Ron had always wanted to own a farm or ranch. While stationed with the army at Fort Huachuca, Arizona, the 19-year-old Wisconsin boy who knew nothing of ranching was impressed by an army buddy's concept of working for yourself. Ron decided he would one day have a ranch. After graduating with a degree in engineering in 1961, he came to Utah for the skiing and mountain climbing.

There he met Dorothy, a transplanted New Jerseyite, in 1975. Fresh out of college with a degree in sociology, Dorothy also came to Utah to ski after two years of being a "ski bum" in Aspen, Colorado. Salt Lake City was also near choice ski areas and afforded greater employment diversity than did Aspen.

The two married in 1978, when Dorothy was winding up work on her M.A. in social work at the University of Utah. Dorothy shared Ron's dream of breaking loose from the 50-hour-a-week city job and carving out a low-level means of subsistence in the country. Both were willing to sacrifice income for free time.

The farm is now developed to the point where it can bring in an income, but nowhere near the six figures the Webers currently earn from their primary professions in Salt Lake City. They plan to continue working at them but to scale back progressively to allow for more time at the farm. Ron recently trimmed his staff down from 6 employees to just himself and does most of his engineering work in an office he installed in a trailer at the farm.

Dorothy, meanwhile, continues working in Salt Lake City, living in the couple's home there during the week and in Ibapah on weekends. She plans to continue along these lines for a while and then establish a consulting practice of her own based at the farm.

Both want to increase the farm's productive capacity, but they don't share a clear vision of the future. Now that the pasture is irrigated, Ron plans to add some cows and convert more acreage to grasses for grazing. Dorothy favors nontraditional commodities, such as chemical-free beef cattle and drought-tolerant experimental crops such as garlic and amaranth. Amaranth grain is increasingly popular at natural foods stores, and its high-protein leaves make good cattle feed. Ron wouldn't mind taking this direction, but only if it has a solid market potential.

The Webers know that investing their money in the 1980s stock market would have yielded a richer financial return and an easier life, but with each year the farm becomes more productive. And nothing else matches the quiet, simple, yet intense moments of pleasure they have enjoyed in the serenity of the sagebrush.

Rural Alternatives

A preference for the smell of sage over the smell of traffic is what unites the people profiled in this chapter. Yet they differ in many ways. Some, such as ostrich breeders Mathew and Deborah Loving, have closed the previous chapter of their lives decisively to plunge into their new country enterprise with a singleness of purpose. Others, such as the Webers, are making the transition gradually. They may let go of their urban careers by retirement or even find ways to move their urban careers to their rural digs.

Here are some facts and trends in the fields of agriculture and hospitality that might interest you if you have your eye out for an enterprise that depends on a rural location.

Agriculture

Ron and Dorothy Weber are swimming upstream in their struggle to break into farming from scratch. They know this and fortunately don't have to depend on their farming income. The hard reality they and other agricultural neophytes face boils down to this: The cost of land, buildings, and equipment is high measured against the low unit cost of the yield.

Bruce Clement, the agriculture agent in Cheshire County, New Hampshire, concurs with the view that it's hard to profit from agriculture if you are starting from scratch. With few exceptions, he thinks, land resources have simply become too expensive to farm. Parts of New York, Pennsylvania, and upper Maine are some of the exceptions to this rule he knows about in the Northeast, where land can still be bought relatively cheaply in relation to its productive capability. If you are lucky enough to find this kind of land, lucky you. Otherwise, Clement adds, you'd best marry into or inherit the land. Even then, your income potential would be modest, at best—which might be enough if your decision hinges as much on lifestyle as dollars-and-cents considerations.

Consider dairy farming, for example. Hank Kenney bought a 250-acre run-down dairy farm in 1972 and has built it up over the years to the model facility it is today. Milk from the herd of 150 (100 milkers) nets Kenney around $25,000 per year. He also derives some income from maple syrup and repairing farm machinery.

To buy a farm of this size, Kenney estimates that you would need anywhere from $300,000 to $1,000,000, depending on location (the higher figure is typical of New England; better deals currently exist in central New York and the Midwest). In addition to milk cows ($1,200 each), figure on three acres of hay or an acre of corn and one acre of pasture for each cow. Kenney advises against total reliance on imported feed unless you are in a big farming area with cheap feed sources.

Milk prices fluctuate widely on the market—they dropped 30 percent last year, says Kenney. And your yield can fluctuate as well. If poor weather in one year reduces the feed crops, the effects show up in the quality and quantity of the milk. When all is said and done, Kenney notes, you might get better return on your investment by putting your money in the bank than the 2 or 3 percent you stand to gain from dairying.

A similar scenario could be sketched out for almost any standard agricultural product, which is why the family farm continues to be edged out by giant agribusiness.

But because big farms can't or won't respond to sudden gaps in the market, particularly if the gaps are small, opportunities will continue to open for small-scale farms producing specialty commodities, such as exotic produce and organic or chemical-free crops and animals, say futurologists Marvin Cetron and Owen Davies.[2] These markets should expand as more Americans adjust their diets to suit healthier lifestyles.

If you pin your agricultural hopes on a plant crop, you will want to track the trend of water availability. Futurologists predict that future farmland will be more costly in the East and Northwest, where rainfall is more predictable, than in the West and Midwest.

Global warming threatens current farming areas with persistent droughts and changing ecological makeup. The change might be slowed but probably can't be reversed. A demand for ways to deal with these inevitable change will create opportunities for small-scale farmers to develop adaptive measures, including growing drought-resistant crops and using water-conserving cultivation techniques.

There are also changes in the markets for agricultural products. A growing demand for low-fat, low-cholesterol meat explains much of the growing interest in fish. Fish farming can provide a low-key business not only for retirees like Bill Hammond but also for entrepreneurs seriously bent on making a profit. Commercial catches have been declining for years at a time when evolving dietary patterns are demanding more fish at the retail level. Farmed trout and catfish should also profit from the increasing contamination of ocean fish by chemicals and heavy metals.

One other agricultural trend is sure to affect big and little farmers alike: the revolution in biotechnology. As the ethical and legal questions of this far-reaching technology continue to be questioned, no one knows where the revolution will lead. Consider gene splicing, for example. Experiments are underway to develop a potato packed with as much protein as beef. If successful, would the product depress the demand for low-fat meats?

Breeding Exotic Animals

Speaking of beef substitutes, let's assume you don't want to compete with Frank Perdue's chicken factories. You dream of a nontraditional agricultural enterprise—or a traditional one that you won't have to depend on completely to put bread on the table.

The old rules regarding farm economics may not apply—at least according to the ostrich and llama breeders described earlier. A chicken takes six months to raise to market weight and wholesales for a few dollars. Raising an ostrich takes two years, a third of an acre of land, and very little in the way of equipment. Ostriches sell for more than $5,000 currently. Can you lose? If you can't, why hasn't every farmer made the switch?

Dairyman Hank Kenney is aware of the "exotics." He points out some things to look into before jumping in full tilt. Llamas, for example, have low fertility, producing one young at a time. He believes that beefaloes have a dubious market and that the high current market price for exotics is based on sales to other breeders. It will drop dramatically when the market is saturated and breeders have to sell their products for feathers, meat, or hide.

Ostrich breeder Mathew Loving doesn't disagree but says that even when saturation occurs, ostriches will still fetch a good price. Ostrich breeding, he adds, is a low-risk enterprise with a rosy outlook. He pegs the amount needed to start as low as $5,000. "If you lost it, it wouldn't amount to more than you might lose on a lemon car," he adds. Even when the market saturates, he estimates the birds will still sell for $1,200 to $1,500, yielding a return on investment of 25 to 30 percent.

Like ostrich breeders, llama breeders are more focused on building up the domestic breeding stock than on selling to other markets. A recent five-year profitability analysis by International Llama Association projected costs and returns for four different economic scenarios. In all cases, the initial investment was $70,000. Breeding stock, six females and one stud-quality male, accounted for $65,000; the remaining $5,000 went for start-up costs. Given the most pessimistic case—10 percent annual decrease in value—average annual return over the five-year period was still 4.5 percent. With an increase in value of 10 percent per year, the five-year average return was 49.1 percent.

Recreation and Hospitality

Most of us have less spare time these days than was available to primitive hunter-gatherer societies—and, some suggest, even less than the inhabitants of the caves in Lascaux, 30,000 years ago. With more people working to make ends meet, fewer weekends will be open for short trips. Recreation will likely center around short-duration activities (much of this home-based) or longer trips during annual vacations.

The quality of ocean beaches will continue to wane because of pollution and erosion. This may motivate more people to seek alternative waterside recreation near rivers and lakes or boost demand for inland sites away from water. The desire to get back to nature will propel demand for camping, an economical form of recreation. Resorts geared to restore mental or physical health should do well, as will dude ranches and other destinations offering back-to-nature experiences.

Look for growing interest in niche resorts. Such facilities will specialize, stretching the resort concept beyond skiing, tennis, and horseback riding to focus on intellectual and cultural activities of interest to a large, well-educated group of aging baby boomers. Checking out local Indian ruins and touring theatrical groups might supplement or even displace high-energy sports.

One example of the alternative resort is the Anderson Ranch, near Aspen, Colorado. It offers classes in photography, furniture making, pottery, and children's arts. Why doesn't someone start a resort for researchers, such as people writing books or doctoral theses? Work stations outfitted with computers, modems, faxes, and copy machines would be provided in some peaceful, out-of-the-way place. Nature walks, hot tubs, and exercise facilities would help keep body and soul together. Hmmm . . .

Part Four

Where Should You Be?

Chapter Seven

You Can Sell Widgets
in Muscatine . . .

Build something, help something, save something. The possibilities are endless.

Jack Lessinger

If you are completely open as to your next destination, this chapter will help you decide how to narrow down your prospects to ensure your best chances of business success. If you already know where you want to go, you may still end up there after reading this chapter and completing the business location worksheet at the end. But you will have, I hope, more solid business reasons behind your decision.

We'll ignore lifestyle issues for the moment and treat possible locations as if their potential for business success was the only thing that mattered. In the next chapter we'll examine the other side of the coin and explore issues important to your lifestyle and personal aspirations. The two come together in Chapter 9 to help you narrow the choices and make a final selection.

The Physical Setting

Climate and geography may be crucial to some businesses but less important or even irrelevant to others. Obviously, if you intend to open up a ski resort, you know you need a place where there are mountains and snow. But you may not know that even though a lot of greyhound breeding is done in areas with year-round warm climates, such as Florida, greyhounds do better where there are cold winters. The reason: Cold winters keep certain parasites in check. Other geographic requirements for a greyhound breeding farm, now that I've got your interest, include at least ten acres of relatively flat terrain (rocks injure the dogs during training).

Climate and geography are also critical factors to consider when starting up agricultural enterprises. They explain why there are more carp farms in Louisiana than Maine, more wineries in California than Idaho, and more potato farms in Idaho than Louisiana. The weather often decides whether some tourist-related businesses have a boom or bust year. Many New England businesses do a major portion of their trade during a few weeks each fall when tourists flock to the region to view the spectacular foliage. They stay away if the leaves drop too quickly or if the weather is too rainy.

Of course, if you want to design computer software, refinish antiques, manufacture optical instruments, or start a mail-order business, you can probably ignore the climate and geography of the area.

Proximities

What do I have to be near and how close do I have to be are two questions that need to be pegged at an early stage in deciding where to locate. Proximity to your market and service base probably comes first. Bruce Hammond relies on a local shipping service to enable him to ship off his weekly batch of comic strips to the syndicate every Wednesday. Telecommuting consultant Gil Gordon needs a major airport within less than an hour's drive to enable him to service far-flung corporate clients.

Necessary proximity to a major city may limit your choices of location if you need to personally reach your clients or supply sources unless you can come up with other ways to do this. If you intend to employ many people, your business should be within reasonable commuting distance for them. But the distance that people are willing to drive varies from place to place and person to person. Even writers who can set up shop for themselves almost anywhere, thanks to rapid electronic and postal communication, may still need to be near public or university libraries, post offices, and office supply stores.

Defining Your Local Market

Who will buy your product or services in a prospective area? Solid market research precedes every successful business venture, no matter where it is located. If your market is national, you may serve it equally well from a beachside cottage in Hawaii as from a mountain retreat in the Adirondacks. But market research becomes a decisive factor in determining your location if you intend to sell your product or service within a specific region. Market research has evolved into a complex discipline in recent years, with the result that today you are likely to find consultants who offer this service even in small towns. Maybe market research, itself, should be your market.

Chances are, though, that you can do your own market research better than anyone else could by tapping into the mountains of published data that lie waiting for you to find them and then following up by investigating the market conditions of prospective locations.

Say you are a New Yorker with a background in big city banking and finance looking for a way to get out of the city. During recent vacation trips to small New England towns, you noticed that there were no pawn shops (a New Yorker would notice that). The idea of starting a pawn shop in a small New England town that came to you as a lark has, over time, taken root and grown into a serious possibility. What to do next?

You obviously want to learn everything you can about the business of pawn shops. Then comes market research. One method, the "market saturation approach," starts by determining the number of people in a market area that it takes to support a given type of business. Stephen C. Harper, in *The McGraw-Hill Guide to Starting Your Own Business*,[1] lists the following as examples:

- Hardware stores—8,000 people per store.
- Bookstores—26,000 people per store.
- Nursery and garden supply—26,000 people per store.
- Eating places—8,500 people per store.
- Women's clothing—5,000 people per store.
- Furniture stores—3,000 people per store.
- Florists—8,600 people per store.
- Barber shops—2,200 people per shop.

Unfortunately, pawn shops aren't listed in Harper's examples, but there are many other sources, such as the Small Business Administration's publication, *Starting and Managing a Small Business of Your Own*.[2] It contains a table listing the minimum number of local inhabitants per store required for success in 46 different types of business. Interestingly, it differs from the above source by a substantial margin for some categories. Restaurants, for example, are listed at 776 people, almost 11 times less than the figure first mentioned for eating places.

Chances are that you won't find statistical data for your business, particularly if it is new or unusual (I haven't yet found how many residents are needed to support a pawn shop). If this is the case, you may find help through professional or trade associations or else make your best guess.

At any rate, when doing market research for particular candidate locations, you'll want to see how many other similar businesses there are to determine if the market is already saturated. If there are no such businesses, you will need to find out why. Has the idea never occurred to anyone or are there cultural, legal, or other locally determined reasons? To answer that, you need to know something about the demographics of the area.

Using Demographics

Demographic data describe a wide variety of population characteristics for a particular area. You can use demographics first to make a profile of an ideal location for your product or service and later to compare alternative locations.

The type of data most useful to you depends on the kind of business enterprise you have in mind. For a sports equipment store, you'll want a place with an abundance of young people. You would do well to steer clear of areas heavy with retirees. But a place with a concentration of older people would be exactly where you should be if you want to sell items geared to their special needs. This market is sure to swell due to people living longer and will explode when the baby boomers move en masse into old age. Demand could soar for such diverse products as large-print crossword puzzles, higher and firmer furniture, TV-screen enlargers, aging-ergonomic kitchen appliances and special healthcare accessories.

To sum up, you first need to ask, "Who is my market?" and then "What kind of area would likely have a high percentage of this type of person?" Here are some of the kinds of demographic information that may be important to the success of your venture.

The Trade Area Population

If you know how many customers or clients you need to support your enterprise and how far they will likely travel to reach you—or how far you can drive to reach them—you can define your trade area.

Say you are thinking of opening a musical instrument shop. Preliminary research tells you that you need a base population of 50,000 potential customers who don't usually drive more than 40 miles to get to a store like yours. Therefore, your primary trade area will contain a population of at least 50,000 within a 40-mile radius and have no other similar stores.

When you apply your criteria to individual places, you may have to redefine your questions to fit locally defined categories. Data from a chamber of commerce, for example, may define the primary trade area as the county with the town listed next, followed by secondary and tertiary trade areas defined by regional logic.

But raw numbers are only the beginning. Whom do you hope to sell to? If your musical instruments are electronic guitars and drums, you will want a high percentage of persons between 15 and 30 years old. For band instruments, you might want an even younger base (most parents start their children on band instruments in the fifth or sixth grade). Pianos and organs are bought mostly by reasonably affluent middle-aged people.

Household Makeup

The type and characteristics of households may play a big part in your success. Your daycare center will probably have a better chance in an area with a lot of children and single- or two-parent households than one with single persons or couples with few children. Published data for localities often list family composition, total number of persons living in households, nonfamily households, married couples, single-parent families, and average household size.

Income

How much the people in a particular trading area make affects their spending patterns and may make or break your business. If you have your eye on a clothing boutique or home accessory shop, steer clear of areas with low per capita incomes. People there are more likely to buy both clothing and home accessories at the nearest K-Mart.

Your intended enterprise may hinge on any of a variety of other demographic factors: home ownership patterns, automobile ownership, the area's main employers, and how long people live in the area, to name just a few.

Keep in mind that demographics aren't static—they change constantly. Look at the ten- or twenty-year trends to see what the future is likely to hold for an area. One of the best sources I've found for spotting what to look for is Judith Nichols's book, *By the Numbers: Using Demographics and Psychographics for Business Growth in the '90s.*[3]

The Local Business Climate

If you are considering establishing a computer software debugging service for a national market, you can ignore the market aspects of the local area. But before you close your eyes to the local business climate, consider the start-up costs, taxes, and local business services you may be in for—they vary from place to place, and all will affect your operation. Here are some factors that may be important to you.

Growing or Declining Local Economy

Whether the local economy is growing, static, or declining affects all locally dependent businesses, but not equally. Products and services for which there is inelastic demand—funeral homes and grocery stores—stand a better chance in a declining economy than products/services whose demand is elastic. I would not recommend New England at the start of the '90s to homebuilders or architects, for example. On the other hand, some businesses manage not only to hold on in a downturn but also to do quite well. My barber reports doing at least as much business in the current downturn (1991) as ever before. He agrees that people could stretch out the time between haircuts, but they don't. Haircuts, he says, give people a relatively cheap way to feel better about themselves.

Nonetheless, most business experts advise choosing an area with good economic health for a locally dependent business. Indicators to look for include how many jobs have been gained or lost in the last five years, how many new building permits have been issued, and how many new businesses have been opened and closed. Look for long-term trends as well as short blips in the business cycle. For example, the northeastern states continue to lose population and jobs to the southern and western states in spite of the boom years of the last decade.

Diversity of Business

The diversity of local businesses is another useful indicator of local business climate. An area with many small, diverse employers is preferable to one with only a few major employers. This was vividly demonstrated by the decay of midwestern towns that owed their existence to auto manufacturing or other heavy industry. When these industries started to slide, so did the fortunes of towns like Flint, Michigan, and Akron, Ohio.

In the last century, mining towns like Virginia City, Nevada, or Park City, Utah, became ghost towns practically overnight when their single economic base was exhausted. Interestingly, Park City rebounded in the 1970s around another single market, the ski industry, but is now becoming a vibrant small community with a diverse economy that includes former urban professionals fleeing the smog and big city woes of Salt Lake City, 40 miles down canyon.

Local Taxes

Local tax structures affect some enterprises much more than others. Businesses that require a large physical plant, such as auto dealerships, are more sensitive to high local property taxes than, say, a marketing firm that operates out of the second story office of a downtown building.

Your enterprise may also be subject to fees and assessments that are not always apparent—or not specifically called "taxes." Some taxes you'll have to pay and not even receive the service! My rural home is just off the newly installed town sewer grid. Though the system doesn't reach my house, I still get socked with the same property tax rate as those who actually get to use it.

As municipalities continue to get squeezed financially, they will come up with more things to tax. New Hampshire has no state sales or income tax presently but instead slams tourist-related businesses with a special tax that affects bed-and-breakfast establishments, bars, restaurants, and ski resorts. Neighboring Massachusetts is flirting with a tax on professional services that will affect everyone from architects to barbers.

Transportation

A thorough survey of the rail, bus, and air shipping options available at your destination is a must if your enterprise hinges on shipping or receiving goods. It's not enough to know whether a bus or train runs through the area; you must know from where and how often. I could, for example, get to New York City or Montreal by hopping on Amtrak's "Montrealer" at Brattleboro, Vermont, 25 miles to the west of my home. Unfortunately, it only passes through once each day (at two o'clock in the morning).

Your business may require regular personal travel away from your base. If so, connections to and from the nearest commercial airport need to be pinned down. Park-and-ride or airport limousine services can save you the hassle of commuting through metropolitan traffic at rush hour.

Many areas boast small municipal airlines that connect to metropolitan airports. The miniplanes that ply these routes are too small to allow you to use your laptop computer. Don't worry—the ride will probably be too shaky to use it anyway. But on a clear day you will be able to see scenery you can't from a 727, so chin up. (See Figure 7-1.)

Communications

A healthy diversity of daily newspapers, shoppers' weekly papers, AM and FM radio stations, television stations, and cable television services in an area augurs well for businesses there. They not only indicate how well-informed the residents are likely to be but are also potential conduits for you to get the word out about your business. You can also tell a lot about the local culture from the region's communications media. If country and western is the main fare of the radio stations, you might want to rethink your plans to open that gourmet coffee bar.

VERY LARGE AIR HUB

LARGE AIRPORT

MEDIUM AIRPORT

1. Seattle-Tacoma	15. Houston	29. Louisville	43. Charlotte
2. Portland	16. Dallas-Fort Worth	30. Indianapolis	44. Raleigh-Durham
3. San Francisco	17. Oklahoma City	31. Cincinnati	45. Norfolk
4. Sacramento	18. Kansas City	32. Dayton	46. Washington
5. Reno	19. Omaha	33. Columbus	47. Philadelphia
6. Los Angeles	20. Des Moines	34. Detroit	48. Newark
7. San Diego	21. Mnn.-St. Paul	35. Cleveland	49. New York
8. Las Vegas	22. Milwaukee	36. Pittsburgh	50. Boston
9. Salt Lake City	23. Chicago	37. Knoxville	51. Providence
10. Phoenix	24. St. Louis	38. Atlanta	52. Hartford-Spring.
11. El Paso	25. Memphis	39. Tampa	53. Albany
12. Albuquerque	26. New Orleans	40. Miami	54. Syracuse
13. Denver	27. Birmingham	41. Orlando	55. Rochester
14. San Antonio	28. Nashville	42. Jacksonville	56. Buffalo

Figure 7-1   Major Airports (*Source: The National Atlas of the United States of America,* Washington, DC: U.S. Dept. of the Interior, Geological Survey, 1970.)

Utilities

If you do have your sights set on a gourmet coffee bar, the flavor and quality of the municipal water is of paramount importance, as we saw earlier with Randy Wirth's coffee consulting business in Logan, Utah.

Steep rates for utility energy sources—gas, oil, electricity—will drive up your overhead costs if you want to open a restaurant or manufacturing facility. On the other hand, those same steep prices might provide just the right market conditions for a business specializing in solar electrical alternatives or home energy conservation.

As the environmental and monetary costs of trash disposal continue to climb, you can't ignore the problem of disposing of any waste your business might generate. You will want to know what facilities exist for waste collection and recycling and what the charges are.

Business Support Services

Once operational, your business—no matter how small—needs steady sources of supplies, shipping, printing, accounting, and legal services. You'll also likely need special help, of one sort or another, when starting out.

If you join a franchise, you can get start-up help from the franchiser. Otherwise, you have to depend on your own resources. Fortunately, many small towns offer various resources to attract small businesses out of a desire to promote a healthy mix of small, diversified, environmentally clean businesses. You may stand to gain from a range of free services. Here's a rundown of the kinds of things to look for—the more available they are, the more anxious the community is to welcome small business.

Chamber of Commerce. Here you'll often find free literature on local services, banks, colleges, schools, demographics, employees and employment agencies, maps, government, and financing.

The Service Corps of Retired Executives (SCORE) offers the expertise of people who have been through it all. SCORE volunteers can help you with the basic necessities of any new business, such as drawing up a business plan, preparing a financial statement, conducting and analyzing marketing studies, and setting up accounting procedures. Beyond basic issues, I rate SCORE's help more useful if you are opening a shoe store than, say, a holographic imaging service, possibly because the retired business executives who make up the membership are more attuned to the past than the future.

Small Business Development Centers (SBDCs), established by the U.S. Small Business Administration at community colleges in many small towns, offer many useful services to small businesses, including help in drawing up a business plan, counseling, training and workshops, help in securing SBA financial assistance, and various information and referral services. One center, based at Midland College, Texas, has published a resource book for small business owners who want to establish businesses in a 17-county area of the Permian Basin of Texas. The book covers such topics as prebusiness considerations; protecting the organization; legal and professional advice; sources of capital; sources of information, including chambers of commerce, colleges, and export assistance centers; permits and registration; and other information.

State or Local Industrial Development Agencies aim to attract desirable industries and businesses to regions and municipalities through a variety of helpful services such as providing start-up information and funneling federal grants and loans. Some even act as developers of certain areas of a town where they hope to attract businesses.

Friendliness of Local Government

No assessment of the local business climate is complete without a sense of how the local government treats businesses. A financial investment firm may get away with an annual renewal of its business license, but a restaurant or healthcare facility not only has to be licensed but is also subject to a myriad of regulations and periodic inspections.

You will want to know what obstacles stand in the way to operating your business and how difficult it is to overcome them. If I were thinking of starting a home remodeling service in Sedona, Arizona, I would want to know if local planning policies encouraged new building permits or discouraged them through inordinate red tape or delays.

When you get down to comparing prospective locations, you'll want to know what changes might be in the wind that would affect an area's business climate. Changes in roads and highways can redirect consumer traffic. Planned major shopping centers can radically change or even destroy established retail businesses. New housing communities, health care facilities, and college expansions also may determine how successful your enterprise will be.

Civic Life

Civic life is an often-overlooked clue to an area's spirit; it definitely affects the general business climate. How many community or service organizations are there, and what are they doing? Look for local chapters of the Lions, Elks, or Rotary Club as well as arts councils, resource organizations for drug and alcohol abuse, mental health organizations, and historic organizations.

If you were sensing the pulse of my town (Marlborough, New Hampshire, population 1800), you would come away with the impression of a place that cares. The garden club plants flowers and green things on every unpaved surface in the village business district and regularly maintains the landscaping at no charge to the town. Kids just starting out on a horn sit next to seasoned musicians in the town band during summer rehearsals for the August concert on the town green. Marlborough has a library board, youth committee, and overseer of the poor. The town bulletin comes off the press four times a year with the latest local scuttlebut. Glancing through a copy leaves the definite impression that this town has a good spirit.

Hidden Alligators

The above list of local factors to consider when testing an area's suitability for your business is not complete. The list could go on and on and still not contain items specific to your type of business enterprise. You'll have to make your own list. When you do, make sure your criteria include things such as local licensing or permits. If you want to develop tourist cabins on a lake, for example, you need to know if development is still possible (recent environmental legislation has put the squeeze on how close sewage-leach fields can be to lakes). Look for local laws or fees that might stand in your way.

Putting Business Location Criteria to Work

Worksheet 7-1a is designed to help you decide what location factors are important to your intended enterprise. The factors discussed in this chapter are listed on the left; the space on the right is for you to write in the local factors you deem important to your business. At the bottom there's a catch-all space for other requirements not listed—the "hidden alligators."

A similar worksheet in the next chapter repeats the process but focuses on criteria important to the kind of life you want to lead in your new locale. You can combine data from both worksheets in Chapter 9 to rate prospective locations.

Worksheet 7-1b presents the example of Sandi Thomas, a 32-year-old computer software engineer who wants to break away from her corporate position in California's Silicon Valley and apply her knowledge to opening a computer store in a small town in northern California.

When Sandi stands back from the completed worksheet, she'll get an overall impression of the type of place that would support her venture. She imagines her storefront shop on a tree-lined street in a small town where her business can prosper and she can enjoy a richer, more rewarding life.

What Is It Like There?
Capsule Profiles Of Five Communities

The people I interviewed for this book live and work in small towns and rural areas from New Jersey to California and from Texas to Montana, places that are diverse by any yardstick. When I asked the residents what their locale was like, I had to revise some of my preconceptions. Here's a brief sketch of five communities ranging in size from Sanford, Florida, population 33,300, to the twin cities of Bryan/College Station, Texas, with a combined population of 120,000.

All five are towns in all the traditional senses of the word and don't depend on a larger metropolitan area for their existence. And they are all

Worksheet 7-1a   Business Location Criteria

Factors	Desirable Attributes
Climate requirements (Temperature, humidity, solar availability)	
Geographical requirements	
Proximities (transportation, urban areas, services)	
Local market attributes	
Desireable demographics (trade area, per capita income, household makeup, education level)	
Local business climate (growth status, diversity, taxes, transportation, utilities, business services, local, government, civic pride)	
Other requirements	

(continued)

Worksheet 7-1b *Continued*

SANDI THOMAS'S WORKED EXAMPLE

Factors	Desirable Attributes
Climate requirements (Temperature, humidity, solar availability)	
Geographical requirements	
Proximities (transportation, urban areas, services)	SHIPPING SERVICE SHOPPING AREA WITHIN 1 MILE. MAJOR AIRPORT WITHIN 100 MILES
Local market attributes	MANY SMALL BUSINESSES. HIGH-TECH BUSINESSES. MANY H.S. & COLL. STUDENTS, PROFESSIONALS
Desireable demographics (trade area, per capita income, household makeup, education level)	MIN. 60,000 PEOPLE WITHIN 3-MILE RADIUS. WELL-EDUCATED POP. WITH HIGH PER-CAPITA INCOME.
Local business climate (growth status, diversity, taxes, transportation, utilities, business services, local, government, civic pride)	LOCAL ECONOMY IN GROWTH MODE
Other requirements	

college towns, though the influence of the college over the community varies. As you read each description, try to picture yourself starting over in a place such as that.

Flagstaff, Arizona

Easterners think of Arizona as a hot, dry place full of horned toads lying in the shade of saguaro cactuses. It has all of these but much more—which is not surprising when you consider that Arizona is a composite of several land forms and at least four distinct climate types. The state has enough room for all six New England states plus Pennsylvania.

Flagstaff is only 130 miles north of Phoenix but is six times colder (measured in heating degree–days). January temperatures average between 14° and 41°F. But who can complain when two of every three winter days are sunny? The high, clear atmosphere makes Flagstaff an ideal site for the Lowell Observatory, where Pluto was discovered in 1930, and a great place to heat your house with the sun's energy.

Perched in the pines at an elevation of 7,000 feet on the Colorado Plateau, Flagstaff is surrounded by the 12,000-foot peaks of the San Francisco mountains, whose slopes contain six of the seven vegetational life zones. The area is the ancestral home of the Anasazi, Mogollon, and Hohokan peoples—evident only from their artifacts at sites such as the Canyon de Chelly—and the present day Pima, Pueblo, Hopi, and Navajo Indians, many of whom live on the adjacent Hopi and Navajo reservations.

Spanish opportunists plundered the region in the 1500s, searching for the fabled Seven Cities of Gold. Missionaries followed and established the first permanent European settlements. Mexico ceded the area to the United States in 1848. The railroad followed, opening the way for mining, cattle ranchers, sheep ranchers, prospectors, and farmers. In 1891, Flagstaff became the seat of Cococino County, the second-largest county in the United States.

Flagstaff owes its economic origins to loggers who tapped the surrounding Ponderosa Pine forest as a source of ties for the coming railroad and spawned a lumber industry in the process. The railroad spurred the town's development as a trading center serving the lumber, mining, and livestock interests.

The economy of the present town of 45,000 hinges on year-round tourism, but Northern Arizona University is the single-largest employer.

The flavor of the indigenous peoples' culture permeates the region, which embraces the small, outlying communities of Sedona, Cottonwood, and Jerome. Native American arts and crafts are displayed in the Museum of Northern Arizona and the Coconino Center for the Arts.

The area abounds in natural wonders: the Grand Canyon, Oak Creek Canyon, Walnut Canyon, Wupatki National Monument, Meteor Crater, Sunset Crater—all within an 80-mile radius. Mountain trails, camping, and hunting opportunities abound, as do fishing and water sports at nearby Oak Creek, Lake Mary, and Mormon Lake. In winter, there's cross-country skiing trails and downhill skiing at the SnowBowl's 35 slopes and trails.

Northern Arizona University, the "mountain campus," offers 130 degree programs to its 16,000 students. As with other isolated college towns, the university boosts Flagstaff's cultural diversity; it has a symphony orchestra as well as dance and theater groups. The historic district houses many quaint boutiques, galleries, and restaurants, while numerous small clubs cater to fans of rock, folk, jazz, and country music.

Sanford, Florida

Like Flagstaff, Sanford is drenched in sunshine. There the similarity ends. Whereas Flagstaff is mountainous, Sanford—and all of Florida—is flat as a pancake. Flagstaff divides its dry climate into four distinct seasons; Sanford is humid and subtropical with two seasons, more-or-less. Average winter temperatures hover around a mild 60°F, whereas summers are "warm and moist" according to the chamber of commerce brochure, which adds, "August's temperatures rarely exceed 95 degrees, dropping 15 or 20 degrees at night." What the brochure doesn't tell you is that the humid, 75° summer nights are uncomfortable without air-conditioning.

Another difference is water. There's water near Flagstaff, but you have to go out of your way to find it. In Sanford, water abounds. The town sits on the shore of Lake Monroe, with the St. Johns River nearby, so aquatic recreation—boating, fishing, water-skiing—naturally abounds. Other outdoor happenings take advantage of the year-round mild climate—golf, a soapbox derby, and riverboat cruises, to name a few.

Sanford is flooded with vacationing seniors and is home to a large number of retirees. One of the year's high points is the Golden Age Games, a chance for the 55-plus set to run, swim, cycle, sail, and sweat their way to honors.

Tourism is a linchpin of the area's economy, but seniors aren't the only target. Twenty miles from Orlando, home of Disney World, Sea World, and the Epcot Center, Sanford is also a mere 30 miles from Daytona Beach, site of the annual, classic auto race and a mecca for those seeking oceanside recreation. Other outdoor amenities include a zoo and Flea World, where 1,500 dealers regularly create the mother of all yard sales. Approximately 250 tourists get off the Amtrak train every day—with their cars. The "Auto Train" starts out in Lawton, Virginia, and comes to the end of the line in Sanford.

Sanford's story started in the early 1800s, when U.S. troops came to fight the Indian Wars. After wiping out most of the Seminoles, the government offered inducements to attract settlers. Two steam boats began plying the St. Johns River to supply Camp Mellon. By 1856 the settlement of Mellonville was a robust trade center. Major Henry Sheldon Sanford acquired 12,000 acres nearby and opened an office in London to lure

English and Swedish families. An amateur botanist, Sanford introduced fruits and flowers from around the world.

The town was all but wiped out by 1895, thanks to a catastrophic fire in 1887, followed by a yellow fever epidemic and disastrous freezes in the winter of 1894–1895. Forty percent of the residents left. The hardy souls who stayed ⊔iversified their agriculture, eventually reviving the local economy. Today the economy is a healthy mix that supports 32,000 inhabitants.

Tourism and light industry now augment the fruit and vegetable truck farms, all helped by a good transportation network. In addition to an Amtrak station, the town has a river port and a municipal airport. Interstate 4 connects Sanford with both coasts, and I-95, which runs up the East Coast all the way to Maine, is within 30 miles.

With the appeal to easy living and all of the tourist glitz, Sanford appears at first glance to lack cultural depth. Not so. The Seminole Community College hosts a continual flux of artists, actors, musicians, and writers and often presents student recitals, art shows, festivals, concerts, and lectures. The Ballet Guild of Sanford-Seminole performs for the public and nurtures aspiring dancers. The Sanford Civic Center seats 1,300 for regular concerts and other cultural events. And don't forget—Sanford is the home base of Triangle Productions, the community theater described in Chapter 4.

Bryan, Texas

Midway between Flagstaff and Sanford is Bryan, Texas, (I know, you expected Texas to be farther west than that). Bryan shares something in common with each. Like Flagstaff, it is sunny. Like Sanford, it has a subtropical climate with mild winters and hot and humid summers. Like both, it is a college town, or—more properly—towns, because Bryan abuts a sister city, College Station. Their relationship is so close that they have a joint chamber of commerce, which sends out a single packet of information on the community.

Located 165 miles south of Dallas and 90 miles north of Houston, Bryan/College Station rated third in *Money* magazine's 1991 list of the best 300 places to live in the United States and scored the highest of all for the local economy—small wonder, with an unemployment rate just over 3 percent when the national average is more than double that. Housing is affordable as well. You can buy an average three-bedroom house for $55,000 to $60,000.

Bryan was founded in 1860 by the Houston and Texas Central Railroads and was named after William Joel Bryan, who sold a tract of land to the railroad. The railroad brought growth, as did oil and fertile lands for agriculture and cattle. In 1871 the town was incorporated, and a land-grant college, the Agricultural and Mechanical College of Texas, was established. The 40,000-student-strong Texas A&M is today one of the country's ten largest universities and the town's largest employer.

Light industry has grown in importance since the late 1960s, when a group of local business interests established the Brazos County Industrial Park. Two hospitals, General Telephone Company of Southwest, and many small companies provide a diversified economic base for the community.

The hometown of the renowned "Aggies" offers a wide spectrum of arts and entertainment. The focus of local restaurants is, as you might expect, steak and Tex-Mex. Clubs feature jazz, folk, rock, blues, and country music. Arts groups range from high- to lowbrow—barbershop quartets and a guitar society, for example. In October over 700 performers and 50 visual artists show their best at a two-day event, FestiFall, held downtown. Other communitywide offerings include an annual jazz festival in Central Park and FolkFest, a three-day celebration highlighting the Hispanic, Czech, and Old West cultures.

Czech?

Fayetteville, Arkansas

Like Bryan/College Station, Fayetteville scored high in *Money* magazine's 1991 rating of the best places to live in the United States. The town of 45,300 rated seventh overall and was among the three highest-rated towns in the category of places with a strong local economy. The town also got high honors in *Kiplinger's Personal Finance* magazine in November 1991, where it was cited as one of the country's top 25 places for job growth and livability. And the American Chamber of Commerce rated Fayetteville's cost of living 10.7 percent below the national average.

The economy, robust even in the recession that began in 1990, owes its vigor to a mix of tourism and the presence of several big companies such as Wal-Mart (which has its national headquarters there), Tyson Foods (poultry producers), and Simmons (mattresses). The mountains, lakes, and rivers of the Ozark Plateau ensure a steady flow of tourists through the region. Many come to visit the Pea Ridge Park, the site of the largest Civil War battle west of the Mississippi, and the National Cemetery in Fayetteville, the final resting place for 1,600 Union soldiers. Eureka Springs, an alpine resort with Victorian architecture, attracts millions of visitors each year who come to see its Great Passion Play.

In the northwest corner of Arkansas, Fayetteville is well off the beaten path. Tulsa lies 100 miles to the west; Little Rock, 150 miles southeast. The area is blessed with a relatively temperate climate and four distinct seasons. Summers are hot and humid. Though chilling winds from the northwest make for cold winters, they are shorter than in the north. Spring and fall can be pleasant.

Fayetteville serves as the hub for outlying small towns in the northwest corner of Arkansas, amid the rivers and lakes of the Ozarks. Its renovated downtown boasts a historic district full of well-preserved buildings from the last century.

The University of Arkansas, founded in 1871, is the town's largest employer. Its 14,200 students come from all 50 states and 75 countries in pursuit of 200 degree programs in 150 fields. Thanks to the university, Fayetteville offers a variety of music, theatre, and arts events that breaks the stereotype of hillbilly towns in the Ozarks.

Missoula, Montana

Up north, another college town sits amid the towering Bitterroot Mountains of western Montana, far from the big cities (about 500 miles each from Portland, Seattle, and Salt Lake City). The indigenous Flathead Indians dubbed the place *Missoula*—"place of fear"—probably to recall the tribe's constant abuse at the hands of the Blackfeet and Nez Perce. Other groups—Salish, D'Oreille, and Kootenai—laid claim to the region during the time the Lewis and Clark expedition entered the valley in 1805. Missionaries came on their heels, followed by the U.S. Army, which established Fort Owen, a trading post, in 1850.

The discovery of gold in western Montana in 1860 led to the success of "Hellgate Village," a trading post that became the nucleus of further development. Flour mills and sawmills were built. By 1864 a logging industry was in full swing, and this continues to be the primary base of the present economy, as evinced by companies such as Champion International and Stone Container Corp. But the economic influence of the surrounding woodlands, including the two-million-acre Lolo National Forest, transcends lumber.

Tourists flock to the area to observe American bison, deer, elk, and bighorn sheep in their native habitat. The diversity of wildlife also makes the region a hunting and fishing paradise. Water skiing and canoeing are popular on the reservoirs.

Unlike other towns that attract tourists (Flagstaff, Sanford, Fayetteville), tourism in the Missoula area is mostly a summer occurrence. Cold, raw winters explain why the two ski areas in the nearby Bitterroots primarily serve the 36,900 hardy souls who live there. Average temperatures in January range between 10° and 28°F. Summers are dry, cool, and pleasant, with average temperatures between 45 and 85 degrees.

At the foot of Mount Sentinel sits the University of Montana, headquarters of the eight-college system. The university provides 11 percent of the area's economic base and brings diversity to an otherwise remote, middle-class town of ranchers and forest-industry workers.

In the winter season, locals can enjoy the String Orchestra of the Rockies and performances put on by the University of Montana's drama, dance, and music departments as well as a repertory theater. Summers feature music events and children's theater at an outdoor circus tent in Caras Park, located downtown.

Wood and paper products industries bring in $87 million annually, accounting for 27.5 percent of the local economic base. Wholesale/retail trade and medical services account for another 19.4 percent, with federal government employment (U.S. Forest Service, mostly) making up 14.5 percent. The unemployment rate as of June 1991 was 6.7 percent, two points below the national average. Per capita income in 1989 was $14,079.

If you are an urban refugee who doesn't mind a cold climate and living far away from big cities, Missoula has much to offer.

We began this section talking about the kinds of things a place should offer for your business success and ended with a sketch of some actual places to give you a bit of the flavor of the places where the people described earlier live and work. Because this book is as much about living as working, the next chapter focuses on how to match a potential destination with the kind of life you aspire to outside of work.

Chapter Eight

But Could You Live
in Muscatine?

In the wake of the tremors that shook Humboldt County in northern California in April 1992, *USA Today* asked readers what they would do if they lived in an area prone to natural disasters. Not one answered, "I'd move."

Moving is a stressful experience to be sure, but it's probably nowhere near as stressful as enduring a major earthquake.

Your choice of location may be limited if you work for others or have a two-career household. Even so, you have more viable choices than ever before, thanks to technology and decentralization. So where *do* you want to live?

For convenience, I classified the case studies of the previous chapters into three groups, according to whether their occupations depended on a local, rural, or in-between market. The real world, of course, doesn't divvy up quite so neatly. Towns meld into each other, as Bryan, Texas does with College Station. Some communities that seem like towns are really satellites of metropolitan areas. Some rural areas like Ibapah, Utah, (profiled in Chapter 6), are so remote as to be rural by any yardstick; others are less remote and may be tied to a regional business center.

So when you are trying to define the kind of area you want to live in, don't think in strict terms of "small town" or "rural." Instead, create a list of attributes, such as density, climate, geography, and the like. In this chapter, I hope to help you define your lifestyle criteria so that you can use them to find the best place for you to live.

Defining Your Ideal Physical Setting

You might come up with a good idea of what your dream locale would be by listing the places you like to go on vacation. But just in case you don't find work in Cancun or Aspen, you can still find a good compromise by isolating what you like about those places and then matching their attributes to viable alternatives. Let's start with the big things—climate and geography—and then work toward the specifics.

Climate

Northern winters are too cold, too grey, and too long for me. Leafing through a magazine one dreary day last March, one of the full-page ads stirred my fantasy. A bronze god and an equally bronze goddess stood on a white beach, gazing out over cerulean waters that turned into deep blue near the horizon. I wanted to be there, feeling the warm sand ooze up between my tocs.

I suppose ads like these prod thousands of winter-weary Northerners to flee southward every winter for an all-too-brief taste of paradise. They return after a week or two to flaunt their sunburns at their pallid office colleagues and complain that their vacation wasn't long enough.

Well, a few days under the tropical sun do pass quickly, especially if you try to squeeze in a lot more than basking in the sun. But to a person from, say, Minnesota, the euphoria comes more from the change of climate than from the climate itself. I doubt whether most Minnesotans could or would want to adjust to unvarying tropical conditions (do I hear you muttering, "try me?"). After the change wears off, you begin to notice that paradise has a few warts.

Four and a half years of living in tropical Africa convinced me this is so. The warmth of the sun-drenched beach, so welcome at first, soon turns into oppressive heat and humidity that you are only too anxious to trade for the comfort of your air-conditioned hotel room. You might also flee there to escape the insects that populate warm climes.

Anyone who has lived close to the equator for more than six months also notices that the days don't change in length very much. The sun comes up at six and goes down at six. If there are seasons, they aren't the familiar spring-summer-fall-winter series, but rainy season—dry season or hot season—hot-humid season or some other variation. After a year or so, many a Northerner feels trapped in a time warp.

I don't mean to suggest that you shouldn't go to these kinds of places for R and R only, that you may not like to live there constantly.

So is there a perfect climate for you? The one that comes the closest for me is the high central valley that surrounds San Jose, Costa Rica. Temperatures hover between 65° and 85°F all year. The year is almost evenly split between a dry and a rainy season, but even in the rainy season the sun shines almost every day.

If you are like many Americans on the fast track, you probably spend most of your time in a sequence of artificial environments—car-to-office-to-car-to-home. You may not have thought much about climate. But climate becomes very important, if a desire for closer contact with the natural world is one of your reasons for leaving the city. If you end up working alone out of an office in your home, you will become much more aware of the daily changes in the weather than you were in the building you used to work in.

Fortunately, you have a lot of choices. Climates in the continental United States range from subtropical in Florida to arctic in northern Alaska. Microclimates within each region make things even more interesting. The absence of green areas in cities makes them both colder in winter and hotter in summer than the rural land just outside them. (Smellier, too.) In winter, cities often become wind tunnels, as anyone who has ever spent any time in Manhattan or Chicago knows.

Microclimates in rural areas differ from valley to hill and, on a hill, from the shady side to the sunny side. I often leave my hilltop house on a sunny autumn morning to drive a few miles into the fog that covers the town of Keene. Like a mini–Los Angeles, Keene is in a valley that traps warm air, creating temperature inversions.

The right climate for you may hinge on physical or emotional factors—or both. Asthmatic people are advised to seek a dry climate. Warm, dry conditions are believed to lesson the pain of arthritis. With aging comes increased sensitivity to cold, an obvious explanation for the appeal of Florida and Arizona to retirees.

Emotional attitudes are harder to get a fix on. Some people don't mind cold winters but tire of their length. Others, such as some of my hardy Yankee neighbors, wouldn't live in any other climate for the world. One of them, a wizened codger, was in his yard sorting through what was left of his winter firewood one morning during the first day in April when it felt warm for the first time. I greeted him with some comment about the nice warm day. "I always hate hot weathah," he replied.

It wouldn't surprise me if my neighbor also preferred cloudy to sunny weather, unlike me, an immigrant from the sunnier West. But that we all need sunlight is just coming to be acknowledged in medical circles.

Psychologists in the early 1980s suggested a relationship between a higher incidence of depression during the winter than during other times of the year. People who suffer from seasonal affective disorder, or SAD, reportedly benefit by spending more time out of doors or exposing them-

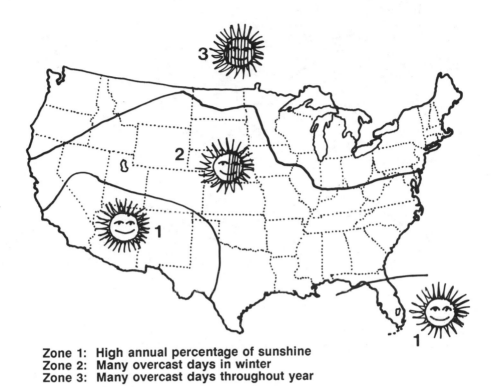

Zone 1: **High annual percentage of sunshine**
Zone 2: **Many overcast days in winter**
Zone 3: **Many overcast days throughout year**

Figure 8-1 Sunlight Distribution

selves to special artificial light sources that imitate the sun's spectrum. If you believe you are among this group and are fortunate enough to have a choice of locations, why not pick a sunny one?

Two factors determine how much sunlight reaches the ground at any given location: the length of day and the clarity of the sky. Figure 8-1 is a sunlight distribution map showing where the sun shines most and least in the course of a year. The southern tip of Florida and the Southwest, extending from southern California to western Texas (zone 1) are the sunniest locales. The Northeast and Northwest (zone 3) get the least.

What else besides sunshine could affect your attitudes toward climate? Well, if you ski, you will want to have easy access to snow. If you want to take up small-scale agriculture, regular rainfall is an asset. Animals, such as the previously mentioned llamas, ostriches, beefaloes, and trout, each have their own optimum ranges of temperature and humidity, as do people.

Most people wearing average clothing are comfortable in temperatures from 70° to 80°F, if the relative humidity is between 40 and 80 percent. Outside of this range, they feel uncomfortable and complain that

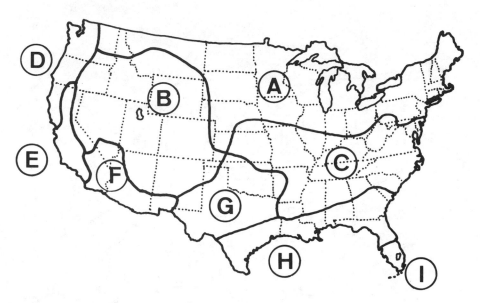

Figure 8-2 Climate Zones (Adapted from *Regional Guidelines for Building Passive Energy Conserving Homes,* AIA Research Corp., Washington, DC: U.S. Government Printing Office, 1984.)

the weather is too cold, too hot, or too muggy. The climate zone map shown in Figure 8-2 sorts the contiguous states into nine zones according to regional similarities. The following is a general description of each climate with representative cities, going from the coldest to the warmest during winter.

- **Zone A:** (Hartford, Madison) Cold and long winters, with the inland states being the coldest overall. Abundant snow. Summers pleasant but uncomfortably hot and humid in July and August, especially in the southern parts.

- **Zone B:** (Salt Lake City, Denver) This zone, which covers much of the inland western states, has cold, windy winters and hot, dry summers. The many mountainous portions of this region contain microclimates that vary depending on local wind patterns, solar exposure, and elevation. Mountainous areas are generally colder, with greater day-to-night temperature fluctuations.

- **Zone C:** (Charleston, Little Rock) The wide area that extends from Chesapeake Bay westward to Kansas is temperate, with four distinct seasons. Winters are mild and rainy near the coast, colder and snowier inland. Summers are long, hot, and humid. Coastal areas are subject to tropical storms—some with high winds. Expect wide diurnal temperature swings in the mountainous areas of Appalachia.

- **Zone D:** (Seattle, Portland) The Pacific Northwest coastal areas are blessed with a mild but very damp climate. Rain falls year round, and there are frequent fogs.

- **Zone E:** (Fresno) Moderately cold, rainy winters lasting from November to April and hot, dry summers mark California's central valley, which extends down to the southern coastal area. Temperatures are more constant near the coast than inland. Summer rain is rare, and droughts have become an increasing concern in recent years.

- **Zone F:** (Phoenix) Extremely hot, dry summers and moderately cold winters characterize the desert areas of southern Arizona and California. Precipitation falling in the winter months of November to April totals less than five inches per year.

- **Zone G:** (Fort Worth) Hot, dry summers, and cool winters in the southwestern portion give way to hotter and more humid summers in the eastern portion of this zone.

- **Zone H:** (Houston, New Orleans) This zone includes the Gulf regions of Texas, Louisiana, Alabama, central Florida, and southern Georgia. Essentially flat and damp, the region gets frequent and heavy rains. The hot, humid summers last from May to October. Winters are usually mild in the western portion that includes Texas and the Bayou country of Louisiana but can be cold enough to require winter heating in other areas.

- **Zone I:** (Miami) Subtropical southern Florida is warm and humid year-round, with uncomfortably hot and humid conditions in summer months.

The Landscape

The continental United States comprises as much diversity in land forms and vegetation as it does in climate. You learned all of that in fifth grade but probably didn't have much reason to care back then, so take a look at Figure 8-3 and bear with me for a short pogo-stick tour across the physiography of the United States.

A lowland coastal plain that begins around New Jersey runs down the East Coast and includes the states that surround the Gulf of Mexico. The very old Appalachian mountains extend from Maine to Georgia, and separate the coastal plain from the Great Plains of the interior. The Ozark Plateau of Missouri and Arkansas rises like an island between the coastal plains of the gulf and the interior plains.

The Great Plains extend westward to the Rocky Mountains. Many of the Rockies' craggy peaks rise up to 12,000 feet, roughly twice as high as the Appalachian peaks, which seldom exceed 6,000 feet.

Figure 8-3 Major Landforms (*Source: The National Atlas of the United States of America,* Washington, DC: U.S. Dept. of the Interior Geological Survey, 1970.)

Between the Rockies and the western coastal range lies a region of intermontane plateaus extending southward from western Washington to the Mexican border. The Great Basin of Utah and Nevada is part of this region. Instead of draining to the sea, the five rivers running through the Great Basin meet their final resting place in the Great Salt Lake, its most prominent feature.

The western coastal mountains begin with the Alaskan range, whose Mount McKinley towers up to 20,320 feet, the highest peak in North America. The coastal range continues southward through Washington and Oregon with the Cascade Range and in California with the Sierra Nevadas.

The Rockies feed river systems that flow in opposite directions from the continental divide to end their journey in the Pacific Ocean (Snake-Columbia), the Gulf of California (Colorado), and the Gulf of Mexico (Yellowstone-Missouri-Mississippi). River systems originating from the Appalachian range flow into the Mississippi via the Ohio or drain into the Atlantic through the eastern coastal plain (Hudson, Delaware, Susquehanna, Potomac, James, and Savannah).

The five Great Lakes, America's inland seas, cover 95,000 square miles and contain the world's largest volume of fresh water. Lake Superior is

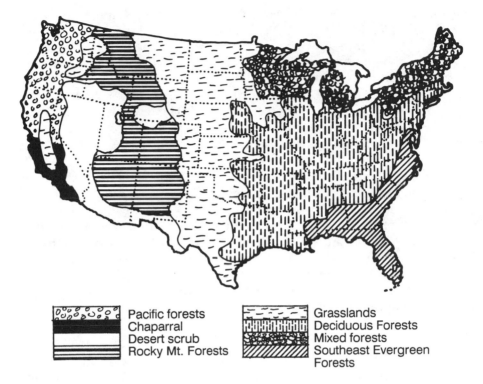

	Pacific forests		Grasslands
	Chaparral		Deciduous Forests
	Desert scrub		Mixed forests
	Rocky Mt. Forests		Southeast Evergreen Forests

Figure 8-4   Vegetation Distribution

1,333 feet deep; Lake Erie, a paltry 212 feet. The lakes are contiguous and connect to the Atlantic via the St. Lawrence River. Thousands of smaller freshwater lakes dot the country, concentrated in regions with the most rainfall. The West contains fewer, but often more interesting, lakes. Lake Tahoe, which straddles the California-Nevada border 6,228 feet above sea level, and Yellowstone Lake, at 8,000 feet, are both deep freshwater lakes set in alpine splendor.

The Great Salt Lake is 1,000 square miles in area but only 13 feet deep on the average. One-quarter salt, its waters are famous for keeping even nonswimmers afloat (everyone should try it, but once is enough). Another salt lake, California's Salton Sea, nestles 235 feet below sea level in the Mojave Desert, one of the hottest places in the country.

Where humans haven't forced nature to conform to their own designs—golf courses in the deserts of Arizona and California come to mind—native ground cover in the United States, whether forest, grassland, or desert scrub, is generally distributed according to temperatures and the availability of rainfall, as shown in Figure 8-4.

Coniferous forests flourish in the regions around the Great Lakes, the Northeast, and the slopes of the Appalachian Mountains. Broad-leafed trees mix in with the conifers at lower elevations and farther south, where oaks, cedar, ash, hickory, and magnolia replace maple and birch. Southern pine forests rule the lowland coastal plain of Georgia, the Carolinas, and the Gulf states. In the swamp forests of Florida and Louisiana's Bayou country grow bald cypress, white cedar, tupelo gum, and brush vines.

The flat, open spaces of the Great Plains are the breadbasket not only to the United States but to much of the world. The few patches unplanted in wheat, barley, or corn contain small stands of mixed forests and grasslands. In the arid Southwest, the grasses thin out to become mesquite grassland.

A lush variety of conifers—fir, spruce, redwood, and cedar—carpet the Pacific slopes of the coastal mountains of Washington, Oregon, and California—a sharp contrast with the eastern side of the range, where lies the driest part of the continent, the Mountain West. Grasses and sagebrush dot the lowland areas, whereas mountainous reaches contain patches of conifer or aspen forest, scrub oak, juniper, and cedar. Farther south, cacti, creosote bush, and other desert plants have adapted to the dry conditions of the stretch of desert that extends from southeast California through Arizona, and New Mexico into Texas.

The Environment

Everyone wants to live where there is clean air and water and you don't have to worry about the kids playing in a toxic waste dump. The maps in this section will help you spot those areas at a macro level.

Cars, still the biggest source of air pollution, have been steadily improved to reduce the amount of pollution they emit. Unfortunately, the improvement has been offset by their increasing numbers. Pollutants from commercial and industrial sources combine to make breathing the air a health hazard in many areas. As you can see from the air quality distribution map (Figure 8-5), there are two worst areas—a broad region fanning out from the coast of California and another stretching out in concentric circles from the Ohio Valley.

Like the air, the quality of the water also varies as to the amount of natural and artifical contaminants. Nature determines whether the water contains minerals like iron, sulfur, magnesium, manganese, copper, flourides, and zinc, most of which are more likely to affect taste and color than health. Some can even be beneficial, such as fluoride, which prevents tooth decay. However, high concentrations of some natural contaminants, such as radon gas or bacteria, can pose a health hazard.

Water is often said to be "hard" or "soft" according to the quantity of calcium and magnesium salts it picks up from the ground. Both types of water have pros and cons. Hard water, high in salt content and low in acid (high pH) tastes better, but makes laundering more difficult. Soft

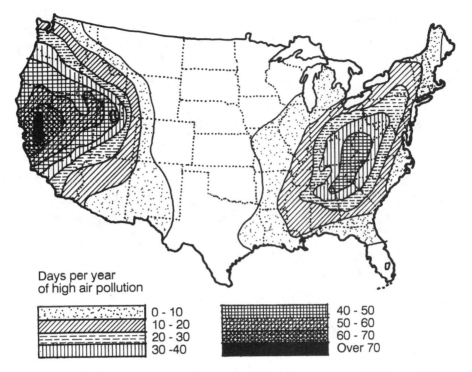

Days per year
of high air pollution

0 - 10	40 - 50
10 - 20	50 - 60
20 - 30	60 - 70
30 - 40	Over 70

Figure 8-5 Air Quality Distribution (*Source: The National Atlas of the United States of America,* Washington, DC: U.S. Dept. of the Interior, Geological Survey, 1970.)

water such as pure rain is acidic (low pH). It tastes worse and corrodes pipes but is better for cleaning.

Artificial contaminants affect the water quality almost everywhere, but the extent of water pollution has decreased in the past two decades, according to a 1988 EPA study. The study cited improvements in water pollution from factories and sewage plants, but runoff from farms, streets, and lawns remained a problem. Still, two-thirds of all river water reportedly meets water-quality standards, as does 44 percent of all lakes and reservoirs. Ground water, the source of drinking water for more than half the population, is threatened by underground storage tanks, landfills, farming, and hazardous waste. (See Figure 8-6.)

Coliform bacteria, PCBs, DDT, dioxin, and lead are some of the culprits linked to diseases that can affect present or future generations.

Water quality, an understandable concern in your relocation decisions, need not override other concerns. It is one of the natural features over which you have some control. The proper kind of filter and aerating device in your home can eliminate or greatly reduce most contaminants and improve the water's taste.

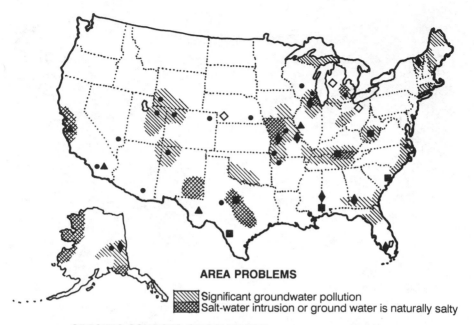

AREA PROBLEMS

▨ Significant groundwater pollution
▩ Salt-water intrusion or ground water is naturally salty

SPECIFIC SOURCES OF POLLUTION

■ Municipal and industrial wastes from oil and gas fields, well drilling, harbor dredging, excavation for drainage systems
◇ Well injection of industrial waste liquids
● Toxic industrial wastes
◆ Landfill leachate
▲ Irrigation return waters

Figure 8-6   Ground Water Pollution (*Source:* Veronica Pye et al., *Groundwater Contamination in the United States,* Philadelphia: University of Pennsylvania Press, 1983. Used with permission.)

The future availability of water may be as big an issue as its quality, especially in the Midwest and West. Cities such as Los Angeles and Phoenix have suffered increasingly frequent shortages. The recent succession of summer droughts suggests a trend for the worse. (See Figure 8-7.)

Hazardous waste (in case you're not utterly depressed by now) is everywhere. According to the EPA, there are 1189 sites in the United States, 116 of which are under federal jurisdiction. New Jersey leads the list with 109 toxic dumps. Nevada has the fewest, with a single site.

Nuclear power plants pose another source of concern in spite of the decrease in "shutdown incidents." It only takes one Chernobyl to ruin your day. The pace of new nuclear plant construction has ground almost to a complete halt. As of 1989, 13 new reactors had construction permits; two more were on order. Nuclear power's future is hard to predict because

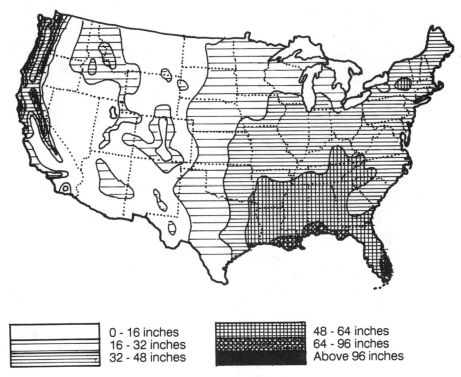

0 - 16 inches	48 - 64 inches
16 - 32 inches	64 - 96 inches
32 - 48 inches	Above 96 inches

Figure 8-7 Annual Precipitation (*Source: The National Atlas of the United States of America,* Washington, DC: U.S. Dept. of the Interior. Geological Survey, 1970.)

of the complicated mix of social, political, and purely energy-related factors that determine energy policy. (See Figure 8-8.)

Natural Hazards

Hazards created by humans aren't the only destructive phenomena to consider if you are completely free to choose your destination. The effects of Mother Nature's regular tantrums cost billions of dollars and extensive loss of life each year. Floods are one of these. We can predict where but not when low-lying areas will be flooded. Figure 8-9 shows how much flooding to expect over a ten-year period anywhere in the 48 contiguous states.

Returning to the natural hazard that opened this chapter, earthquakes, we can predict neither the location nor time of an earthquake, though measurement technology continues to improve. Seismic activity results from the movement of the earth's tectonic plates, and the areas with the least stable plates are found in the western states, near mountains.

Though minor earthquakes occur regularly in all earthquake-prone areas, California has taken the lion's share of major hits so far. The famous

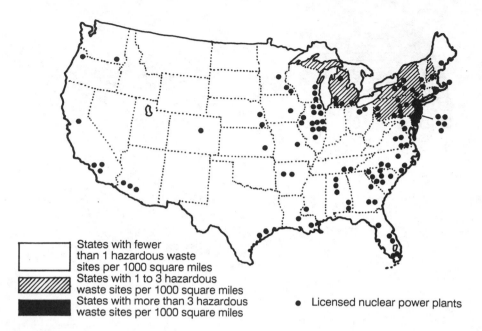

States with fewer
than 1 hazardous waste
sites per 1000 square miles

States with 1 to 3 hazardous
waste sites per 1000 square miles

States with more than 3 hazardous
waste sites per 1000 square miles

● Licensed nuclear power plants

Figure 8-8   Hazardous Waste and Nuclear Power Plant Sites (Compiled from data in the *1992 World Almanac* and U.S. Council for Energy Awareness.)

1906 earthquake that destroyed San Francisco was immortalized in a movie. In October 1989, the Loma Prieta Earthquake, which measured 7.1 on the Richter scale, killed 67 people and caused an estimated $680 million in damage. A series of tremors with hundreds of aftershocks occurred through the spring and summer of 1992 in various parts of California, making residents wonder if "the big one" would soon follow.

The Rocky Mountains are also due for a major earthquake. A 1959 earthquake near Yellowstone National Park caused a massive landslide that dammed up the Madison River and created an entirely new lake.

Architectural design codes classify the United States into four seismic zones, according to the intensity of earthquakes measured or predicted.

Unfortunately, the most dangerous areas of potential seismic activity include major population centers. Many of the heavily populated regions of California fall into one of these. Another hot spot includes three of Utah's biggest cities; Ogden, Salt Lake City, and Provo-Orem. If you want to locate in an area with the least risk, consider the Dakotas, Minnesota, Wisconsin, Texas, and the Gulf states. (See Figure 8-10.)

But the Gulf Coast will land you right in the path of another natural hazard: high winds. Hurricanes rake the Gulf and Atlantic coastal areas every summer and fall with winds often exceeding 90 miles per hour.

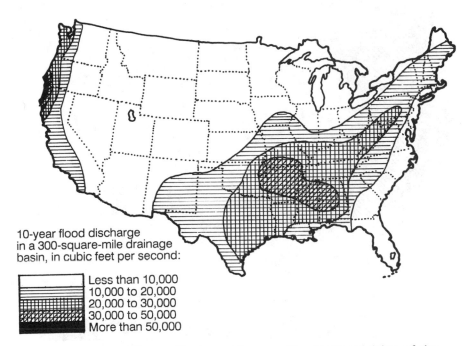

10-year flood discharge
in a 300-square-mile drainage
basin, in cubic feet per second:

Less than 10,000
10,000 to 20,000
20,000 to 30,000
30,000 to 50,000
More than 50,000

Figure 8-9 Flood-Prone Regions (*Source: The National Atlas of the United States of America,* Washington, DC: U.S. Dept. of the Interior, Geological Survey, 1970.)

Meanwhile, their inland cousins, tornadoes, rise up unpredictably to sweep across the Midwest from the Texas panhandle northward to the Canadian border. Though they are much smaller than hurricanes, tornadoes can generate winds exceeding 200 miles per hour and often level everything in their path. Figure 8-11 will give you an idea of where you are likely to be threatened by high winds.

Fire is another natural hazard that endangers human settlements, but areas at risk are harder to pin down with accuracy. Recent droughts have made vast areas of the West virtual tinder boxes waiting for disaster. Yellowstone Park caught fire on 20 August, ("Black Saturday, 1988"). A week later, when most of the 300-foot-high flames were under control, 706,277 acres inside the park and another 285,002 outside had been incinerated. On 20 October 1991, the worst fire in California's history reduced 3,000 homes to charcoal and killed 22 people on the hills above Oakland.

If you overlay each of the preceding maps, you may conclude that there are only two places free from artifical and natural hazards: Fort Rock, Oregon and Las Vegas, Nevada. On second thought, maybe there is just one. If you move to Las Vegas, you may escape nature's wrath and get wiped out anyway.

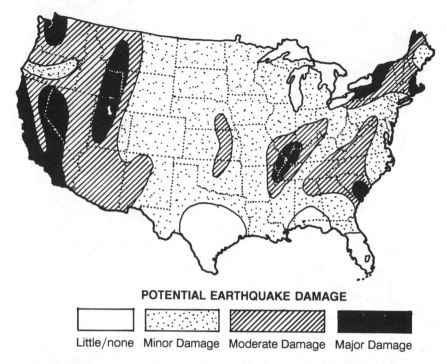

POTENTIAL EARTHQUAKE DAMAGE

Little/none   Minor Damage   Moderate Damage   Major Damage

Figure 8-10   Area of Earthquake Hazard (*Source: Earthquake History of the United States,* Revised ed., Boulder Colo.: U.S. Dept. of Commerce, National Oceanic and Atmospheric Administration, 1973.)

Lifestyle Criteria: It Takes More Than Green Trees to Make a Life

Away from the Madding Crowd

Does anyone really want to live in a crowded environment? According to a 1985 Gallup poll of 1,557 persons who were asked where they would like to live, only 7 percent preferred cities with a population of one million or more. Fifteen percent opted in favor of a medium city (100,000 to 1,000,000). Fifty-two percent preferred small cities or towns, and 25 percent favored rural areas (1 percent reported "don't know"). John Herbers argues in *The New Heartland* that many of those who had to live in big cities were never truly urbanized in the way that many generations of Europeans were. They fled as soon as the opportunity arose.[1]

Their first flight outward was to the suburbs. Many towns that sprang up after World War II such as Levittown, Pennsylvania, were sterile at the

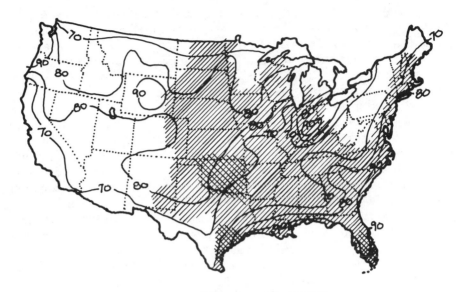

ANNUAL PROBABILITY OF TORNADOES

Areas with at least a 50% chance of one or more tornadoes per year

Areas with greater than 50% chance of one or more tornadoes per year

MAXIMUM AVERAGE WIND SPEED

 Maximum expected wind speed in miles per hour at 30 feet above the ground

Figure 8-11 Wind Hazard Areas (*Source:* Adapted from *The National Atlas of the United States,* Washington, D.C.: U.S. Dept. of the Interior, Geological Survey, 1970.)

outset—row upon row of monotonous little boxes stamped out of the same mold. In time, the owners added their own personal touches—a porch here, a wing there. Trees grew. Eventually, the developments matured into attractive communities.

By the 1970s urban decay had spread into the suburbs, bringing with it drugs, crime, deterioration of facilities and services, and traffic congestion on the arteries connecting residential neighborhoods to shopping areas and central city cores.

Today, new residents in the suburbs are likely to be formerly urban-based minorities who can now afford to leave the central city but still work there.

But how dense is dense, and how close to your neighbors do you want to be? We know from animal studies that you can stuff only so many rats into a cage before social organization breaks down and they eventually destroy each other. No one to my knowledge has put a figure on how densely packed cities can get before similar things happen. Some very thickly packed cities, such as Amsterdam and Hong Kong, seem to work. In others, such as New York and Los Angeles, the urban fabric appears to be unraveling, but is it due to population density or other factors?

Whether or not population density affects the breakdown of society, it has been linked to how satisfied residents are. A 1979 survey by urbanologist Mark Baldassare revealed that overall dissatisfaction was greatest in high-density neighborhoods and that satisfaction with local institutions, housing, traffic, and public safety also declined with increasing densities.[2]

The average population density of big cities was 3,005 persons per square mile, according to the 1980 census. Watered down to include the suburbs, the figure was still around 300. But density can be misleading. Consider Utah and New Hampshire—two states very different in size but close in the total number of inhabitants. Utah's average density is 21 people per square mile (land area only), whereas New Hampshire's is 123. Yet Utah is really two worlds: a 90-mile-long, 30-mile-wide strip along the western slope of the Wasatch Range containing 900,000 people (300 persons per square mile) and the rest of the state, barely inhabited. New Hampshire's population, scattered around the hundreds of small towns and villages throughout the state, makes any one place feel uncrowded.

Density may be as much a function of perception as of people per unit of land. Take the physical arrangement of housing. Apartment buildings are higher in density than the row housing of the type built by the thousands in the 1980s. But as Joel Garreau points out in *Edge City*, the two types simply trade one kind of adjacency for another.[3] Row housing, he suggests, is what you get when you tip an apartment building on its side. Instead of neighbors above and below you separated by a floor or ceiling, you have them stacked side by side, separated by a wall. Even the dinky private yard space allotted each unit for summer barbecues isn't much bigger than the balcony of an apartment. In the end, you may feel more crowded in row housing than in vertical apartments.

If the perception of crowding rather than density alone is a truer measure of people's satisfaction with their locale, it favors rural rather than urban locations. A recent Roper Organization survey of 1,010 adults found that 66 percent of rural residents said they were optimistic about their community's future, compared to 54 percent of the total public. The rural respondents also rated the friendliness of their area good to excellent. Only 59 percent of the total public did so.

Commuting/Travel

If you ask a commuter "How far do you live from your work?" you may be more likely to hear "one hour" than "45 miles" in reply. People have always measured commuting distance in terms of time, writes Joel Garreau in *Edge City*, and the maximum distance they have ever been willing to commute has been 45 minutes. Cities like sixteenth-century Istanbul were rarely wider than people could traverse in 45 minutes, when walking was the state-of-the-art transportation mode. Manhattan in the twentieth century was about 45 minutes by car or train from the outlying suburbs of Long Island, Westchester County, southwestern Connecticut, and northern New Jersey. Today that's all different. Two-hour commutes from central New Jersey and Connecticut are common.

Los Angeles was born and bred to be enslaved to the automobile. Each year, its 6.5 million cars waste 485,000 hours, 72 million gallons of gas, and $507 million in lost productivity, commuting, or crawling through gridlock. Average speeds, now 35 miles per hour, are predicted to slow to 19 by 2010.

The availability of housing and quality of life have always determined how far people would commute. They still do, but the choices are different than when cities, suburbs, and rural areas were more easily identified. Today's office workers may have to go 60 miles from the city to find affordable housing, but instead of commuting back into the city, they commute to an office park maybe only a few miles down the freeway. The new scene creates a wild variety of commuting times and distances, ranging from self-employed professionals who work out of home offices to others who willingly endure long commutes to obtain the desired quality of life.

Many of the entrepreneurs mentioned earlier are able to work where they choose to live because they are willing to travel occasionally on buying trips, to visit clients, or attend trade shows. Even if you are able to reduce or eliminate daily commuting, carefully consider how frequently you may have to make such trips and how long it takes to get to the nearest major airport.

Cost of Living

The cost of living is generally higher in cities than in outland areas. A move outward will probably trim your housing and food costs. Everything else is an unknown to be discovered through research just like other local factors. If your work depends on a national market, you might choose to locate in a low-cost state such as Florida. You'll have to be more selective if you aim to cater to a local market.

Moving to a small town or rural area will probably mean an increase in your transportation budget even if you base your business in your home. You will likely be removed from mass transportation services or at least won't be able to depend on them to meet many of your transportation needs; you'll be forced to rely on one or more cars. You may not be commuting as far to work yet put a lot of miles on the car ferrying yourself and other family members between school, church, shopping, and recreation.

Some additional costs may not show up in local cost-of-living data. Your telephone bill may grow substantially, because most of your calls will likely extend beyond the local calling area. If you don't intend to give up TV with your move, your choices may be to pay a monthly fee for a cable service or else invest in a satellite dish.

Then there are local and state tax structures, which are sure to affect your cost of living. The total number of taxes may not be as important as how they affect you, given your occupation, family size, and housing. New Hampshire, for example, neither taxes income nor retail sales (with minor exceptions). I'm still not used to getting a penny back when I fork over a $5 bill for an item marked $4.99. But schools and local services still have to be funded. This is painfully apparent to me every six months when the town socks me with a property tax bill seven times larger than my monthly mortgage payment.

Housing

Whether you seek better-quality housing, lower costs, more space, more distance between you and your neighbors, or simply a chance to own your own home, you will have more opportunity in the outland than inside a metropolitan area. Two criteria should weigh into your thinking about housing when you compare prospective destinations: availability and cost.

If you are part of the great baby boom generation, you may need more space for a growing family. The stock of three- and four-bedroom homes in small towns is much better than in large cities where apartments predominate. If you intend to buy cheap and fix up, I'd look for an area with a good variety of old homes. A good range of home sizes will ensure you a decent chance to suit your family requirements.

As to costs, the purchase price will likely be your first concern. Look for areas that offer houses in a variety of cost ranges. Here, too, you will do better than in a metropolitan area. During the boom years of the 1980s, housing costs soared to unattainable levels in many cities. One study reported the 1989 cost of a typical 1,800-square-foot house at $290,000 in Boston, $244,400 in San Francisco, and $150,277 in Washington, D.C. The same houses in nonmetro areas were half that or less, but you had to go farther out to find them.

When considering cost, don't forget the ancillary costs of home ownership, such as property taxes, operation, and maintenance. If you locate in an area with cold winters and high fuel costs such as the Northeast, the cost of winter heating can be as much as $1,200 for an uninsulated house with no exposure to the sun. Houses in hot or warm climates may need upgrading to cut down the heat gain and reduce the operating cost of air conditioning. Repairs and maintenance add still more to your overall housing costs but can be minimized if you do the work yourself.

Access to Goods and Services

Wherever you end up, you won't be out of reach of the material goods and services that make a good life. But outland living may require a shift from buying out of stores to buying out of catalogs. Or instead of running out on impulse to buy one or two items, you'll need to consolidate them on a list and wait for a major shopping trip to the nearest supply source.

Access to services may be more limited. The nearest repair center for my ailing Sony reel-to-reel tape recorder is Weston, Massachusetts, 90 miles away. It's still waiting for service. Some specialized services, such as piano tuning, may not be available at all.

Before you begin comparing prospective destinations, it might help you to consider the material things and services that really matter in your life. List each of them according to importance. Then next to each, write down the number of times per year you are likely to need that product or service. In another column, indicate whether you can get each item through the mail. A glance at your finished list should tell you how far out you can relocate without radically changing your lifestyle.

Health and Personal Care

When rating a prospective location's personal care and healthcare facilities, you'll be interested in variety and quality. You could begin by listing your personal care needs. Almost everyone needs a barber or beauty shop, and these are available even in the smallest villages—though the variety may shrink. If you are a male used to sweet-smelling unisex salons where they shampoo you first, you may have to make do with "men's" barbershops where you read dog-eared copies of *Field and Stream* while waiting.

What healthcare services might you or your family regularly need? A family practice doctor, a dentist, and an optometrist are probably a must for most people. Other possibilities might include an orthodontist if your teenager needs braces, an obstetrician-gynecologist if pregnancy is nigh, a chiropractor if you have a chronic back problem, and maybe a therapist (if country life starts to get to you).

There are specialists for every condition, but they locate according to their own desires, not your convenience. It's no accident that specialists cluster around big cities. That's where the major hospitals are and where the amenities are diverse enough to accommodate a specialist's income level.

Hospitals are where people go when they have an illness or need medical attention. As such, they are more oriented towards illness care than healthcare, or preventive maintenance. Big hospitals, squeezed by rising costs in recent years, are being gradually displaced by well-equipped clinics run by groups of physicians with complementary skills. You can't predict if and when you might need a hospital's services, but rather than trying to locate yourself near a major hospital, you might do better to locate near an all-purpose clinic that can handle anything from a sprained ankle to cataract surgery.

Which brings us to another question: How do you get to a hospital or treatment facility in an emergency? Wherever you end up, you should have access to an ambulance service—public or private—that can reach you in short time and get you to the right facility.

There's no single yardstick for rating the quality of health care in an area, but combining many measures paints a reasonably accurate picture.

One of the best indicators is the infant mortality rate—how many babies of one year or less die for every 1,000 live births. Another is the communicable disease index—a composite number of cases of venereal disease, tuberculosis, and hepatitis per each 1,000 inhabitants.

A frequently used indicator of local health care is the number of physicians per 1,000 people. Of course, the number won't show whether those who need medical attention are getting it.

If you do use hospitals and clinics to measure the level of care available to unwell persons, what could you use to measure a region's concern for wellness? You might tally the number of commercially run fitness centers or public facilities such as the YMCA and YWCA or the number of alternative care options aimed at prevention rather than treatment. You might ask what kinds of public outreach programs are offered by local hospitals and clinics regarding prenatal care, obesity, substance abuse, AIDS education, and other medical concerns.

Public Safety

Crime is on the mind of almost every urbanite these days. A 1990 Gallup Poll revealed that a surprisingly high number of Americans regard several of the largest and most popular tourist cities as unsafe places to live and work. New York headed the list, with 85 percent of those responding feeling it was unsafe, followed by Miami (76 percent); Washington, D.C. (71 percent); Detroit (68 percent); Chicago (65 percent); Los Angeles (64 percent); and San Francisco (43 percent).[4]

Though crime is no longer just an urban problem, moving to the outland will improve your chances of escaping both personal and property crime. I have always sensed this but was shocked to find how much difference there actually is. The FBI Uniform Crime Reports annually list the crime rate in the form of a crime index total—the number of property crimes (burglary, theft, larceny, and arson) and assault crimes (rape, murder, and aggravated assault) committed per 100,000 inhabitants. The 1989 crime index total for the communities profiled in the last chapter ranged from 2,727 in Sanford, Florida, to 5,012 in Bryan, Texas. Now look at how big cities fared: 70,003 in Boston, 319,097 in Los Angeles, and 712,419 in New York City—261 times that of Sanford. Until this pattern is reversed, it will be no wonder that people who can are fleeing big cities.

Crime statistics don't tell you the whole story of how a community addresses public safety. The number of police officers per 1,000 inhabitants indicates if the area is adequately staffed. The number of fire fighters and the location of the nearest fire station would also be worth knowing.

Education

Some say that Americans are the most schooled and least educated people among the industrial countries. Are our schools really getting worse, or is education a convenient scapegoat for American inability to compete with foreign manufacturers? The answers are complex and political. Although few will deny that inner-city schools have been on the skids for some time, more disagree on the state of the nation's schools as a whole. Comparisons to Japanese or European schools conveniently ignore the differences in mission. American schools, reflecting our democratic ideals, have always sought to provide an equal measure of education to all citizens, regardless of race or economic status.

Schools of other countries—Germany, for example—are rooted in an elitist system that sorts students early on into one of two classes. After completing the equivalent of public school, bright students go on to college-track secondary schools; the rest go to technical or vocational high schools or drop out to join the work force.

With no general agreement as to what exactly our schools should be doing, what should you look for when you rate the educational quality of a place you are considering for residence? Here are some criteria that appeal to me.

First, make sure there are schools available and accessible for the age range of your children. High schools in rural areas can be few and far between. If the high school is far out, expect a lot of driving to get your children to and from after-school activities.

As to rating quality, I'd start with the school dropout rate. If students are leaving the schools in droves, you can infer that the schools are not meeting their needs and that the schools' influence in the community is less than optimal.

A third yardstick is the amount of public money expended per pupil. Although this doesn't guarantee quality, it does tell you something about how much the community values education. You can use other corollaries of the numbers game, such as the average number of pupils per class, the number of students that go on to college, and level of teachers' salaries.

Subjective factors also tell a lot about local schools but are harder to qualify. The age and condition of the buildings indicate how well the district addresses the physical requirements for learning. I'd want to know the type and range of available extracurricular activities—sports, drama, music, and special clubs. Classes or programs offered to the community at night speaks of commitment beyond merely teaching the three R's.

Your Social and Cultural Life

On a typical Friday, Mark leaves the office at 5 P.M. (remember Mark from the introductory chapter?). He joins a group of friends at O'Reilly's bar, three blocks away. Over the course of an hour or so, the friends unwind. Here Mark can freely air the ups and down of his workweek and talk of plans for the weekend. Later it's off to dinner with Diane. They choose among a dozen interesting eateries within a short radius of downtown Boston—everything from stand-up oyster bars to sit-on-the-floor Japanese restaurants. Tonight they'll settle for one of the creative sandwiches and black beer at a German restaurant, so they will have enough time to make the 8 P.M. performance of a Nigerian group at the Wang Center.

For all of the woes of urban life—no need to repeat the litany here—Mark likes the amenities that only big urban areas offer. He worries that culture shock will set in if he leaves. His concern is justified. Small towns and rural areas simply don't get many symphonies, ballets, and national theater troupes. Nor will you find the diversity of restaurants, clubs, libraries, and museums in Fargo that you enjoyed in Minneapolis.

If you want to maximize your chances for cultural amenities, look for small towns that are homes to major universities. Missoula, Flagstaff, Fayetteville, and Logan, Utah, all offer cultural opportunities you wouldn't expect to find in their region were it not the home of a state university.

Even if you end up in an area without a university, you might not be so far away from a metropolitan area that you can't get to the big city three or four times a year to visit the museum, eat Thai food, and see the big city lights. For the rest of the time, there are other options, as we'll see in Chapter 11.

Sports and Recreation

As with arts, the type of sports and recreational opportunities you enjoy or pursue are sure to change when you leave the big city. Rooting for a major league team from a grandstand with several thousand other frenzied fans will be a thing of the past or limited to your occasional visits to the city. Will watching your local bush league team battle the one from the next town compensate?

If your outland locale is deficient in facilities for major league sports, it may compensate with other outdoor opportunities. As I write this in the waning weeks of winter, I take frequent breaks from my word processor to gaze out the south windows of my studio at kids skating on the pond across the road. When Lucie comes home later in the afternoon, we'll leash up Ralf for a three-mile walk on a road rimmed by maple trees and stone walls. Last week they attached taps to the maples, which were connected by plastic tubing to plastic tanks that collect the sap for syrup. Ralf stops now and then to sniff out a cranny between the stones, wondering how recently the chipmunk was there.

Come June, we'll start swimming in a lake two miles up the road. The sand for the small beach was trucked in, but everything else is genuine. The water is clean enough to drink, and even after several years of acid rain, it's still home to sunfish, frogs, and salamanders.

Depending on your bent, you can locate in an area that will be close to fishing, hunting, camping, or simply walking. Hell, just being away from city lights will mean you can see the stars at night. And it's so nice to hear crickets chirping instead of sirens wailing.

Chapter Nine

How to Select the Best Location

How many of your previous places of residence did you pick through a methodical process? Few, I'll bet, if you are like most people (myself included). Like balls on the pool table, we tend to get bumped around without benefit of conscious choice or a grand plan. Maybe not knowing where you will be five years from now is better than knowing. It certainly makes life interesting.

But where would you go if you had the chance to pick the perfect place to live and work? Does such a place exist, or would you find that you want to live in Tahiti but could better run your business in Peoria? In this chapter, you'll have the chance to find out. Whether you end up moving or not, you will have been through the process of making an examined choice. It might even be fun.

The method I propose starts by examining the big factors that affect why you prefer some regions over others and then zooms in on specific sites within a target region for detailed consideration. After researching data you deem important for your lifestyle and business needs, you can rate several candidate sites against each other and narrow the choice down to a final few.

Methods and systems can be useful but they don't always make the final decision. Some overriding personal factor—an allergy or penchant for wind surfing—may determine where you end up. Or maybe you'll get frustrated and base your decision on a gut feeling or the toss of a coin. In any case, you'll be better prepared by undertaking a rational process of gathering and evaluating information than if you rely on shortcuts at the outset.

Factors That Decide Your Fate

The many factors that decide your destination, if you move, can probably be grouped under two headings: preference and freedom—where you want to go and where you are free to go. I'd like to address the first by showing ways to apply the location criteria of the last two chapters. But first, let's see what factors limit your choice of location.

Your freedom of movement, at any given time, is limited by factors outside your control and by you yourself. The need to be near an aging parent is an external factor. Fear of the unknown is internal. I suspect most people are controlled by a combination of the two and that the proportion is constantly changing. When we view the pattern of our lives over time, the image may recall the balls on the pool table. Age itself may be a limiting factor.

Young children are naturally free and curious about the world. At some point their culture begins to close them in, telling them what they can and can't do. "Don't waste your time playing around with that piano, Christie, just practice the stuff for your lesson." Thus, Christie's opportunity to learn to improvise has just been squelched. Successive signals of this sort dampen children's natural curiosity about the world beyond their immediate setting. With the loss of curiosity goes the perception that they can change their circumstances. They soon learn to prefer the comfortable, if imperfect, world they know to the unknown.

Of course, not everyone gets narrowed down to the same extent. Just as Lucie feared putting down permanent roots in one location, we now have neighbors who have lived in this small New Hampshire town all of their lives and can't imagine ever leaving.

What kinds of barriers have you set for yourself? Are there places you can't imagine living because of preconceptions? If so, finding out about what it is really like there may open many doors and extend your world of possibilities. For example, if you had asked me about Fayetteville, Arkansas, before I started researching this book, I probably would have said it was backwater, full of yokels whose highest cultural expression was Johnny Cash. The real Fayetteville, as we saw in the last chapter, has a diversity I never dreamed of.

Are there places such as Fayetteville yet unknown to you where you might be happy? If so, I would like to suggest a four-part method you can use to find and evaluate them. It begins by matching your lifestyle and business requirements to select a broad region and then helps you narrow down areas within this region to result in a short list of candidate locations. The third step is to find out as much as you can about each candidate without actually going there. Last, I'll give some tips to help with your on-site research of final contenders.

Finding Your Perfect Region

Figure 9-1 shows the United States carved up into 12 areas according to broad similarities (to keep the exercise manageable, I arbitarily left out the states of Alaska and Hawaii as well as Puerto Rico and the U.S. Virgin Islands—any of which may be a candidate region). I took another liberty in the way I set the boundaries around each region. But I feel these boundaries best define the broad commonalities that people usually associate with each region. For example, Region 1, (New York and New England) is an area with strong cultural, geographic, and climatic similarities. The largest, Region 10, contains six western states marked by wide open spaces of mountains and plains and low population density.

Filling out Worksheet 9-1 is the first step of the four-part method of selecting the best site for you. Simply pick from the 12 regions of the contiguous United States shown in Figure 9-1 using the general criteria listed.

You can obtain some of the data for this first step from the discussion of regional features in the previous chapter. Other data may require a trip to the library or a few phone calls. It might help to fire you up if you think of yourself as an explorer, which is what you are.

The first category, lifestyle factors, lists climate and geography. The object is to combine the type of climate you prefer living in with any climatic requirements of your business. For example, agriculture, recreation, or hospitality may work in some natural settings better than others. Geography follows a similar pattern.

For the second category, business factors, list important features of a broad region that are important to your business. "Growth mode" and "diversity" are listed as examples. Demographic factors might include breakdowns by age group or other factors you choose, such as the percentages of families, working women, and the like.

Selecting Specific Candidate Locations

On to the second step: finding candidate destinations within the region you favored in Worksheet 9-1. You can approach this procedure as an art (stand back and throw darts at a map) or as a science. Here's the scientific approach.

Say Region 11, comprising Washington, Oregon, and northern California, garnered the most check marks. Or perhaps you are determined to end up there, in spite of the damp, gray climate of the Pacific Northwest.

Because this region contains communities of every size and type, you need two or three initial limiting factors. Pick important considerations

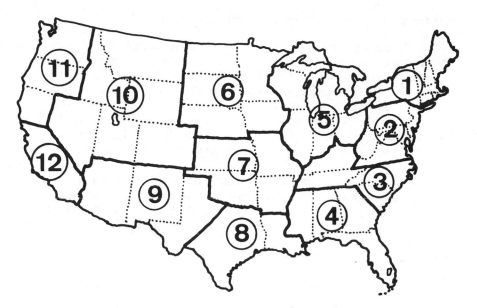

Figure 9-1 Map of Regions

that you can quickly evaluate from a good map. Let's say you settle on the following three requirements:

1. You want a town of between 15,000 and 50,000 people.
2. You don't want to live in or near Seattle or Portland, but business trips from time to time require you to be within, say, 100 miles of a major airport.
3. One of the factors that determined this region (from Worksheet 9-1) is your desire to be near mountains.

Start with the map of each state in the region, say California. From the airport data in Figure 7-1, you'll note that Sacramento is the only major airport serving northern California. Use a compass to draw a circle representing a 100-mile radius on the map, centered on Sacramento. Using the compass, you can determine the size of the circle from the scale that appears somewhere on the map.

A good atlas or state road map will key the size of the town to the size of the dot representing it. If you need to find out the economic relationship of the community to the surrounding area, locate an economic atlas such as the *Rand McNally Commercial Atlas* (you'll find it in the reference section of your library), which differentiates between towns with populations between 25,000 and 100,000 and "principal business centers" of less than 25,000 people. In this example, however, we'll assume that

Worksheet 9-1   Which Region Should You Locate In?

This worksheet matches general criteria from your business and lifestyle
needs against the 12 regions of the United States shown on Figure 9-1.
Indicate how important each factor at the left is (1 = minimal, 2 =
moderate, 3 = very). Rank how well each region meets each criterion, from
0 to 3. Multiply this figure by the degree of importance and enter the result
under each region. For example, If climate is very important and region 1
has an unacceptable climate, its score is 2 x 0 = 0. Add the scores at the
bottom of the form to get the best region(s) for further investigation.

Criteria	Import.	Score for candidate regions
		1 2 3 4 5 6 7 8 9 10 11 12

Lifestyle Factors

Climate	
Near rivers, lakes	
Near ocean	
Near mountains	
Other:	

Business Factors

Growth economy	
Diversified economy	
Demographics:	
Other:	

Totals	

your market is national and that you've chosen a target size for other reasons.

The northeast portion of the circle falls within the Sierra Nevadas. Chico (26,600) and Yuba City (18,740) are two towns near the Sierras within the population parameters.

The next state in the region, Oregon, is served by one major airport in the Portland area. Most of the cities and towns within a 100-mile radius of Portland are also within the western slopes of the Cascade Range. You pick Corvallis (40,960), Tilamook (21,160), and Astoria (10,000).

Most of Washington State is within 100 miles of the Seattle, Spokane, Yakima, or Portland (Oregon) airports. You avoid towns in the southwest corner of the state, which is flat, rather than mountainous. Yakima (49,826), Longview (31,050), and Wenatchee (17,260) grab your attention.

You now have eight candidate locations for further investigation. Limit them further, if you want, by considering criteria such as proximity to water. Then list the survivors in the columns at the right side of Worksheet 9-2. The items listed on the left of the worksheet are suggested criteria you might consider, but feel free to ignore as many as you want and add your own. If you need more spaces than provided, then make an enlarged form, using this as a model.

To compare the locations you listed on Worksheet 9-2, you need information about each. Step three of the process enables you to find this data without having to visit each site.

How to Find Out What It's Like Without Going There

You can obtain some of the data you'll need for Worksheet 9-2 from the maps and information in Chapter 8. Other information will require deeper digging. Your public library and nearby college or university library are the best places to start. They contain reams of information if you know where to look for it. If it has been a while since you last dogged through the card catalog for a college research paper, you are in for a few surprises. Even small libraries are swiftly joining the electronic age. The card catalog is being replaced by electronic databases.

For general information on places, start with the large atlases in the reference department. (I've found that the quickest path to success in the reference department is the reference librarian.) Also in the reference department you may find a collection of phone books from around the United States. They probably won't have hard-copy listings for the smallest towns you are investigating, but they may have them on microfiche. If you have the time, call the customer service representative of your phone

Worksheet 9-2   Comparing Specific Locations

Write your list of candidate locations in spaces under "Candidate Locations." Under "Factors," write any additional factors important to you. Rate how well each location satisfies each factor in terms of 0 (unacceptable), 1 (acceptable), or 2 (well). Finally, add the scores of each in the subtotals, and then add those for the total scores.

Criteria	Candidate Locations					

Lifestyle Factors

Climate:	Sunshine						
	Temp., humidity						
Geography:	Rivers, lakes, ocean						
	Mountains						
	Forests						
Environment:	Safety from flooding						
	Safety from earthquakes						
	Safety from high winds						
	Safety from hazardous wastes						
	Air quality						
	Water quality						
	Quality of built environment						
Cost of Living:	Local taxes						
Housing:	Cost advantage						
	Diversity/availability						
Necessities:	Availability/diversity						
Repair Services:	Auto						
	Equipment (appliances, etc.)						

(continued)

Worksheet 9-2 *Continued*

Healthcare:	Hospitals/clinics							
	Doctors/dentists							
	Ambulance/emergency care							
	Fitness facilities							
	Community wellness programs							
Public Safety:	Low crime rate							
	Adequate fire protection							
Education:	Adequate no. of schools							
Cultural:	Symphony/theater/arts							
	Churches							
Recreation:	Outdoor recreation							
	Spectator sports							
	Restaurants/clubs							
Child/eldercare:	Childcare facilities							
	Eldercare facilities							

Subtotals, lifestyle						

Business Factors

Proximities:	Near an airport							
	Near major highway							
	Accessible to major city							
	Accessible to hub city/town							
Demographics:	Least competition							
	Per capita retail sales							
	Per capita income							
	Low unemployment							
	Diversity							

Subtotals, business						

Totals						

company and order a copy of the phone book for each candidate location on your short list. They will mail you a copy of any phone book you request and add the charge to your phone bill. This time and effort spent will be repaid many times over in the savings you make tracking down data.

Small-town yellow pages are a gold mine of useful information. Many begin with an overview of the community—its history, economic base, and cultural and recreational amenities. Individual categories tell you what the community offers. Just look what you might glean from the A's alone:

- **Accountants.** The number of accountants in a community tells you how high the business activity is and what services you may want to use in your own business.
- **Air Cargo, Package Express.** If your enterprise depends on regularly shipping goods, you will need convenient access to land and air delivery services.
- **Ambulance Service.** You may never need one, but it could save the life of a family member in a medical emergency.
- **Antique Dealers and Restoration Services.** If you are going into the antique business, you will probably stand a better chance in an area with a critical mass of antique dealerships that attracts customers from other regions.
- **Architects.** Unlike antiques, the fewer the better if you are looking to establish an architectural practice. A given area can only provide a market base for so many architects (some say 1 per 20,000 population). Beyond that ratio, you will probably have to seek markets beyond the local area.
- **Associations.** The abundance of community organizations such as United Way, Alanon, arts groups, and historical societies auger well for community services.
- **Auto Repairs.** Getting your car fixed is not a high-satisfaction service, such as getting a haircut, so it will minimize the pain if you at least have a wide selection of repair services.

Phone directories also list health services, schools, colleges, banks, real estate agencies, the chamber of commerce, daycare facilities, and other indicators of a well-rounded community.

Now let's take a more detailed look at some of the local area criteria you may want to list on Worksheet 9-2 and how you can get the facts from where you are now.

Lifestyle Factors

Climate and Geography

You thought you had finished mulling over climate/geography issues when you homed in on a region, didn't you? Well, not quite. In some regions, such as New England/New York (Region 1), the climate is similar enough overall to consider it one type. Others, such as Region 10 (which contains six western states), have overall regional similarities but climates can vary from place to place. St. George, Utah, for example, is considerably warmer and sunnier than Cour D'Alene, Idaho. Check the respective maps on climate, geography, and vegetation in Chapter 8 for general information. If you need more specific data, you might obtain it from an atlas or the chamber of commerce. If your business enterprise requires more extensive data, you can find it in the *Comparative Climatic Data for the United States*, published annually.[1]

Environment

You can find general data on areas subject to flooding, high winds, earthquakes, hazardous waste, and air pollution in the maps in Chapter 8. Specific locations can vary widely, though. For example, Salt Lake City's valley accumulates air pollutants, which reach health-threatening levels in winter. I used to drive up into the canyons east of the city and look down on the lid that hovered over the valley floor. If your target location is anywhere near a metropolitan area, you can probably get regional pollution data from the appropriate state agency or city department. Environmental statistics for the state are published in two annual reports by the Government Printing Office, Washington, D.C., 20401: *Environmental Quality: Annual Report*, by the U.S. Council on Environmental Quality; and the *National Air Quality and Emission Trends Report*.

All but the smallest cities and towns have maps that show where the flood plains are and the likelihood of flooding within 10- and 100-year periods. You should be able to get help on this one from the town's building or planning department.

Hazardous waste sites are everywhere, as was pointed out in the previous chapter. Those prioritized for cleanup under the Superfund provisions—1001 of them as of this writing—are listed in the Federal Register, which is available in most libraries. All Superfund sites and other waste sites under evaluation are listed in a database called CERCLA (Comprehensive Environmental Response Compensation and Liability Act). To get the current printout of sites within the state you are interested in, contact the regional office of the Environmental Protection Agency (EPA). For the location and phone number of the branch office for that region, call (800) 424-9346. If you hit a dead end with the EPA, try contacting the appropriate state agency, such as the public health, natural resources, environmental protection, or water resources department.

The built environment (everything beyond nature) will matter to you if one of the reasons you want to flee a metropolitan area is to be surrounded by more attractive stuff to look at every day. Unfortunately, you won't escape urban ugliness by merely choosing a smaller community. Many once-attractive town centers have become tawdry. The route into the center of town is likely a commercial strip of low-rise fast-food joints, car lots, and road signs. Brochures from the chamber of commerce won't show these parts of town, so look for other indications. The presence of a historic district is a good sign. Look for specific references such as "many well-preserved Victorian houses." You might try phoning the town's planning department to ask what the town's visual setting is like. If the official doesn't understand what you mean by "visual setting," you're in trouble.

Cost of Living

You'll have a leg up on cost-of-living information if you know someone you can rely on in the area. Ask them to send you the Sunday edition of the largest newspaper in the region and copies of any shoppers' weeklies. But odds are you don't know anyone there, so lean on a local real estate broker as suggested in Chapter 3 in the section on job hunting.

You can learn a lot about the costs of area housing from the real estate sections, but the wide variation in types of housing makes it hard to put this data into a form suitable for a quick-and-dirty appraisal of how areas compare. I suggest you give up on housing as a cost-of-living indicator. Instead, use groceries. Make a short list of, say, ten items you buy every week. Make a total and repeat the process for each area, using the same items. This is a reasonable figure to use at this stage for comparing the cost of living from one area to the next.

An annual index of the cost of living appears in the *Statistical Abstract of the United States*, available in the reference section of your library.[2]

Housing

Between the broker's advice and the local newspaper's Sunday edition, you'll get a good overview of what's available. You may get distracted by falling in love with a specific listing, so remember that at this stage you are only interested in general information for comparing this area with other candidates. A real estate broker friend offered a good tip: disregard the houses in the bottom third of the price tier—the picture has likely been framed to exclude the service station or busy street next door.

To assess housing availability in the area (vacancy rate), divide the number of vacant units by the total housing units. If the friendly broker you phoned earlier has this data, use it. If not, rate the area, from 1 to 5 to measure how easy you feel it might be to find housing there.

Consumer Goods and Services

As with housing, you'll get a good overall picture of the cost and availability of goods and services from scanning the candidate town's newspaper and yellow pages. Heed one caveat, though: Directories for low-density areas often include several small regional towns in the same book. You can easily be misled into believing two computer stores listed consecutively are close by when, in fact, they may be in opposite ends of the county. It will help to use the directory in conjunction with a map.

To compare candidate areas in the worksheet, you might use the two suggested categories, grocers and department stores, or create your own. Most people buy groceries at least once a week and need general merchandise sold at department stores. From the yellow pages, count up the number of retail grocers and department stores in the same area or within a reasonable driving distance and use this to compare candidates. For the next blank in the form, services, pick a frequently used category such as auto repair or plumbing (or a composite) and make a similar index.

Healthcare and Personal Care

Five items mentioned in Chapter 8 are listed on Worksheet 9-2 as general indicators of healthcare and personal care in a community. You may add or substitute others, depending on your individual and family needs. Determining the number of hospitals, clinics, and specialists is easy if you have the town's phone directory. Similarly, you can find out how many facilities offer fitness conditioning by looking under listings for "gymnasiums" and "health clubs."

The total physicians per 1000 people is a good figure for comparison with other locations. If you can't get this with a call to the county or state health department, you can come up with a figure by counting the physicians listed in the yellow pages, dividing that number by the area's population, and then multiplying the result by 1000. If you do get a friendly ear from the health department, you might also ask them for the infant mortality rate and communicable disease index.

Public Safety

Of the various indicators of public safety mentioned in the previous chapter, the two simplest and easiest to obtain are the number of police officers and fire fighters per 1000 people. You should be able to get these figures by calling the personnel department of the area's police and fire departments.

Of course, just knowing the number of police officers won't tell you much about the area's crime rate or types of crimes committed. The *Uniform Crime Reports,* published by the FBI each year, will. Available at your library, this compendium rates all but the smallest towns for crime rates of murder, rape, robbery, aggravated assault, burglary, larceny, theft, motor vehicle theft, and arson.

Education

For a quick indicator of the educational setup in a candidate town, you might phone or write the public school board or district administrative office and ask how much the district spends on each pupil and what the dropout rate is. Make sure you don't enter the rate itself in the worksheet; use it to see how low each area's rate is and then rank them, with the lowest area receiving the highest ranking.

A good library source of educational statistics is the *Digest of Educational Statistics*, published annually by the U.S. Center for Educational Statistics, Government Printing Office, Washington, D.C., 20401.

The number of colleges and universities in the area will probably be indicated in the material you receive from the chamber of commerce, or else you can quickly look it up in the yellow pages.

Cultural Amenities

Area information supplied by the chamber of commerce is sure to tout cultural amenities in the area, such as live theater, dance, and the arts. You may not give a damn about ballet but crave contra dancing or barbershop quartet singing. Since these are not commercial enterprises, they may not appear in the phone book. Specifically ask about them when you phone the chamber of commerce or other sources you may talk to who are willing to share regional lore.

Recreation

Your easiest source of information concerning the area's outdoor recreational facilities will be the chamber of commerce data. Look for restaurants and clubs and other items of interest to you in the yellow pages. You can create an index number for use in the worksheet in various ways. Look under "restaurants" and count the number of different categories rather than using the total number of establishments (who wants to live in a town with 18 pizza parlors and not a single Thai restaurant, anyway?).

Business Factors

Proximities

From a good detailed source such as an atlas or road map you should be able to determine the distances important to your business or lifestyle, such as the distance from the center of town to the nearest airports, interstate highways, seashores, lakes, as well as the nearest big city. A quick and easy way to quantify the distances is to use an economical compass (the kind you draw circles with), obtainable at dime stores.

Demographics

Chapter 7 explored some of the kinds of local demographic data that can influence the success of your enterprise. The rapidly shifting population patterns over the last few years caused by changes in the national economy make tracking down reliable current demographic data a daunting task.

Start with general information and move toward the specific. For good sources of national demographic trends, check your library's recent issues of magazines such as *American Demographics, The Futurist,* and *Inc.* The following books are packed with helpful information: *By the Numbers: Using Demographics and Psychographics for Business Growth in the '90s; Megatrends 2000; The New Corporate Frontier: The Big Move to Small Town USA; Edge City; The New Heartland; and Trend Tracking* (listed in the Appendix).

The U.S. Bureau of the Census publishes detailed reports on the demographic makeup of various population centers including specialized breakdowns of the population by sex, race, and age; types of households; number of rooms in each household; presence of household appliances; and number of automobiles per household. The types and availability of reports are listed in the *Bureau of Census Catalog.* Look for this catalog and any pertinent specialized reports in the reference section of your library.

You may get adequate demographic data from the chamber of commerce. If not, check with the state or regional planning agency or industrial development bureau.

Local Economy

As with demographic data, start with general sources (the easiest to find) and move toward specific data applicable to your enterprise. The best single source I have run across is *The Rand McNally Commercial Atlas,* which contains economic statistics for hundreds of cities and towns according to their economic importance to the surrounding region.

Another general source for economic statistics is the *Almanac of the Fifty States,*[3] an annual listing of state-by-state statistics on transportation, real estate, retail trade, and other data.

You might find all of the local economic data you need from the *State and Local Statistics Sources,*[4] published by Gale Research, Inc. The last part of the book lists hundreds of sources for further searches of state and local facts. If you prefer the phone to library research, check with the area's planning agency or industrial development bureau, as with demographic data.

Business Services

The area branch of Senior Corps of Retired Executives (SCORE) can tell you what kind of business services you are likely to find in any of the towns where they maintain branch offices. The Small Business Administration operates a national network of area centers. Locate the SBA field office nearest the area of your interest through the white pages of the local telephone book by looking under "United States Government, Small Business Administration" or by writing to the agency's headquarters, Washington, D.C., 20417.

On-Site Research

The two worksheets, when completed, will help you pick a region and specific candidate locations within it and then compare each candidate to arrive at the final choice. Your final decision should be made after a visit to each destination under serious consideration, step four of the selection process. No amount of off-site research can tell you what it is really like there. No matter how diligent you were in collecting data from a distance, you may be surprised to find that the flavor and feel of the place isn't exactly what the chamber of commerce brochures promised. Qualities such as community spirit, so necessary to your fitting in and getting your business going, are hard to assess from a distance.

Chapter 8 suggested you find out as much as possible about your dream destination from where you are now, through phone books, chamber of commerce propaganda, and the like. If you were lucky in your preliminary fact finding, you obtained a cost-of-living index for your target area. Now you can fine tune the data with some spot checking.

How many trips should you make? How long should you plan to spend there? Unfortunately, there are no one-size-fits-all answers to these questions. It all depends on your circumstances; you alone should decide.

The next section pegs specific things to look for on your fact-finding visit and how to go about it. We'll assume that this trip is exploratory. Your aim is to gather data, not to look for specific houses to buy or rent; that alone could consume all the time you allotted for the trip, so your time and efforts will be better spent in scoping out the type, availability, and general cost of housing. If you then decide in favor of this place, you can make a a serious housing search on a second or third trip.

First, some general tips. Arrive at your motel or other temporary base of operations with a car. The car and a phone will be your best friends during the short (and maybe hectic) time you spend here. Have a good map of the area and study it in advance to get a general feel of where things are and the distances between them.

Two more helpful tools to have on hand are a camera and a tape recorder. I suggest you buy three or four rolls of black-and-white film to record your impressions of the setting. If you run across serious candidates for housing, photograph them. Use the tape recorder while driving around to record your impressions. When not using your tape recorder, turn on the car radio to a local A.M talk radio show. An hour of learning what ticks off the natives might be all it takes to turn you off to this area. If you had been listening to the talk shows in my area today, you would have heard hunters ranting in protest of a bill currently before the state legislature that would expand the distance between houses and free hunting area from 300 to 1000 feet. I had no idea the law allowed someone to shoot within 300 feet of my house!

If you are staying at a motel, get friendly with the management. Ask them where the locals go for meals, such as diners and coffee shops, and then eat there yourself rather than at a restaurant that caters to travelers. You may have to grit your teeth over the "blue plate special," but it's worth the price if it connects you with folks who can fill you in on the local scene—the pithy stuff you didn't read about in the chamber of commerce literature.

Scoping Out the Real Housing Scene

Housing is likely your single biggest expenditure, and housing costs vary widely. The initial visit will be your best chance to find out the type, cost, and location of available housing.

Before your trip, you might phone one or more real estate brokers in the area. Tell them the kind and size of house you are interested in buying or renting and ask them to mail you current listings. They may send you a "relocation package" containing listings plus other information, some of which may even prove useful. You may have enough data to estimate the housing costs without visiting the broker, but you may want to do so anyway to fine-tune your facts. It may be hard to keep from getting drawn in at this point. You may fall in love with the town the minute you first see it. Then, if the broker happens to show you the perfect house, it will be tough to stay noncommittal. If this happens, you will have to be prepared to put down a deposit in the form of earnest money, if you buy, or a month's rent, if you rent (more about finding, buying, and renting in the next chapter).

If you will be buying, you will want to know the cost and availability of getting a mortgage to finance your new home. A quick way is to phone or visit a local mortgage lender to nail down the interest rates, minimum down payments, and specific limits that may apply to your situation.

As the federal government has shoved the burden of supporting the schools onto municipalities in recent years, property taxes have skyrocketed in some areas. So the community's property tax may figure in as a major part of your overall cost of housing if you intend to buy. As previously mentioned, New Hampshire, has no general sales tax or state income tax. It is not uncommon to fork over annual property taxes of $3,600 on a home valued at $100,000. Pin these costs down with the broker or banker if you haven't already.

Basic Supplies

Use your first visit to get a feel for what consumer goods are available and how far you'll have to drive to get them. If you don't have an idea by now of how much things cost in this area, use the list of ten items suggested in the last chapter to check out actual prices at a nearby supermarket. Use the same kind of list for clothing, hardware, and other items you regularly buy.

Superfluities

It's easy to get caught up in necessities if your visit is short. But don't neglect the other things that make life whole, such as hobbies. Because I usually have one or more remodeling or furniture construction projects in progress, I need constant access to well-stocked building suppliers. If you are an amateur mechanic, you will want at least one good auto parts store. Other members of your family may benefit from cloth or yarn stores, arts and craft outlets, or home brewing suppliers. How many music stores are there? Do they sell tubas and oboe reeds as well as electric guitars?

An abundance of hobby outlets will not only enrich the lives of you and your family but also tell you something about how the natives spend their free time—an important point to consider in relation to your social integration in the community.

After-Hours Amenities

Your first visit can get you a firsthand glimpse of the cultural and recreational opportunities that were touted in the area's promotional literature. "A constant extravaganza of live entertainment at downtown clubs" may turn out to mean Saturday night performances of Harry Horsefly and his Gritty Sidewinders at the American Legion hall or Wayne and Wanda accompanied by a battery of electric instruments at a motel lounge.

Transportation

If you are moving to an area of lower population density—and you presumably are if you are reading this book—you are probably leaving an area with good mass transportation for one which, at best, has some sort of bus and taxi service. For better or worse, the automobile will be your major means of getting around. Although the cost of buying a car might not be critical because you can buy a car outside of the area, the cost of owning and driving will. If you haven't succeeded in pinning these costs down before your visit, do it now. Check first with an auto insurance agency to find out what insurance the state requires and then ask for a quotation based on your circumstances (number and type of cars, number and age of drivers, etc.).

The cost of fuel will be apparent the first time you fill the tank of your rental, but check out whether there is much variation between the cheapest and most expensive stations.

If you will need to fly out of the nearest major airport on business trips, you will do well to check out the options for and costs of getting from your home to the airport, which may include a bus, limo service, or a flight from a local airport. Find out what transportation links there are with the nearest metropolitan area. For the three or four trips we make annually to Boston, 85 miles away, we rely on a good bus service from Keene, 5 miles away. This choice may not save any time but definitely eliminates the anxiety of driving in downtown Boston—a madhouse by any standard.

Schools and Daycare

By the time of your first visit to the area, you will probably have an idea of the costs associated with education, both public and private, as well as the amount spent per student in the public schools. You may have gleaned some idea of the quality of education by examining the dropout rate and other statistics. Your visit to the area will give you a golden chance to get a real feel for the schools—even if it's a snapshot image.

Before you leave, contact the school district's headquarters to arrange a visit to a school. If someone at the school shows you around, take in all of the canned presentation but also keep your antennae tuned to the subtle signals. If it is an elementary school, is it an atmosphere that encourages or stifles a child's natural curiosity and enthusiasm? What do the displays in the hall tell you? What accommodations are there for special students, those who are gifted as well as those with some kind of handicap? Is the high school big on extracurricular programs? How does it stack up in sports, music, and drama?

Business Support

If you intend to start a business at your new location, you will naturally have an agenda of items to chase down, ranging from possible businesses to buy to scouting for locations and suppliers of materials. Consulting or working out of a home office will require computer and office supplies. Can you get these by mail order? Architects and engineers need periodic access to blueprinting services. Check into other services you might need in this locale, such as computer and equipment repair and other consultants.

To get a sense of how friendly the local government is to business, you might start with personal contacts you have already made—a real estate broker or banker, for example. They can give you a general idea. You will have to be more creative to find out just how the governmental policies of the city, town, or county affect your type of business. An architect or builder might find out about the building permit process during a visit to the town hall, ask the building officials how long the usual application process takes and how appeals are handled, and then get the other side of the story by talking to a few architects, engineers, or surveyors.

So now you have systematically picked out your Shangri La, if you followed the four-step process as described. In the next section we'll tally up the costs of relocating there to enable you to start planning—if you decide to make the move.

Part Five

How to Do It

Chapter Ten

Estimating the Costs
of Change

Think back for a moment to Mark, the disenchanted group manager from the introductory chapter. Imagine that he has finally had it with his urban job. In the course of a looser-than-usual Friday night happy hour, he suddenly sees with complete clarity why his career seems to have stalled and what is missing in his life. Having risen to his present position through his competence as a software writer, he no longer writes software. Nor does he have much power or control over how or what his group does. His suggestions for product improvements and innovations have fallen on deaf ears.

Mark has been thinking in increasingly serious terms of starting his own software company and seizing on the product opportunities his company has rejected. He even has a list of potential client companies that he can serve mostly by mail, enabling him to locate pretty much where he wants. Mark and Diane would like to move away from the Boston suburbs to upstate New York, where they could be close to skiing in the winter and lakes and woods for the rest of the year. The move will, they hope, enable them to become a more closely knit family and to forge ties to the community—something they miss at their present residence.

The idea was sparked on that fateful fall morning when Mark happened to glance up at the rustic picture on his calendar. It has since caught fire. Now he can't eat, drink, or sleep without thinking of striking off on his own. But he wakes up at two in the morning with anxiety attacks. "What are my chances of success?" he wonders, "how much money will I need, and where will I get it?"

Mark's concern is well placed. More than half of the 700,000 new businesses started this year won't survive the first three years. Only one-fifth will see their tenth year.

Although business writers differ on the exact ingredients for small business success, they seem to concur that a solid grasp of the financial aspects of business is a basic requirement. To determine if you can afford to dump your job, move to the outland, and start a business, you will need to thoroughly examine your financial circumstances. Even if you decide not to make the leap, it's something you should do anyway from time to time.

This chapter will give you a chance to estimate the consequences of a career change in a new location by completing a series of worksheets. The aim is to estimate the total costs at the end of six months, but you can extend it as far into the future as you like. Because there's no way to address all of the individual variations, two assumptions are in order:

1. You plan to relocate. You know where your destination is and have done some basic research about the area.
2. You plan to start a small business. You know enough about the business to estimate start-up and operating costs.

How Much You'll Need

The money you'll need to relocate and start a business can be broken down into four categories:

1. The amount you need to relocate your household to the destination of your choice.
2. The cost of disposing of your present home and getting housing in the target area.
3. Six month's living expenses.
4. The costs of starting and operating a business for six months.

Moving Costs

The cost of moving your household furnishings can vary a lot, depending on the total weight carried and distance. In 1992 the average household could be moved across town for around $500 and from one coast to another for $6,000. Movers can transport almost anything, from candlesticks to cars. But if the distance is very far, moving time is a good occasion to decide whether you really want to keep that tent you bought ten years ago and haven't used since. Why not consign all of that stuff you have forgotten about to the yard sale or charity? Your donations will make you feel warm inside and trim the cost you have to pay the mover.

To get an accurate figure of how much moving will set you back, ask interstate moving companies for estimates. They will send a representative to your house to walk through every room with you, recording the items you say will be moved. Their *estimated cost of service* may or may not bind the company, depending on how the estimate is qualified.

Housing Costs

Pulling up stakes and heading out will incur all sorts of expenses, some of which are easier to estimate than others. The more of these you can identify at the outset, the better prepared you'll be to deal with the unexpected, such as the possibility that you have to move before your present home is sold. During the time it awaits a buyer, you'll have to continue making mortgage and property tax payments.

You won't know the exact cost of your housing until you locate a specific house or apartment, but you can come up with a solid guess based on the preliminary research you did from a distance and, possibly, your visit to the area (you want to estimate only initial costs here; the monthly payments are covered in the next section, living expenses).

To get a fix on the cost of buying a house, start with your best guess of the purchase price. You may be able to dodge a high down payment through creative financing or having the seller carry the contract, but for now assume you'll be applying for a conventional real estate loan that would finance 80 percent of the purchase price. Your up-front costs will be the down payment, the remaining 20 percent, and closing costs—a laundry list of additions the lender tacks on, including title insurance, mortgage fees, transfer taxes, settlement fees, recording fees, credit reports, appraisal, and loan fees. If you can't tie these down with a call to the real estate loan officer at a bank in your destination area, throw in another 3 percent to 5 percent of the loan amount to get a rough figure.

When you move into a new place, you'll likely face additional expenses to get the place operational, such as paying for repairs, painting, and decorating as well as equipment you will need but not be taking along, such as a refrigerator you decide to leave behind. Add the approximate cost of as many of these as you can pin down. When you get there, you may find that you don't have to pay for these expenditures at one time but can schedule them on a priority basis.

Selling your own home will cost you either a lot of time and effort if you do it yourself or a commission of 6 percent or 7 percent if you engage a real estate agent. When you are researching the area, find out what local or state quirks may add to the selling costs, such as deed preparation, notaries, or other expenses. Connecticut, for example, requires you to hire an attorney to handle the contract.

Your Living Expenses for Six Months

One of the most common bits of advice offered by the entrepreneurs portrayed earlier was "Have enough to live on until your business becomes profitable." There seems to be little agreement on how much that ought to be, but the range suggested by these entrepreneurs and other sources is three months minimum for retail businesses and six months or longer for service enterprises and manufacturing.

If you are moving out of a metropolitan area, your odds favor moving into a lower cost of living. You probably have an idea of the difference already from preliminary fact finding about the area. But because long-term advantages will be offset to some degree by short-term contingencies—all of the little settling-in costs you won't be able to estimate at the outset—it might be best to assume that your cost of living will continue at the same rate as last year.

To get a quick figure, dig out your checking account records for the last six months. Write down the balance of the first statement; let's say it was $5,000. Now add up all deposits made in the six month period, say $30,000, and add them to the opening balance for a total of $35,000. Subtract the balance at the last statement, say $8,000, and you end up with a net figure of $27,000. That is the amount you spent in the last six months. If you try this procedure, make sure you throw out any large, uncommon expenditures, such as cash paid for a new car or the $6,000 you lent your nephew for college expenses. Also add in amounts transferred to savings accounts or investments, because those are not actually a living expense.

If your expenses were not all paid out of one account or you want a deeper understanding of where you are spending your money, cull your records and itemize them as shown in Worksheet 10-1.

Business Expenses for the First Six Months

The cost of establishing and operating your business for six months can range from a few thousand to several hundred thousand dollars. A writer or consultant working out of a home office can start with little more than a computer, a few office supplies, a phone, and a spare room. Retail businesses require much more up-front investment for space, inventory, and a variety of start-up accessories. Manufacturing enterprises usually entail the highest initial expenditures. Detailed analyses of start-up costs, beyond the scope of this book, are available in some of the excellent reference sources listed in the Appendix. The aim here is to help you get a ballpark

Worksheet 10-1   Living Expenses for Six Months

Expense	Monthly x 6 = Total	
Housing		
Rent or house payments	_____	_____
Insurance	_____	_____
Utilities	_____	_____
Property taxes & fees	_____	_____
Maintenance and other expenses	_____	_____
Food and groceries	_____	_____
Transportation		
Car payments	_____	_____
Insurance	_____	_____
Car upkeep, parking, gas, misc.	_____	_____
Federal and state income taxes	_____	_____
Personal expenses, nondiscretionary		
Loans	_____	_____
Doctors, dentists, drugs	_____	_____
Health insurance payments	_____	_____
Life or other insurance	_____	_____
Education, childcare	_____	_____
Other	_____	_____

Subtotal, nondiscretionary expenses   _____   _____

Personal expenses, discretionary		
Vacations, travel	_____	_____
Entertainment	_____	_____
Gifts, contributions	_____	_____
Newspapers, magazines, books	_____	_____
Other	_____	_____

Subtotal, discretionary expenses   _____   _____

Total of all living expenses for six months	_____	_____

estimate of how much you'll need to get into business before you take the plunge.

So where do you start? Research. Find out everything you can about the enterprise. From the library you can borrow books on small business in general and about your field in particular. You may discover the latest developments through trade magazines and other periodicals. If the library has a good resource department, you might find a trade association that publishes regular newsletters. Think of this stage as fishing; at the outset there's no knowing what exactly you might catch. In time, your efforts will prompt questions that will focus your research and help you answer basic questions such as: What is the market for my product or service? What is its profit potential? Is the market saturated? Am I too early or too late? Is it sensitive to national or local economic dips?

These and other questions will eventually have to be addressed in a business plan if you seek financing from outside sources. Preparing a business plan will not only help you persuade lenders to help finance your operation but also help you clarify your goals and intentions, as well.

What you present in your business plan depends on the type and size of the operation. Starting a small retail store might entail explaining how you intend to make your operation a competitive force in its market area and where you will get supplies. Someone looking to finance a manufacturing enterprise should focus on such matters as licensing, research and development, means of production, and the like. In addition to the introduction, table of contents, and any supplemental information, the bare bones plan for a small business start-up should cover the following points:

Business Concept
- Description of product or service and the market niche/opportunity
- Overall goals for earnings and growth
- Form of ownership
- Experience and qualifications of you and other key personnel
- Organization and management, number and type of employees
- Location, physical facilities (leased or rented)

Marketing and Promotion
- Target customers and market area
- Competition—who, where, and how many
- Marketing strategy (why will customers buy from you rather than the competition)
- Projected sales

Financial Considerations
- Projected earnings, monthly and annual
- Projected cash flow for first and subsequent years
- Opening balance sheet (initial position, assets the business will have, and how much will be needed to finance)
- Collateral sources, including market value of each item
- Personal financial statements
- Names of your accountant, attorney, and insurance agent

You can get free help preparing a plan from the local chapter of the Service Corps of Retired Executives (SCORE) or through the business books listed in the Appendix. When you get down to working up the final plan, a few hours with your accountant will be a worthwhile investment. Before you get to that stage, however, you should know where you stand financially.

The worksheets that follow will help you look at your financial picture so you can better decide whether to go through with your plan and, if so, what additional financing you might need.

Worksheet 10-2 is designed to help you tally up your business expenses for the first six months (this is a reasonable period of time to assume you'll need before profits start coming in, but you can pick any time horizon you want). Individual line item costs vary from business to business, but every business has a bulge in costs at start-up, followed by more predictable monthly operating costs. You can use the form as a model and tailor it to your own business requirements.

What Are Your Resources?

Estimating the costs of moving, setting up a business, and living for six months helps you set a financial goal for yourself. To determine how much additional money you'll need, you will next want to examine your personal resources.

You may have already done a net worth evaluation, perhaps many times. It's a useful exercise even if you don't plan earth-shaking changes in your future. But the net worth assessment in Worksheet 10-3 is a little different. Rather than lumping all your assets together, it isolates those you can or want to sell off from those hard to liquidate or that you want to keep. After all, you would probably choose to borrow a little more if interest rates are favorable rather than cash in IRAs or retirement funds at a severe penalty. And you may not want to sell stocks if their current market value is too low.

Begin by listing all cash assets you have access to—checking, savings, and cash buried in the rabbit holes out back. Next, enter stocks and bonds

Worksheet 10-2   Business Expenses for First Six Months

One–time expenditures	Amount
Opening inventory (retail only)	_____
Deposits	
Lease	_____
Utilities	_____
Licenses	_____
Other	_____
Equipment and fixtures	_____
Leasehold improvements, remodeling	_____
Opening promotion, advertising	_____
Other start-up expenses	_____
	_____
	_____

   1. Subtotal, one–time expenses   _____

Monthly operating expenses	Monthly
Inventory maintenance (retail)	_____
Wages	_____
Payroll (wages plus taxes)	_____
Rent	_____
Advertising, marketing	_____
Insurance	_____
Accounting, legal, other services	_____
Supplies	_____
Transportation	_____
Telephone	_____
Utilities	_____
Other monthly expenses	_____
	_____
	_____

   2. Subtotal, monthly expenses x 6 =   _____

Total of all business expenses for first six months (1 + 2)   _____

along with their market value at the time of your evaluation. The first two categories represent funds most easily converted to cash, though you may suffer some penalties for early withdrawal or a currently low share price.

Worksheet 10-3   Personal Resources

PART IA – LIQUID ASSETS

1. Cash

Bank	Account	Date	Balance
_____	_____	_____	_____
_____	_____	_____	_____
_____	_____	_____	_____

Total cash > _____

2. Stocks and Bonds

Stock/bond	Shares	Price	Balance
_____	_____	_____	_____
_____	_____	_____	_____
_____	_____	_____	_____
_____	_____	_____	_____

Total current market value > > > > > > > > > > > > > > >_____

3. Real Estate to be Liquidated

Name of property	Date	Current Equity
_____	_____	_____
_____	_____	_____
_____	_____	_____

Total value of liquidated real estate > > > > > > > > >   _____

4. Personal Property to be Liquidated

Item	Date	Value
_____	_____	_____
_____	_____	_____
_____	_____	_____

Total value of liquidated personal property > > > > >   _____

TOTAL LIQUID ASSETS (1 + 2 + 3 + 4)   _____

(continued)

Worksheet 10-3 *Continued*

PART IB – NONLIQUID ASSETS

---

5. Life Insurance and Annuities

Name of instrument	Mkt. price	Date	Value
_____	_____	_____	_____
_____	_____	_____	_____
_____	_____	_____	_____

          Total value of life insurance and annuities > > > >   _____

---

6. Real Estate to be Retained

Name of property	Date	Current Equity
_____	_____	_____
_____	_____	_____
_____	_____	_____

          Total value of retained real estate > > > > > > > > >   _____

---

7. Misc. Loans, Trust Deeds, Accounts, Notes Receivable

Description	Date	Value
_____	_____	_____
_____	_____	_____
_____	_____	_____

          Total value of accounts owed you > > > > > > > > >   _____

---

8. Personal Property to be Retained

Item	Date	Value
_____	_____	_____
_____	_____	_____
_____	_____	_____

          Total value of retained personal property > > > > >   _____

          TOTAL NONLIQUID ASSETS (5 + 6 + 7 + 8)   _____

          TOTAL ASSETS (1 through 8)   _____

(continued)

Worksheet 10-3 *Continued*

PART II – LIABILITIES

9. Notes, Credit Accounts, Personal Property Loans You Owe

Loan and Creditor	Terms	Monthly Payment	Balance Owed
_____	_____	_____	_____
_____	_____	_____	_____
_____	_____	_____	_____
_____	_____	_____	_____

Total you owe >   _____

10. Real Estate Loans and Mortgage Payments

Loan and Creditor	Terms	Monthly Payment	Balance Owed
_____	_____	_____	_____
_____	_____	_____	_____
_____	_____	_____	_____

Total you owe >   _____

11. Other Personal Liabilities

Bank	Terms	Monthly Payment	Balance Owed
_____	_____	_____	_____
_____	_____	_____	_____
_____	_____	_____	_____

Total other liabilities > > > > > > > > > > > > > > > > > >   _____

TOTAL LIABILITIES (9 + 10 + 11)   _____

PART III – NET WORTH

Total Assets   _____
Total Liabilities   -- _____

NET WORTH   _____

In Section 3, list real estate you plan to sell to accumulate capital for your move, including your home, undeveloped land, and any other properties. But remember that real estate is liquid only if it can be sold.

List any other personal property you would like to (and believe you can) sell in Section 4, such as surplus vehicles, furniture, and appliances. Be conservative here. Enter real market values, not what you think these items ought to be worth.

The total, so far, gives you a target figure to use in figuring the net cost of your change.

In Part 1B you will list all assets that have value but aren't as easily liquidated or that you will sell off only as a last resort.

List all retirement accounts in section 5—IRAs, KEOGHs, annuities, and life insurance. Be sure to list the surrender value of the insurance and annuity policy (what they would be worth if you could convert them to cash today). Check with the agent if you are unsure.

After you itemize the real estate you want to retain in section 6, enumerate all money owed you in section 7: loans, trust deeds and mortgages, accounts, and notes receivable. Loans might include the $5,000 you loaned to your nephew to help him pay for his car. Trust deeds and mortgages could include a second mortgage you hold on another property. Write in the monthly payment and most recent balance owed for each item.

Section 8 is a catch-all, where you can list all personal property that could be converted to cash if necessary. Separate the big items—cars, boats, or grand pianos—but lump small things such as miscellaneous furniture together. As in Part 1A, use real market value, not sentimental value.

Add up the above for a total of your nonliquid assets and then add in the amount from the first part, Liquid Assets, for a total of all assets you hold or have an equity in. To find out how much equity (or your net worth), complete the next section, Part 2, Liabilities.

In Section 9 list all accounts for which you owe a balance. Start with personal notes and loans. Be sure to include any loans you have taken out against insurance policies. Enter each credit-card account, the average monthly payment, and the total amount owed.

Real estate (mortgage) loans can be enumerated in section 10. Write in the bank and then the terms, which, for a mortgage loan, might read something like "fixed rate, 9.75%, 20 years, ending in 2005." Include your monthly mortgage payment and the total remaining to be paid (you should find this figure at the bottom of each monthly statement).

Section 11 is where you list all other debts that don't fit neatly in any other category, such as past due tax liabilities, loans to relatives that may not have rigid terms, fines, those traffic tickets gathering dust, outstanding bribery payments, and so on. Now total all your liabilities.

To figure your net worth, subtract your total liabilities from your total assets. This bottom-line figure is useful when you write up your business plan to apply for loans. It is the most optimistic amount you can marshal toward realizing your dream.

The Bottom Line

You can figure out the financial consequences of your move on Worksheet 10-4, which is based on a six-month time line—the assumed period before your business enterprise produces a positive cash flow. Your bottom line will show a surplus, if your resources exceed your anticipated costs, or a deficit, if not. Part of the deficit may be split between a real estate loan to finance your next house and additional financing needed to establish and run your business for six months.

The worksheet is designed to allow you to go through several iterations to reflect different scenarios. Copy the form for as many iterations as you need and then list the assumptions of each iteration at the top. For example, let's consider how our hypothetical urban refugees, Mark and Diane, might use the form under two scenarios, A and B.

The couple would like to sell their present home, appraised at $125,000, and buy a home of similar price at their new locale. They don't want to move until they actually have the proceeds from selling their house in hand. These are the assumptions Mark writes in at the top of Worksheet 10-4 and labels "Scenario A."

From Worksheet 10-3, Mark and Diane estimate their liquid assets to be $113,000 if they can sell their home for $125,000 ($8,000 in cash, $30,000 in stocks and bonds, and $75,000 equity in their home). They have excluded retirement investments valued at $35,000 from the list of assets to be liquidated, but they are willing to sell off other investments consisting of stocks, bonds, and money market accounts. Diane has locked up a teaching job at their destination, from which the couple can count on a net six-month income of $17,000. Their total available resources for the first six months thus amount to $130,000.

They estimate moving costs at $10,000 and the cost of selling their present home at $8,750 (7 percent of its sale price of $125,000). Because they will apply all proceeds from the sale of their former home to the purchase price of the new one, they list $125,000 on the line for down payment. In the following line, they write in the closing costs, $3,750. From Worksheet 10-1, they estimate their cost of living for the first six months to be $15,000, which does not include house payments because the house was paid off. Total living and housing costs thus total $162,500.

Worksheet 10-4 Your Finances for the First Six Months

Scenario: _____

....

....

....

....

PART I – AVAILABLE RESOURCES

	Amount	S.Total	Total
1. Liquid Assets (Worksheet 10-3)		_____	
2. Other Sources			
Spouse's 6-month income	_____		
Your part-time 6-mo. income	_____		
6-mo. Interest/dividend income	_____		
_____	_____		
Subtotal, other sources		_____	
3. Total available for use > > > > > > > > > > > > > > > > > > >			_____

PART II – ANTICIPATED COSTS FOR 6 MONTHS

	Amount	S.T.	Total
4. Living/housing Costs			
Moving expenses	_____		
Home selling costs	_____		
New home closing costs	_____		
New home down payment	_____		
6-month living expenses	_____		
_____	_____		
Subtotal		_____	
5. Business Expenses (Worksheet 10-2)		_____	
6. Total Costs for first 6 Months > > > > > > > > > > > > > > > >			_____

PART III – SURPLUS OR DEFICIT

Surplus or Deficit (line 3 minus 6)	_____	- _____	=	_____

(continued)

Worksheet 10-4 *Continued*

Scenario: (A)

1 - BUY $125,000 HOME
2 - SELL PRESENT HOME BEFORE MOVING
3 - APPLY PROCEEDS TO COST OF NEW HOME
  ($125,000)

PART I – AVAILABLE RESOURCES

	Amount	S.Total	Total
1. **Liquid Assets** (Worksheet 10-3)		113,000	
2. **Other Sources**			
Spouse's 6-month income	17,000		
Your part-time 6-mo. income	~		
6-mo. Interest/dividend income	~		
	~		
Subtotal, other sources		17,000	
3. **Total available for use** >			130,000

PART II – ANTICIPATED COSTS FOR 6 MONTHS

	Amount	S.T.	Total
4. **Living/housing Costs**			
Moving expenses	10,000		
Home selling costs	8,750		
New home closing costs	3,750		
New home down payment	125,000		
6-month living expenses	15,000		
	~		
Subtotal		162,500	
5. **Business Expenses** (Worksheet 10-2)		10,000	
6. **Total Costs for first 6 Months** > > > > > > > > > > > > > > >			172,500

PART III – SURPLUS OR DEFICIT

Surplus or Deficit   (line 3 minus 6) 130,000 - 172,500 = (42,500)

(continued)

Worksheet 10-4 *Continued*

Scenario: (B)

1- BUY $125,000 HOME
2- SELL PRESENT HOME BEFORE MOVING
3- FINANCE NEW HOME THROUGH REAL ESTATE
    LOAN

PART I – AVAILABLE RESOURCES

	Amount	S.Total	Total
1. **Liquid Assets** (Worksheet 10-3)		113,000	
2. **Other Sources**			
Spouse's 6-month income	17,000		
Your part-time 6-mo. income	—		
6-mo. Interest/dividend income	—		
_____	—		
Subtotal, other sources		17,000	
3. **Total available for use** >			130,000

PART II – ANTICIPATED COSTS FOR 6 MONTHS

	Amount	S.T.	Total
4. **Living/housing Costs**			
Moving expenses	10,000		
Home selling costs	8,750		
New home closing costs	3,750		
New home down payment	25,000		
6-month living expenses	23,400		
_____	—		
Subtotal		70,900	
5. **Business Expenses** (Worksheet 10-2)		10,000	
6. **Total Costs for first 6 Months** > > > > > > > > > > > > > > > > >			80,900

PART III – SURPLUS OR DEFICIT

Surplus or Deficit (line 3 minus 6) 130,000 - 80,900 = 49,100

Because Mark's business can be operated out of an office in the home, his start-up and operating costs will be a modest $10,000, from Worksheet 10-2. Total costs for the move and first six months will be $172,500.

Subtracting this figure from their anticipated available assets, they end up with a net deficit of $42,500, which will have to be financed somehow.

The couple wonders what the bottom line would be if they applied the proceeds of their home sale to a down payment and other expenses and financed their new home through a conventional real estate loan. On to Scenario B.

Part 1 stays the same. In Part 2, the new home down payment decreases to $25,000 (20 percent × $125,000). But living expenses increase by $5,400, the amount of six months of house payments, which they figure at $900 per month. Their total costs for six months now amount to $80,900, resulting in a bottom-line surplus of $49,000.

But what happens if Mark and Diane can't sell their home by the time they have to move out to allow Diane to start her teaching job on time? They get out their calculator again to work up Scenario C. They can use the form to trace through this and other scenarios to reflect various other assumptions, such as:

D. Not being able to sell their present home before they move and having to continue making house payments until it sells (another scenario might reinclude monthly rent of the house if they can rent it in the interim).

E. Reducing the bottom-line surplus of Scenario B by taking out a smaller real estate loan.

F. Rent, rather than buy, a house at the new location.

Mark and Diane know that successfully changing career and location is fraught with uncertainties. One of the biggest challenges is making the numbers work. They will scheme some more until they come up with one or more workable scenarios. With a firm grip on the financial aspects of their venture, they will have removed one of the biggest sources of worry and be one giant step closer to realizing their dream.

Chapter Eleven

Settling In

A Place to Live

Moving out of the city or suburb to an area of lower population density will mean a change not only in your living accommodations but also in the way you relate to your neighbors. Because both kinds of changes have potential for positive and negative outcomes, it's to your advantage to understand as many of the implications as possible before you make hard-to-reverse choices.

More affordable housing is one of the first things you will likely notice. Small towns and rural areas beat out metropolitan areas hands down when it comes to price and variety. You'll find a much better stock of detached, single-family houses—both new and old, an appealing prospect if you are looking for an alternative to a small and expensive inner-city apartment.

Socially, you are likely to trade anonymity for repute. In a small town your life will become everyone's business for better or worse, but more about fitting in later. For now, let's explore the issues you will face in finding the right housing in the outland.

Rent or Buy?

Owning a home with a yard may be one of the engines driving your move out of the city. Home ownership, ever part of the American dream, has also been a reliable monetary investment in the past, particularly in the early 1980s. You could pay for a home with a loan with an interest rate of of 8 or 9 percent and then watch your home appreciate at the rate of 10 percent or more.

Today the call is closer. The recession of the early 1990s created a glut of unsold homes. In some areas, prices declined; in others, prices stayed high but the homes stayed on the market longer. Meanwhile, the rate of appreciation of houses shrank to under 5 percent.

Still, real estate has outpaced other forms of investment since the 1970s. Even with a down payment of 20 percent, home ownership is a leveraged investment that you can finance over a term as long as 30 years. If you are in a high tax bracket, the deduction for mortgage interest and property taxes you receive on your federal income tax is a substantial advantage. Your increasing equity, in time, becomes a reservoir of savings that you can use as collateral for loans.

Whether or not you intend to buy a home in your new location, consider the advantages of renting a house in the area for a while as an intermediate step. The current glut of unsold homes has left many on the market for several months. Because the owners continue to pay for property tax and upkeep, they are inclined to rent them out until they find a buyer.

Renting will give you a chance to "test drive" a candidate house and get a feel for the neighborhood while freeing up your cash flow to help you get your business established. If you need more time to find permanent quarters, it will provide a base from which to conduct your search.

Ample time is an ally when house hunting. You will have a better chance of finding the right housing—and keeping your peace of mind—if you begin before you relocate and follow a methodical process such as was suggested in Chapter 9. Alas, things don't always line up in the order you want, forcing you to act on the spur of the moment. They still work out if you keep your cool—they did for us when we faced a tight schedule in our last move.

When we moved to rural New Hampshire in the fall of 1983, we had only two one-day visits to the area to search for a home for our family of four. We looked for a home to rent, using the office of my new employer as a base of operations. Knowing nothing about the rural region surrounding the headquarters in the quaint village of Harrisville, we tracked down housing prospects from newspaper want ads and area real estate listing brochures, then scouted them out over the phone.

Nothing at all was available in Harrisville, and two full days of chasing down prospects turned up nothing within a 25-mile radius, the maximum distance I was willing to commute (everything is relative—my previous office in Salt Lake City was five blocks from the house).

Utterly discouraged by the end of the second day, we were driving to our motel when I spotted a real estate office on Main Street in Marlborough. Thinking "What do we have to lose?" we stopped to ask if they knew of any homes for rent in the area. The agent told us about a three-bedroom home that a Connecticut couple had bought for their retirement but wouldn't be moving into for a year or two. They might be interested in renting it out temporarily.

The home was a nice, if compact, Dutch Colonial frame home in a valley surrounded by trees—too many goddamn trees. In winter we seldom saw the sun (there isn't a whole lot here anyway). The constant gloom and lack of a vista depressed me.

We walked our dog on a circuit that took us up a hill on one side of the valley we lived in. At the top, my attention was always drawn to an aging but once proud red Colonial farmhouse with a for-sale sign almost hidden in the unmowed grass. Attached to the rear of the house was a huge barn in even worse repair, and attached to it was yet another, smaller barn. The home overlooked a pond to the south and the hills of Marlborough to the north. To the northeast, the vista extended all the way to Vermont's Green Mountains.

One of the things that most attracted my attention was the unbroken access to the sun on the south side. I dreamed of sitting in the new sunspace I would build where the decrepit porch now was, drinking a cup of coffee amid tropical plants while the sun heated the house. Would this house be a handyman's dream or turn into a bottomless money pit?

After a year in our rented house, we bought the home on the hill at a good price and spent the next five years pouring money and effort into transforming it into the home of our dreams. Today, the big barn has been razed, and the sunspace graces the south side. The home fits our family's personality like an old shoe.

But I'm glad we rented for a year. The time not only gave us the opportunity to investigate the problems and potentials of the house on the hill but also allowed us to consider other houses without being pressured.

Scoping Out Country Homes

When you get around to serious house hunting, be prepared. Know what to look for and systematically record your findings. After you have checked out two or three houses, their features tend to get muddled in your mind. A camera and tape recorder or a clipboard for taking notes will help you recall the differences later when you are comparing candidates.

Find a method that suits your style. I can record much more data on a walk-through inspection by speaking into a small tape recorder than by trying to take notes on a clipboard, though this method isn't without embarrassing moments. If the broker is within earshot, you may not feel comfortable making statements like "The kitchen wallpaper sucks and the bedrooms smell like cat piss." Say it anyway.

Use your camera to document visual impressions as a supplement to your recorder or clipboard. You can increase your camera's utility in small and dark interior spaces by equipping it with a wide-angle lens and a flash.

Two additional tools can be very helpful: a flashlight and a 25-foot measuring tape. Don't try to measure out each room unless the broker's poop sheet doesn't give the dimensions. Instead, use the tape to measure any feature with weird dimensions, such as a bedroom doorway that you suspect is too narrow to get your antique chest of drawers through or the headroom in the basement (it may be the key to converting it to a home office or TV room).

As you go from room to room, record basic data first and then your subjective impressions. Include the finishes on the floors, walls, and ceilings; the state of repair; heat sources; and special features ("The second bedroom has a wonderful little oriel window that overlooks the backyard"). Your subjective impressions, which are just as important, go beyond whether you can fit a double bed into the room—they describe how you feel about the space ("The living room seems too long and narrow, the kitchen feels dark and gloomy").

You may see the home as a jewel in the rough, just waiting for the right touch to bring out its potential. Be sure to record as many opportunities as you spot ("By punching out the wall between the kitchen and living room, I could flood the kitchen with sunlight") and limitations or changes likely to be costly ("Unfortunately, the wall between the kitchen and living room includes a chimney and is probably filled with plumbing").

If you are handy at remodeling but short on design skills, arrange to visit the house a second time accompanied by an architect, designer, or competent home remodeler. The few hours' fee will be well worth it. A professional can also spot serious construction flaws that will be costly or impossible to repair and raise other questions that may not be apparent. Whether or not you engage help from a professional, here is a short list of potential danger spots. If you notice any of them, get an expert's opinion before closing a deal.

- **Basements.** Look for any signs of water and insects—both are potential sources of trouble. Major cracks in the foundation are a major problem. Joists and floor beams should be solid. Small holes foretell insects. Bang on any beams that seem to be wasting away with a screwdriver or hammer. If the sound is hollow or if the tool sinks into the wood, dry rot lurks.
- **Plumbing.** Water pipes should be consistent in type, free of leaks, and appear well organized. A bad example would be something akin to what we encountered: a water pipe starting out as steel, then meeting a section of garden hose, and finally ending in copper. If the water system is operating, turn on taps in each sink to see what kind and how much water comes out and if the fixture leaks. Leaks can be repaired, but they do cost money. If a well supplies water, you will want to check out whether the supply is steady and the

quality of the water as well as the condition of the pump. If the sewage flows into a septic tank/drain field, you should know the capacity and age of each. Replacement is a several-thousand-dollar proposition.

- **Electrical.** Look for exposed wiring in the basement and attic. Wiring should be of one type, preferably single cables encased in white plastic (romex). Then look for the main panel (fuse board) in the basement or imbedded in a wall on the first floor. If it has fuses rather than circuit breakers, the system needs modernizing. Likewise, if the wiring coming out of the panel is other than white plastic (romex), it, too, probably needs to be replaced.
- **Heating/cooling.** Two things are of concern: the condition of the system and its efficiency. You could have a local heating system contractor evaluate the condition of the system or include a provision in the sales agreement to warranty the system for the first year. Finding out how much it costs to operate the system will be harder. Ideally, the prior owner would turn over his/her fuel bills for the previous year. But because most people aren't that organized, you can evaluate (or have an expert evaluate) the system in regard to the availability and cost of fuels. If the home's only source of heat is wood stoves, you are in for many hours of managing wood. If your heating system is electric in an area with high electrical rates, such as New England, beware. Look for weathertight, well-insulated houses with their long sides facing south. If a prospective house is poorly insulated, reserve up to $10,000 for weatherization. The investment will pay back within five years in most cases.
- **Walls.** Look for mildew, fungus, or other signs of dampness on interior and exterior walls. Wet areas—kitchens and baths—are rooms where moisture can cause real damage. Check the condition of walls surrounding tubs and showers and in back of toilets for rot and decay.
- **Windows and doors.** Double-glazed (insulated) windows are a minimum requirement these days in areas requiring winter heat. Single-glazed or deteriorated windows will need to be replaced to keep heating bills down. Sliding glass patio doors—even good ones—are hard to weather-seal. If energy savings is a concern, plan on replacing them with french doors or solid walls.
- **Roofing.** Unless the roofing is really shot, you probably won't be able to assess its condition by looking at it. Keep an eye out for signs of chronic leaks inside, such as walls with suspicious streaks or stains on a portion of an upstairs ceiling.

Buy a Farm?

Are sheep grazing in the front meadow and apple trees on the ridge part of your dream of rural living? There's no reason you can't, or shouldn't, have these. But the economics of agriculture are such that it's next to impossible to start from scratch and make a decent income, as was pointed out at the end of Chapter 6. So first be clear about your motives and what you hope to gain in the way of financial rewards.

What kind of farm should you look for? That depends on the intended use. If you want to raise sheep or rutabagas, learn as much about sheep husbandry and rutabaga culture as you can before you look for a site. Each crop has its own requirements for space, type of soil, and water availability.

If you fall in love with a farm property but don't know how best to use it, the nearest county agricultural agent can help you find the best use or advise you on feasible alternatives for the region. The U.S. Soil Conservation Service (part of the U.S. Dept. of Agriculture—see the Appendix) can be another source of useful information. The agency maintains aerial maps and data of soil types throughout the United States.

Most of the previous advice on home buying applies as well to farm houses. But there are many types of farm buildings—some little more than simple roofed affairs suitable for general storage and keeping the rain out of supplies and others specialized for certain animals. When you understand the needs of the animals and crops you will be raising, you can judge the adequacy of the buildings on a candidate farm property.

Adapting Your Home

"I have found the perfect country house—well, it needs just a bit of remodeling." These words have lured many a home buyer into a bottomless money pit and have run as many marriages into the ground. Unless you are a seasoned remodeler, call in an expert to put a dollar figure on the planned changes before you sign the sales agreement. Even with an estimate, you won't know the final costs, because contingencies lurk under every item. Many of these are explained scientifically by "Germer's Law of the Missing Substrate." Here's how it works.

Say you want to tear out that hideous wall paneling in the master bath—the plastic laminate material that tries to imitate marble—and install ceramic tile over the substrate, the plaster beneath. When the first panels are pulled off the wall, you notice that the plaster is too crumbly to support tile. It has deteriorated over the course of ages of escaping moisture and should be removed. You first try to remove it but save the wood lath; then you say, "what the hell," and pull off the lath. Now down to bare studs, you notice that the insulation is damp and some of the studs are rotted. Before you are through, you have replaced some studs, all of the insulation, and a new interior wall substrate—all in addition to your original target, the ceramic tile.

These are the kind of surprises that await you at every turn when you start to tear into an old house—especially one in the country where the quality of carpentry hidden from view was the best you could get with a chain saw. To minimize the damage to your cash reserves and marriage, heed the following suggestions.

First, get the best preliminary advice as to the feasibility and probable costs of changes you want to make and upgrades that are necessary to make the home livable.

Have the work done before you move in (ideally) or prioritize the work in a way that will minimize disruptions to ongoing family life. A mistake that people make time and again is trying to do everything at once and then ending up living with unfinished work. The longer it remains unfinished, the less likely it will get finished. A better way is to seal off each room or area to be remodeled, and then finish *all* work in that room, down to the painting and carpeting. If you are doing your own remodeling, don't bite off more than you can chew within a reasonable time (here defined as the time before you say, "The hell with it; we can live with unfinished drywall for a week or two").

If you can't do the work, or parts of it, yourself, pulling in the right outside specialists can help you escape getting stuck living in unfinished drywall indefinitely. Here are some of the possible services you might need to bring a country house in line with your lifestyle requirements and the pros who can help you (I assume you already know about carpenters, plumbers, and electricians).

- **Building inspection.** Architects and structural engineers are qualified to assess the structural integrity of foundations, beams, joists, and columns. Builders can also give valuable advice, but be aware that the basis of their judgment is practical experience rather than academic training. For a thorough assessment of the condition of the house, consider employing a home inspection service.

- **Chimney.** If there are wood stoves, you will need to have the chimney inspected as insurance against fires from creosote buildup. Look in the yellow pages under "chimney sweeps." If there are no listings, call in a brick mason or roofing repair service for an opinion.

- **Construction.** Builders, home builders, and contractors all do home construction. They charge on the basis of a firm bid, if you have detailed plans and specifications, or cost-plus-expenses, where you pay them the actual cost of materials and labor plus a percentage for profit (15 to 20 percent).

- **Design and planning.** Architects and home designers meet with you to determine your objectives and then conceptualize a scheme. Their final product, construction drawings and specifications, contains enough information for a builder to give a firm estimate of project costs. Architects and designers charge a fixed fee, a percentage of expected project cost, or an hourly rate. Locate candidates through referrals or the yellow pages and then interview two or three over the phone.

- **Interior design.** Architects also do interior design, but if your requirements are complex, call in an interior designer to help you with colors, materials, and finishes. They charge a fee for their services and/or a percentage of the cost of items they specify. Some home furnishings stores provide interior design services on the condition that you buy your furnishings from them.

- **Kitchen design.** Kitchen design is done by architects or interior designers for a fee. Some home improvement stores and kitchen and bath showrooms offer design service and bury it in the total cost of the equipment sold.

- **Landscaping.** Landscape architects are the design professionals best qualified to create a unified scheme to enhance your yard. Landscape services actually install the work and often offer design services as an adjunct.

- **Septic system.** Plumbers and septic system installers can evaluate the state of the septic tank and drain field. Try to have these items inspected before winter, when access to the septic tank may be difficult or impossible.

- **Surveying.** If you need to establish site boundaries or create a site plan as a basis for remodeling or landscaping, call in a registered land surveyor. A surveyor should be able to give you a firm fee estimate from the services you require and size of your property.

- **Water quality.** Look in the yellow pages for water testing labs. You can order tests for health-threatening contaminants such as lead, radon, mercury, and bacteria as well as benign but taste-affecting impurities such as iron and sulphur. If your new country home has a drilled or dug well with a pump, you should know which plumbers and well specialists you can call on for advice and service.

Adjusting to Rural Life

Life away from the crowd undoubtedly has its rewards. It also has pitfalls. One of the first ones to come to your attention is that nobody comes to pick up your garbage. You have to hire a collector or spend part of Saturday morning carting it to the dump. Just when you are thinking how great it is to be able to have a dog that you can turn out into the yard for his evening "do," he gets "done" one night by an encounter with a skunk. The odor is guaranteed to perfume the house for months. Or maybe he returns with his snout full of porcupine quills.

During your first winter you notice that the gravel road you live on doesn't get plowed until midafternoon. In March it turns into a quagmire.

But even with the occasional unwelcome surprise, the change was worth the move to me and most of the urban refugees I have talked to. You can minimize the number of unpleasant surprises by finding out as much as you can about the location before moving there.

Chapter 8 described some of the things to look for when you set out to match your lifestyle needs to outland locations. Even in remote locations, the material things you depend on are probably not too far away or else available through the mail. Services are scarcer in the country. I cited the example of the scarcity of specialists such as piano tuners. If you end up in an area without certain services, you may need to rethink your need for the service or come up with another way to meet the need. Maybe you could trade in your piano for an electronic keyboard. You might do well to get a wrench and learn to tune it yourself; it may turn into a profitable sideline.

Is There Culture Away from the Bright Lights?

Your cultural life won't end when you move out of a metropolitan area, but it will surely change. How it will change depends in large part on how creatively you exploit the possibilities there. Live theater you see will more likely be put on by a local college or civic troupe than a national-class company. Instead of concerts by the Los Angeles Philharmonic, you may have to settle for the Grass Valley Community Orchestra.

Here's where the creative part comes in. Because the quality of the arts groups are a notch or two below their urban-based counterparts, they are more accessible to nonprofessionals. With more time on your hands than you had in the urban rat race, why not throw yourself into an amateur theater group or a community orchestra or chorus? If one doesn't exist, find a few like-minded amateurs and start something.

Back in Salt Lake City, we regularly attended performances by top-notch groups such as the Utah Symphony, Ballet West, and various theatrical groups. A professional pianist in college days, I had not played since, except at home. It had been years since my wife, Lucie, had played her flute. In spite of—or perhaps because of—the variety of professional arts companies in and around Salt Lake, we felt we weren't good enough to compete and had far too little time to seek out amateur groups to join.

When we moved to rural New Hampshire eight years ago, we became painfully aware of how much we had taken for granted back in Salt Lake.

We retooled. I dragged out the clarinet I hadn't played in 30 years and learned bassoon and tuba from scratch. Lucie dusted off her flute and then took up trombone. Today, I am a regular member of a college-community concert band. We both belong to the town band as well as a five-piece variety ensemble that plays everything from Dixieland to oompah. So far, we have serenaded nursing homes (because they have "captive" audiences, they are a good place to start), and performed concerts on the village green and at garden parties, a First Night celebration, and Oktoberfest at a ski resort. Both our teenage children are involved in local music groups of one sort or another.

As with music, you can also compensate for the lack of big-time spectator sports by falling back on your personal resources. The shift can propel you from being a spectator to a participant—something you couldn't do back in Philadelphia or Chicago. Join the bush league team or coach a little league team.

Getting Established Socially

On one of my New Hampshire T-shirts, a moose sprawls lazily in a hammock, a weed poking out of one corner of his mouth. Out of the other, he drawls, "Ya ain't from around heah, are ya?" A local bumper sticker reads, "Welcome to New Hampshire, Now Go Home." Both characterize the parochial Yankee. As is often the case, the stereotype may contain a grain of truth. But since coming to New England eight years ago, I have found the inhabitants no more or less open than those of my native Utah (except they don't say "howdy" here). We fit in, I think, because we are sensitive to local quirks and customs and are willing to go the extra mile.

At a social gathering one night, a man from a neighboring town was working himself into a lather complaining about the local hunters. A recent arrival from New York, he had bought a home surrounded by 80 acres of woodland. In his zeal for privacy, he had posted the land to prevent hunters from trespassing. They utterly ignored his signs.

The newcomer recounted how he had tried in vain to get the local police to take action. The next chapter of the struggle, he warned, would be played out in the courts.

Of course the hunters saw things differently. They had been hunting in these woods for years, just like their fathers before them. Now they weren't by God going to let a few warning signs put up by an outsider stop them.

On the way home, Lucie interpreted the conflict from her perspective as an anthropologist. The conflict, she said, was a clash of cultures—urban and rural. The landowner played by the rules of crowded urban environments, where people who don't know each other use the law to mark their turf. But in rural regions personal relationships, tradition, and custom are often the arbiters of rights. Neither party understood the other's point of view.

Describing a culture-clash situation is easy enough for an anthropologist to do as an observer; it's quite another matter if the anthropologist is one of the actors. During our first winter here, some parents objected to an annual religious display in the elementary school during the holidays. The school board, fearing a civil rights suit, ordered the display removed.

This enraged a very vocal group of supporters. One of them, a close neighbor, was passing out leaflets one day as Lucie walked by. When Lucie complimented her for standing up for her principles, she took this as a vote of support and asked Lucie to sign a petition of protest. Lucie declined, explaining that although she admired the neighbor's activism, she disagreed with her position. "Why don't you just pack up and go back to Russia?" retorted the neighbor. Several years went by until the two understood each other enough to become good neighbors.

Some rural areas have long-established protective barriers that make fitting in difficult, such as established class structures, moral attitudes, or religious viewpoints. But the process of integrating is a two-way street. What barriers do you bring?

Now in their tenth year here in a small town not far from us, two acquaintances I'll call Marlene and Warren have yet to claim any friends in the town. The reason, they feel, is Warren's former career as a scientist in the defense industry. Marlene says, "When Warren tells people what he used to do, they say, 'Oh, you made weapons of destruction.' " Warren sees no necessity to downplay a career he is proud of. Besides, it was a good opener in the last place they lived, a community that was home to many retired military and defense industry professionals.

You don't need to dump your past to fit into the eccentric social world of a small town—just shift the emphasis. Open your senses to find out what the natives respond to and then reach into your own background to find something that resonates. I am constantly surprised at what people warm up to. I gained more respect from my rural New Hampshire neighbors than I probably deserved by rescuing the run-down house on the hill. The respect came, I think, because of the value folks in these parts place on doing almost everything yourself without calling in outside experts (that same trait makes it harder for me to convince people that they would be better off having an architect designing their home). Similarly, Lucie gained a lot of respect by telling stories to the children at the town library.

When you open your ears to the local pulse, you, too, may discover unplanned keys to acceptance. Ron Weber operates a de facto pawn shop for Goshute Indians living on the reservation just south of his farm in Ibapah, Utah. It is not uncommon to see the dust from one of their pickups in the distance as it wends its way up the long gravel drive to the farmhouse. A Goshute man gets out with a chain saw in hand. Ron asks him what it is worth. They settle on a loan amount. In two or three weeks, the man returns with the money and picks up his chain saw. No one has yet defaulted, and Ron never charges interest.

A more universal way to gain entry to the community is by getting involved in local organizations, suggested earlier as a way to create cultural and sports outlets. Dave and Alice Cadwell, the urban transplants-turned-rural restaurateurs, got deeply involved in their small Connecticut community. Dave found a way to harness his experience as a medic in Vietnam by getting qualified as an emergency medical technician and then joining the town's volunteer rescue service. Now second in command of the 12-person squad, his dedication over the last three and a half years has won the respect and gratitude of the town. Alice has found her key to the community though devoting several hours each month as a board member of the town's parks and recreation committee.

Almost every community has organizations of one sort or another that could benefit from your contributions and that could, in turn, help you build a social network. You'll have more to give and gain by involving yourself in a group that centers around a personal interest or area of expertise. If you are good at planning, keep your eye open for a position on the town's planning board. Like books? Become a trustee of the local library. Tired of singing in the shower? Join an amateur chorale, the church choir, or the local chapter of the barbershop quartet association.

Opportunities to work with youth abound—from volunteering at the local elementary school to coaching a little league team. Service clubs, community associations, and churches provide still further opportunity for social outreach.

If there is no local group that fits an interest of yours, start one. Groups form around the damndest things. My brother-in-law belongs to a Miata club—a group whose only requirement is that you own a Mazda Miata sports car. Imagine the possibilities. A writers' group, amateur mushroom-hunting group, exotic cuisine club, or woodwind quintet are just a few of the kinds of groups you could start. And once you start participating, you will really start to see what attracts people to make a life in small towns and rural locales. And you'll no longer be an outsider.

Chapter Twelve

Doing Business in the Outland

There are many roads to becoming your own boss in a small town or rural area, whether you intend to deliver a service or a product. Assuming you don't plan on starting something on the scale of a steel mill, I would like to explore three routes to a minibusiness (one person or one person and a few employees): buying an existing business, becoming a franchisee, and starting a business from scratch.

Buying an Existing Business

What am I looking for? How can I find prospects? How can I tell if they are any good? How can I finance the purchase? These are some of the questions you face when you buy an existing business, whether in the outland or anywhere. I haven't hit upon pat answers from the people I have talked to, but their experience yields useful insights. Consider the Cadwells and Biff Mahoney.

The Cadwells illustrate how two out-of-towners found and bought a business property far away from their original home.

A visit to rural northwest Connecticut in 1986 charmed Dave and Alice Cadwell (Chapter 6) into moving there from Florida and starting a business. On one of his business trips to New York City, Dave took a side trip through northwest Connecticut to revisit the area and sniff out local business opportunities. He discovered a run-down restaurant property in West Cornwall through a local realtor. Absentee owners from New York City had run the greasy spoon at less than full commitment. Their asking price for the property, $275,000, included restaurant equipment and a

1600-square-foot apartment above. When they offered to carry the loan, the deal was too attractive for Dave to pass up. The Cadwells scraped the down payment together through the help of their parents and were on their way to pumping new life into the enterprise.

Through patience, creativity, and lots of effort, the Cadwells established their business relatively smoothly. Biff Mahoney's story also had a happy outcome, but not quite in the way he had planned.

Biff had recently quit an unrewarding job as a car salesman to start a business of his own. He scanned the want ads in regional newspapers and local digests each day in the fall of 1991, searching for prospects within reach of his home in Richmond, New Hampshire.

When he spotted an ad for a printing shop in nearby Peterborough, he got really excited. Biff had spent most of his 50 years working in the printing business. The ad claimed that the shop had raked in an annual gross over $225,000. Included in the $135,000 asking price was all equipment, inventory, existing accounts, a promise not to compete for ten years, and good will.

The seller rejected Biff's first offer of $110,000, but—ironically—accepted his second offer of $89,500 "because they were afraid my next offer would be still lower," he surmises. Biff next applied for an SBA-backed loan but hit rough shoals when he tried to get the financial records from the seller, who had been running the business from a checkbook. Undaunted, Biff set about digging out his own data from whatever sources he could find and recording it on a spreadsheet. The previous year's gross, he found, was $40,000 less than advertised. By this time, the SBA was jittery. Biff was advised to back off of the deal.

He did. But somewhere along the way Biff's dream of owning his own business had irrevocably narrowed to owning his own print shop. "I sat down and did some real soul searching, and said, 'Well, I have this three-car garage out here, and when I put it up, I knew in the back of my mind that would be a good place to [someday] put up a shop.' " He insulated and finished the walls and added a darkroom and a small gas furnace all for less than $2000. "The $800 a month I'll be saving in rent translates to $5 an hour production time," says Biff proudly.

Biff expects to lay out no more than $15,000 to buy used printing equipment he finds through newspaper ads and industry sources. What if it breaks? "I have been in the business long enough to know that if something breaks, I can fix it," he answers. His entire start-up costs will be lower than the $20,000 down payment he would have had to make on the Peterborough print shop. And it couldn't be much closer to home.

Both of these examples have a happy ending—one reached by following a deal through, the other by knowing when to steer clear. Buying an existing business is risky, say experts. In the words of Edward M. Moldt of the Wharton School of Business, "You have to kick all the tires and look under the hood." Here are some tires to kick:[1]

- Look for offerings in unlikely places, such as "blind" ads, a trade network, or through brokers. Many businesses avoid open advertising for fear of driving away employees.

- Be familiar with the workings of the industry you are considering. Use this knowledge to rate your candidate (Biff Mahoney knew printing; Dave Cadwell was new to restaurants but knew his way around the food service supply industry).

- Think of how resalable this business will be if and when you want to (or have to) get out.

- Try to determine whether the owner is selling for personal reasons— an illness or retirement—or because of a fundamental problem with the business or industry.

- Hire an accountant to help you evaluate the company's performance over the past five years to see if it is more solid than the current sales would indicate. Look for at least a 20 percent annual return on investment rather than a break-even proposition. Order a Uniform Commercial Code search to find out if there are unreported liens against the business. Also look for outstanding loans, ongoing audits, or tax liabilities.

- Check inventory to see whether it jives with the asking price.

- Hire an attorney to review the contract and lease agreement and the status of any trade secrets that may affect the future of the business. Your attorney should also have an eye out for undisclosed sales contracts, noncompetition clauses, restrictions on transfer of stock, and other legalities that may lie hidden.

Franchises

It may be unfair, but when I hear the word "franchise," I see long strings of tacky little buildings lining the way to an urban area. The Colonel looks down from his revolving fried chicken bucket, which abuts the golden arches. The scene is much the same in Portland, Oregon, as in Portland, Maine. These well-known symbols have not only homogenized the cities and towns of the United States but are now making inroads as far away as China. You know how that Big Mac will taste, regardless of where you buy it.

But architectural quality aside, the unvarying predictability of the product may well be why franchises are so successful. The $775-billion-a-year industry accounts for one-third to one-half of all domestic retail sales. And the industry encompasses more than mere fast-food joints and muffler repair shops. Over 2000 franchisers span nearly every type of business. In a recent three-page newspaper special I spotted ads for franchised golf supply stores, pet stores, shipping service, children's computer education, steel home construction, and catering. Air Boingo of Park City, Utah, even franchises steel towers for bungee jumping.

You might be a good candidate to join the 500,000 other franchisees if you dream of becoming your own boss but aren't sure of your expertise or don't want the risk of starting a business from the ground up (and many businesses succeed or fail on how well the operators grasp the nuances). Randy Wirth (Chapter 4) is considering starting a specialty coffee franchise based on his knowledge of such subtleties as how to get just the right kind of water or grind for a gourmet coffee.

Fewer than 5 percent of franchised outlets fail each year, says the International Franchise Association. The House Small Business Committee, in a 1992 study of fraud in the franchise industry, put the failure rate closer to 35 percent.

If joining a franchise does indeed reduce your risk, the tradeoff is a shorter leash. Though you'll own your own business, you won't be free to run it as you want to.

In addition to reduced risk, a franchise offers you a chance to get into your own business without a lot of experience in the product or service you deliver, although it helps to have managerial experience (about one-third of franchisees had previously been corporate managers). But training and management specifically tailored to the product or service is one of the things you should expect from the franchiser. In some cases, financial assistance comes with the deal—no small matter, because the costs of getting into a franchise can easily exceed the cost of starting your own small business.

Entry fees of *Money* Magazine's ten top-rated franchises for the 1990s ranged from $650 (Jazzercise fitness studios) to $66,000 (McDonald's). Total start-up costs ranged from $5000 (Jani-King International commercial cleaning) to $400,000 (Petland). After upfront expenses, you'll pay 2 percent to 6 percent of gross sales to the franchiser. Your return on investment may not come in for three to five years.

Success with any franchise depends on a product or service high in demand and a franchiser who will back you completely. Before you commit yourself to this path, it might be well to reexamine your motives. If one of your goals was more free time, franchising may not be a good choice. On the other hand, it could help bring your family closer together if you make them part of running the business. Here are some other tips that business writers often suggest to potential franchisees:

- Choose a franchise that appeals to you and that you believe in (why hasn't anyone come out with a natural fast-food franchise?). Your chance of success is proportional to how much you know about the product or service. You can get a feel for the range of available franchises by attending one of the franchise fairs staged by the International Franchise Association (its address is listed in the Appendix).

- Get the contract and full financial record of any prospect you select, including the franchiser's audited financial statements and litigation history. This should be included in a Uniform Franchise Offering Circular, which the FTC requires the franchiser to provide you. Go through these with your accountant and attorney. Things to look for include the chain's failure, termination, and turnover rates as well as whether the franchiser depends on start-up fees rather than continuing royalties (a bad omen).

- Visit several of the company's franchises that have been operating for a year or longer to get a feel for what you will be in for. Ask about sales performance, profitability, and unexpected obstacles or windfalls they encountered along the way.

- Keep an eye out for scams. If the franchiser asks for a fee before sending you a disclosure statement, it should send up a red flag. Some fraudulent franchisers use "singers" who pose as successful franchisees over the phone. If you suspect dishonesty, check with the Better Business Bureau.

Starting from Scratch

Buying an existing business or getting into a franchise are two ways to become self-employed in the outland without having to grow a business from seed. Neither may be right for you. If you itch to develop a new idea—or just burn to do things your way—you won't like being hemmed in by the constraints of a franchise or existing business.

Starting from scratch will give you the freedom you want, along with some tough challenges. To begin, you'll need a viable business idea, as we saw in Chapter 3, and a source of financing, explored later in this chapter. I'll leave matters such as detailed advice on legal structure, business plans, pricing strategies, and the like to books about starting small businesses, such as those listed in the Appendix. They are a *must read* if you want to beat the odds and succeed. I wish to mention only a few of the challenges not addressed by these books that you may face as a first-time entrepreneur in the outland.

Finding a suitable base of operations is one of these. A space in your own home might be a good choice for temporary quarters to hatch your business or as a permanent site if the fit is right. A home office serves the needs of many of the people in this book, such as writer Don Best, cartoonist Bruce Hammond, and nanny referral service owner Karen Ryan.

Because this option appeals to a growing number of professionals—20 million by a recent estimate—it is the subject of most of the next chapter.

But a home office isn't right for everyone. It wasn't for Barbara Blackburn when she hung her shingle as a business consultant on her home in Sedona, Arizona. "I found it hard to start working again after taking the dishes out of the dishwasher or laundry out of the washing machine," she confesses, adding, "It was just too easy to sit around in my bathrobe." Barbara found a place to relocate her office in an old high school. The 2500-square-foot space was more than she needed for her staff of three, but panoramic views over the Verde Valley toward the red rocks on the other side made it too hard to pass up.

Many outland entrepreneurs find suitable quarters for their businesses in sites even less likely than high schools. Steve and Lisa Carlson (Chapter 5) fell in love with a former summer camp overlooking Vermont's Lake Iroquois. They bought it and built a house that included a space for their nascent small press publishing business. The garage provided warehouse space until the business outgrew it. Jim and Pat Lee (Chapter 6) converted a 200-year-old colonial home on a 250-acre spread in Vermont into a country inn and beefalo ranch.

Converted buildings often come with perks missing in newer facilities. Savvy developers in the 1960s converted a group of run-down industrial buildings on a San Francisco wharf to house upscale boutiques and restaurants. The success of Ghirardelli Square soon inspired other, similar developments such as the converted bus barns that have become Trolley Square in Salt Lake City, Larimer Square in Denver, and Boston's Quincy Market. Lofts in old factories or mills are preferred office sites for many designers. Why? The old buildings exude a charm or character lacking in modern buildings—even when they try to capture the charm of a bygone age.

But converted space isn't necessarily cheaper space. To avoid unforeseen expenses consult with a competent builder or architect before undertaking a conversion.

Getting your first work is another major hurdle for first-time entrepreneurs (we'll talk about maintaining a steady work flow a bit later). There are as many strategies as there are kinds of businesses. Some folks walk away with business contacts cultivated during their former employment. When he left his editorial position at *Solar Age* to become a freelance writer, Don Best had a list of potential clients cultivated over the course of his contacts in the magazine industry.

Gil Gordon got his first corporate client for a new area of consulting through his efforts promoting his first specialty: telecommuting. He gave seminars and workshops and wrote articles for trade journals to create visibility. At a break during a seminar in New York City, he got into a conversation with a representative of an Atlantic City casino who complained of high employee turnover.

Gordon made a proposal to the casino. It was accepted, and he had his first client for employee retention. He now credits his network as his main source of work. Each client has had a specific personnel problem or someone on the staff who was interested in taking a chance on telecommuting. "Pain and vision are the great motivators for the 90s," he observes.

One suggestion Gil Gordon thinks will benefit all first-timers is to have a hook. If you want to start a word processing business, he suggests, don't become the 50th word processing service in Mapleton offering the same service. That's suicidal. Instead, find out what the other 49 firms offer, what their rates are, their turn-around time, and so on. Then do a little market research on potential users to find out what they need. Maybe you'll end up specializing in scientific papers because the other 49 love to do text but hate tables and graphs. Or you could offer a two-tier pricing arrangement. "I think it's possible to find a special niche even in fields we think of as generic," he points out.

Because Gil Gordon was onto a new thing, he often got publicity in the form of news coverage—a boon to any neophyte business. Many of Mathew and Deborah Loving's first customers heard about their metamorphosis from New York stockbrokers to ostrich farmers the same way: through coverage in newspapers and on television. If your business isn't as exotic as ostrich breeding, it may have an unusual twist you can use to make it newsworthy. Any start-up business can usually get an announcement in the local newspaper, just by being new.

Support for Your Outland Enterprise

If you sought out the local small business support agencies to help decide where to locate (as suggested in Chapter 7), you already know what services are available at your destination. Before you hang your shingle, however, why not get all the free help you can from area support agencies such as SCORE, the nearest Small Business Development Center (SBDC), and chamber of commerce? This kind of help costs you nothing more than your time and effort.

Financing a Start-Up in a New Location

If financing is what you worry about most, take comfort in the results of a recent survey by the National Federation of Independent Business. Only 4 percent of the respondents said financing was the hardest part of running a small business, compared to 22 percent a decade earlier.

You'll have a good idea of how much you'll need to both start and run your business if you completed Worksheet 10-2 or have written a business plan.

But even with a good plan and impeccable credentials you may have a tough time borrowing in these days of tight money. As Barbara Blackburn puts it: "The amount of effort [required] to borrow money is pretty absurd these days. Even four years ago, it was real easy putting together a good package if [you] had good credit, a worthwhile business or a business with a track record, or Auntie Gertrude would co-sign . . . [Now] the banks out here are not lending money, period."

If you are starting from scratch, Barbara suggests you stash away one or two year's operating expense and enough capital to buy your own equipment—a tall order, unless you have a sizable store of liquid assets or were lucky enough to make a killing on the sale of your last home. How to find capital is a constant theme of the excellent books on small business listed in the Appendix. Here are some of the choices that in my opinion offer the most potential for starting a *very* small business.

Starting Small

You may not need any capital beyond what you can scrape together out of savings if you start small enough. Service businesses are in the best position for this approach, but even product enterprises can start out on a shoestring with creative planning. If you want to breed ostriches, for example, you don't need a flock of ostriches—just a breeding pair and a house for them.

Begin with your list of start-up requirements. Ask these questions about each item:

1. Do I really need this?
2. If yes, how can I get it without buying it?
3. If I have to buy it, can I get it used?

For office-based professionals, the office itself is first on the list. Many firms of one or two people can work effectively and save a bundle by deciding to set up in a home office. The decision need not be permanent. If you keep the spatial modifications to a minimum, the space can easily revert to another use when you move to other quarters.

Office equipment is the next candidate for savings. Jim Jones, the producer of audiovisual materials in Bryan, Texas, advises, "Go find yourself a desk at a garage sale, check the papers for your computer hardware, go buy used equipment." Jones learned the hard way. After investing several thousand dollars of borrowed money to equip his office, he was squeezed on repayment a few years later when a souring economy in Texas caused his business to flounder.

For equipment such as you might need for construction or manufacturing, Barbara Blackburn suggests exploring leasing or lease-purchase arrangements. Many equipment suppliers carry their own financing for lease-purchase agreements.

Explore arrangements to rent or share equipment too costly for you to buy or lease but that you need only occasionally. One day while I was ordering business stationery from a local printer, I went gaga over a state-of-the-art copy machine standing in the corner. The proprietor agreed that the machine could do everything but scratch your back. Unfortunately, he didn't get enough use out of it to support the lease payments. I suggested he might increase his volume by offering the machine for use by one-person businesses such as mine. He agreed. Today, I go in to make copies, indicate the number on a piece of paper nearby (we use the honor system), and pay my tab monthly at a rate less than that charged by the nearest commercial copy service, five miles away. It's a win-win situation.

Another way to start small, if you are buying an existing business or a building, is to persuade the seller to carry the sales contract. This is how Randy Wirth and Sally Sears bought their first natural food business in Logan, Utah, and—five years later—bought the building that housed the business.

Tapping "Angels"

So you pare start-up costs to the bone and still come up short. You are left with the options of borrowing or selling equity to investors. Before approaching banks, Barbara Blackburn suggests you consider borrowing from friends or relatives ("angels") who might have underused money sitting around. Urge Aunt Helen to cash in some of her certificates of deposit that may now be earning 4 or 5 percent and loan you the money at 8 or 10 percent. You'll both come out winners on the deal.

Barbara Oakley (Chapter 3) started her educational flashcard company, Fireside Flashcards, after securing a $60,000 loan from her father. Your family and friends know you best, so they are the most likely to loan you money on the basis of your character. But misunderstandings can result if you don't explicitly spell out the terms of the loan in writing. Here are some things to consider before approaching a friend or relative for a loan:

- Be sure the loan won't jeopardize your nonbusiness relationship.
- Clearly define the rate of interest and repayment terms.
- Don't promise other favors as a condition to the loan (or otherwise let yourself in for emotional blackmail).
- Have a friend or relative cosign.
- Be sure your lender won't need repayment before the agreed life of the loan.

- Be sure that your lender can afford the loss if your enterprise flops and that he or she understands the risk.

Persuading Banks

You may increase your odds of obtaining loans from banks by heeding Barbara Blackburn's advice. First, do your homework thoroughly. Make up a detailed business plan that specifies how much you are seeking, what it will be used for, and how long you need the money for. Your own credit history will be of primary importance to a banker, so make sure you supply records of all charge accounts and loans you have taken in the past.

Your best bet might be the bank you currently do business with. You will have the advantage of a long association and good credit risk, all the more so if you have established yourself as a dependable debtor. If your home bank is reluctant to issue a loan for a business outside its area, see if it has a branch in the area you plan to move to.

As a last resort, get your home bank to write you a letter of recommendation before you relocate that you can use when applying to a new bank.

Other Financial Institutions

In addition to commercial banks, consider approaching savings and loan institutions or credit unions. Burned badly in the last decade, S&Ls now operate more responsibly, making them as unlikely as banks to be sources for start-up capital. You'll have to be a member to get a loan from a credit union, and you may not be able to use the money to fund a new business enterprise outside the institution's home turf.

Help from the Government

Two factors make banks or S&Ls hesitant to loan you money to start a business: The limited supply of money to loan and the perceived risk of you not repaying it. You can't do much about the first because it depends on policies beyond your control. You may buck the second issue with help from the Small Business Administration (SBA), a federal agency created in 1953 to provide advice and financial assistance to small businesses.

Your chances with the SBA are best if you are looking for funds in excess of $50,000 and if you are a member of a minority group or a woman, according to Barbara Blackburn, who summarizes the application process thus: First get a list of SBA-approved lenders. Apply to a bank on the list. If you are refused, apply to a second, then a third. With three formal declines in hand, you can fill out a 38-page application and submit it to an SBA bank. If you are then approved, the SBA will take a pledge on your real estate and guarantee 80 percent of the principal balance.

Trading Equity for Cash

If you can't find start-up money anywhere else, you might try selling ownership in your venture in the form of limited partnerships, syndication, or stock. Setting up these arrangements, which falls beyond the scope of this book, should be done with competent financial and legal counsel. Having more than 19 investors will land you under the regulations of the Securities and Exchange Commission.

Trading equity for cash is trading one assortment of money-hunting woes for another, as Barbara Blackburn sees it. "If I had cash I would rather loan it to you than invest in your business these days, unless I had a lot of confidence in your ability to manage and be successful . . . or [if] I'm in a tax bracket where I'm looking for a tax write-off," she says. In the latter case, she would rather invest in a "Subchapter S" corporation, where the losses would pass through directly to the shareholders.

Insurance

Books about running small businesses always stress the necessity of having adequate insurance. The question you will face is this: Just what constitutes adequacy? The proliferation of malpractice suits that started in the 1970s has left few professions unscathed—even some who thought they were covered to the hilt. Healthcare costs keep soaring, in large part, because of the astronomical rates doctors have to pay for malpractice insurance. The cost of liability protection has increased for other professions as well.

The cost of liability coverage for architects, for example, is so dear that as many as half of all architectural offices "go bare." Some even believe having insurance actually invites lawsuits (the "deep pocket" effect). Uninsured architects compensate by exercising extreme care in the way they work.

And liability is only one of the possible types of coverage you may need. Your business may also need insurance for business property, computers, business interruption, disability, errors and omission, product liability, or partnership. Other than workers' compensation insurance, which is required if you have employees, the type and extent of protection you'll need isn't etched in stone; it depends on how much risk you can live with.

Health insurance is the perk you'll likely miss most if you are a corporate refugee. With few employees to spread out the actuarial risk, small businesses are hit hard when they buy healthcare coverage, paying as much as 20 percent more than big companies, according to Kelleen Jackson of the National Federation of Independent Business.[2] If you have employees, here are some things that may help you trim your health insurance costs:

- Educate your employees on healthy living by distributing a monthly newsletter with health tips and bringing in speakers for topics such as quitting smoking and reducing stress.
- Arrange discounts for employees' memberships in fitness centers.
- Create incentives for employees who maintain healthy lifestyles.
- Maintain a high deductible of $200 or more for claims.
- Look for insurance with a higher deductible ($200 or more) and 80 percent rather than 100 percent coverage.

Because they can't take advantage of group rates, one-person businesses get hit hardest with health insurance costs. So before you start looking for an individual policy, see if there is a group policy for which you are eligible through membership in a trade, professional, or college alumni association. The way out for many dual-career couples is to ride on the group insurance of a nonself-employed spouse.

Where to start your journey through the insurance maze? The entrepreneurs I know to suggest first finding an agent you can trust. An independent agent that represents more than one insurance carrier is in the best position to find you the best rates. Keep an eye out for savings through discounts or increasing your deductible.

Operating in the Outland

The main difference between operating a business in downtown Oakland and operating one in downtown Oak Leaf is the scale—there's simply less of everything outside metro areas. Jim Stiles's antique shop in Fayettville, Arkansas, or Janis and Robert Atkins's natural foods store in Bryan, Texas, don't seem to differ much from their big city cousins. But if you end up outside a city or town or working out of a home office, expect radical differences.

Suddenly you are cut off from close proximity to clients, suppliers, services, and—for better or worse—other people. The tradeoffs may or may not be worth it in the long run. Blue jays squabbling outside your window may be a welcome change to honking horns and sirens. But you may have to change the way you deal with suppliers, services, and clients.

Promoting Your Business

Keeping clients coming in isn't much different than attracting them in the first place, except that you're now no longer newsworthy and can't continually rely on free news spots in the media. Unless you get surprised like Dave Cadwell did.

Tom Brokaw, the NBC news anchor, lives up the road from Cadwell's Corner Restaurant in West Cornwall, Connecticut, and drops in when he is in town. In the spring of 1992, Brokaw planned to use the restaurant and town for a human interest spot on the evening news. Then major rioting broke out in Los Angeles in the wake of the Rodney King verdict. Dave thought that the network would no longer be interested in the restaurant, given the magnitude of the story. "But next Saturday, in walks the camera crew and there's Tom," he reported. "They put a microphone to me and I'm cookin' and we're chattin' and we ended up on the nightly news."

Cadwell's Corner may gain some new customers from the one-time spot and word-of-mouth advertising, but tourists who come back to see the autumn leaves and covered bridge are still the primary promoters.

Word-of-mouth advertising also served Karen Ryan's nanny referral service until recently, when she decided to augment it with a listing in her trade association's national directory.

Mike Lee promotes his Montanan llamas through paid ads in three national llama magazines (I cease to be surprised—there must be a trade magazine for belly button lint-pickers). Jim Lee spreads word of his Vermont Inn through listings in over 20 travel books dealing with country inns. Ads he tried in the *New York Times, Yankee, Capitol,* and *Vermont* magazines proved too expensive for the return. He estimates that past clients and referrals account for 40 percent of his business.

Direct mail serves the marketing needs of some entrepreneurs. Jim and Mary Alinder keep 2000 past and prospective customers abreast of new showings at their Gualala, California, gallery by mailing them flyers and a quarterly newsletter. The flyers are of high quality, printed on card stock. (If they were a bit larger, I would frame them and hang them on the wall.) Jerry Ragen (Chapter 4) attracts business for his Fairmont, West Virginia, bulk-mailing service by sending out—what else?—direct-mail flyers to area hospitals, insurance companies, and universities. But Gil Gordon thinks direct mail is pretty much a waste of time and money in an age inundated by junk mail.

Involvement in community service organizations heightens the visibility of some entrepreneurs in remote locations. You will be able to select the right channel for communicating your message when you decide who you are trying to reach and how much of your operating budget you can afford to spend on reaching your target. If you are like the entrepreneurs I have talked to, you'll make midcourse corrections with experience.

Advertising is far from an exact science. Randy Wirth and Sally Sears tried the usual mix of print and broadcast media to promote their natural food store and cafe, with middling returns. Then they made a video and aired it on the local cable TV station. "We just assumed that our customers would not watch television," says Randy, "and it really had some of the best market impact we have ever seen." They also extract public interest through visual and aural devices. Tables outside their cafe under a colorful awning catch the eye of passers by, while the aroma of coffee roasting helps draw them inside.

Service Networks

Rural entrepreneurs often cite isolation from basic services as a major problem, according to *Venture* magazine.[3] Advertising and legal advice may be more than 50 or 100 miles distant. Other common deficits of the outland include capital, an entrepreneurial climate, information networks, and innovation.

You can do something about certain of these shortcomings. Take supplies. For items you don't need daily, look into mail or delivery services. You can get office supplies from furniture to computer forms from any of several national mail-order companies (Quill, NEBS), and their prices are frequently lower than what you'd pay in stores. For example, I would have to drive 85 miles to Boston to reach Charrette, the nearest major source of architectural supplies. Fortunately, Charrette sells by mail order from catalogs published quarterly. Orders I phone in today will be delivered tomorrow by UPS.

For other items, you may have to drive to the nearest city. But you can save time by resisting the temptation to run out the door every time you need some white-out. Maintain a list of things to do and buy and then go only when you have to.

You will have to consider each service you might need to find the most cost-effective answer to the question of how to get it, and the answers are not always easy to come by. Take copying. To support my writing and architectural practice, I require copies almost every day, most of which are of text I produce on a word processor. For these, I rely on my laser printer. It produces beautiful copies in a variety of fonts. But from time to time I need to copy material not created by my word processor or need to reduce, enlarge, collate, or copy in color. When I need these options, I share the leased machine from another local business, mentioned earlier.

I have held off buying a copy machine in part because I can't decide which features I absolutely need. And technology is changing rapidly enough to make anyone fear buying a machine that will be obsolete next year.

Overcoming Disconnectedness

Face-to-face contact with clients, peers, and business contacts is another loss to be dealt with when you move to an area of lower population density.

Some contacts will go out of their way to reach you, wherever you are (I have no problem getting architectural sales reps to swing by my office on their forays through the boonies).

Start networking. If you are not already a member, join the trade or professional association for your type of business. You'll be able to keep up with state-of-the-art advances through their newsletter or journal. Attend their business meetings, seminars, and workshops when possible, even if it means driving 50 or 60 miles.

Barbara Blackburn suggests linking up through interactive computer media, pointing out the incredible information networks available through modems such as America Online and CompuServe. "I was doing a search for a client the other day . . . within 48 hours, he had four pages of responses from people all over the country saying 'Don't do this, don't do that.' "

Online computer networks had caught the fancy of 2 million users by 1992, reports Joan Warner in *Business Week*.[4] If there are 20 million home-based businesses as is estimated, the potential for online networks to connect this far-flung grapevine has barely been scratched. CompuServe, Prodigy, and GEnie, the three most favored currently, offer access to stock market quotes, travel reservations, weather data, news, encyclopedias, and other information, but the feature that enables entrepreneurs across the country to connect to each other is the electronic bulletin board. When you log onto a "chat session," you communicate with others in much the same way as in a telephone conference call, except you type instead of talk. The beauty of this is that you end up with a written record of your conversations, a real boon if you use the information in your business.

Of course, interacting with others via modem isn't the same as speaking face to face. Barbara Blackburn misses the business meetings she used to have over drinks or lunch, which were a normal part of her workweek back in San Francisco. But she doesn't miss them enough to trade them for the ten weeks of vacation she takes every year to backpack or run rivers in her Arizona paradise.

We have been talking about disconnectedness in the business sense. Urban refugees who move to sparsely populated locales to work by themselves also face another aspect of breaking the ties to their former milieu—loneliness—one of the topics of the next chapter.

Chapter Thirteen

One Person in a Home Office

Boxes filled with reader's letters line her living room. The dining room serves as a conference room and work area for her employees: an assistant and a marketing director. Her office is crowded with small-business tomes and a computer, for which she battles her husband, Joe, who's also a writer. Her son's closet doubles as a filing cabinet. The only room in the house that's off-limits to the business: 10-year-old daughter Jeanne's bedroom.

Judith Schroer[1]

The arrangement described above sounds like a textbook example of home office "don'ts." Ironically, the occupant of this seemingly chaotic home is Jane Applegate, the author of *Succeeding in Small Business: The 101 Toughest Problems and How to Solve Them*[2] and a weekly newspaper column on small business. Applegate's office space probably began humbly enough as a desk in a spare room—a pattern common to many home office workers. But rooms that seem so large and empty at first soon fill up. Applegate reached the crisis point and is in the process of moving the office into her remodeled garage.

But it doesn't have to be that way. If you regard a home office as an office that happens to be in your home, you will be able to plan and organize the space more professionally than you do the rest of your home. Planned right, your home office will serve your business needs superbly while you reap the benefits of low overhead, higher productivity, freedom from the hassles of commuting, and the freedom to work how and when you please.

Setting up can be as simple as spending a few hundred bucks to install a desk and business phone in a spare bedroom or as ambitious as investing several thousand dollars to remodel or add on to your home. The proper scale depends on your needs, your financial resources, and how long you plan to stay in the house. I know, the 1880s Victorian house you just bought has a fantastic corner turret on the second floor with curved windows on three sides. You marked it from the start as the space for your future office. Sure, the round walls will be a bit tricky when it comes to fitting in rectangular equipment, and clients will have to walk through the kitchen to get there, but the space is too appealing to pass up. Maybe so, but before you lock yourself in to this decision, back off and consider all of the issues—it may save you many regrets later.

First, decide if basing your office in your home will keep you within reach of your clients and suppliers. Will they be able to find you? An address that requires a map to guide visitors is probably impractical for a designer who expects clients to come to the office but would be perfectly acceptable, even preferable, for a freelance writer who never meets clients on his or her own turf.

Keep It Legal

Most municipalities set restrictions on the use of residential properties. To find out if you can legally operate an office out of your home, obtain a copy of your local zoning ordinances. Many such ordinances permit "home occupations"—a carryover from the days when certain types of professions were common in residential areas. Even if a home office is legally allowed, you may still have to formally apply to your local planning or zoning board for a "permitted use" or similar provision.

Permission, if granted, will likely restrict your operation, limiting the kind of signage you can install outside (if any), how many employees you can have, the extent of outdoor lighting, and the number of parking spaces.

If the ordinance makes no provision for home offices, you may be able to get permission by applying for a variance. In such a case you will have to apply in writing, demonstrating that you have enough off-street parking and that the office won't disrupt the residential character of the neighborhood. You'll likely have to present your case in person before the planning and zoning committee and hope your neighbors won't use the hearing as an occasion to object to your plans.

Condominium associations and certain housing developments sometimes have their own "protective covenants" that you may have to get around even before approaching any hurdles created by the municipality's ordinances.

Tax Issues

A home office may offer tax advantages, but tax laws have recently been tightened. The IRS even introduced a separate form, "Expenses for Business Uses of Your Home," in 1991. After struggling with it for more than two hours, I finally gave up and turned it over to my accountant. To satisfy current IRS rules, your home office has to be used *exclusively* and *regularly* for *activities related to a trade or business, and be either a) the principal place of business, b) a place to meet and deal with patients, clients, or customers, or c) located in a separate, free-standing structure.* If you intend to use your home office part-time for take-home work, expect a hard sell, but most full-time professionals will have little trouble as long as they keep living space separate from office space.

As far as space planning is concerned, the more physically distinct and businesslike the space, the easier it will be to convince the tax folks it's truly an office and not just an amenity to your home.

How Much Space Do You Need?

The smallest office can be little more than a closet just large enough to house a desk. With some shelves above, it can be closed off from the adjacent room with folding or accordion doors that open to allow you to sit out in the room to use the desk. A space this small would naturally suit only the simplest needs and would eventually provoke claustrophobia in almost any normal person. I wouldn't want to face working eight hours in a space this small.

At the other end of the spectrum would be an office of 400 to 500 square feet (two good-sized rooms), which is ample space for a couple of work stations, a computer, a conference area, and a separate entrance. This sounds big, but you quickly grow into the space. Most home offices probably fall somewhere between these two extremes, with an area of, say, 150 to 200 square feet.

Many people pick out a space and then try to make it work. This is like buying shoes by the style and then trying to make them fit your feet. A better approach is to first find out how much area you will need by adding up the space required for equipment and functions.

Start with a list of equipment that will take up permanent space on the floor. Omit things like chairs that move around and items that will be placed under or above other items, such as bookshelves or wastebaskets. Don't list a computer or copy machine, but do list the table on which it will perch. Next to each item, write down how much square footage it will take up. A desk measuring 2.5 feet by 5 feet occupies 12.5 square feet. Get the dimensions of items you don't know from office supply catalogs or take a measuring tape to an office supply store for some field research.

To the total square footage required for floor-based equipment, add an equal amount for circulation—space required for moving around. Very efficient plans may get by with less circulation space, but this is a good ballpark figure to use at this stage of the game.

How Should the Office Relate to the House?

To help narrow the choice of possible office locations, consider the following factors.

- **Visitors.** If you plan to do graphic paste-up, sales, or telecommuting work, you will probably use your office as a base of operations from which you will contact clients by phone, or else you'll go to them. Other occupations, such as interior design or various kinds of consulting, require clients occasionally to come to you. In these cases image is important. Clients may not take you for a serious professional if they have to walk by your dirty laundry to get to your office. A separate entrance is a must.

- **Family distractions.** The need to oversee small children may be the main reason you decided in favor of a home office, but watching them will undoubtedly get in the way of your work. In their book, *Working from Home,*[3] Paul and Sarah Edwards offer sound advice: "Keep your home a home and your office an office." Hiring a baby-sitter for a few hours each day or finding another childcare arrangement will grant you a valuable chunk of unbroken time to work and the freedom to locate the office in a remote part of the house. Using a physical barrier separating your office from the rest of the house signals other family members that you are at work and shouldn't be disturbed. It can also help you shift gears into "work" mode when you enter the office space.

- **Sounds and smells.** Other reasons for physically isolating the office from the rest of your living quarters are sounds and smells. Privacy from the usual din of the household will be best if the office is not only separate but remote. If smells from a nearby bath or kitchen are a problem, consider installing exhaust fans in those rooms.

- **Access to amenities.** If clients will be visiting your office regularly, some provision for coffee or refreshments and a place to hang coats will be worthwhile amenities to have. Access to a rest room is also a must. If the office is in the house, you can probably get by with using the kitchen for coffee and the bath as a rest room. If the office is in a converted shed or garage, it may be well to install a small toilet facility unless doing so is prohibited by cost or zoning ordinances, which often restrict plumbing in accessory buildings to prevent a single-family home from becoming a multi-family home.

- **Personal needs.** It's your office, so it should suit your style of working. I can sit only so long at a drawing board or computer before I feel the need to get up and move around. I take several minibreaks to pace and stare out the windows. My office, located in a converted attic above a garage, has a "pace space" and ample windows opening onto country vistas that make for good staring. If I had to set up in the basement, I might get the same relief from the work routine by staring into an aquarium or group of plants under grow lights. However your office relates to your home, it has to be primarily a workspace. When you are in the workspace, as telecommuter Donna Cunningham puts it, "you can't also be 'at home'—I don't live in my office; I don't work in my home. I work in my office that happens to be in my home."

- **Think of the future.** Most homeowners eventually sell their house and move. What becomes of your office space at the time of resale? It might add to the house's sales appeal, but you should probably hedge your bets by not doing anything that would permanently lock the space into office use.

Costs

A firm idea of how much you can spend to create an office space and knowing where you will get the money will help guide you in finding the best location. In general, the most economical space is one converted from a space already finished, such as a bedroom or family room. An unfinished space such as a basement or attic would cost somewhat more. Still costlier is space gained by adding onto the house. A separate structure is the most expensive but offers the most flexibility for planning.

Small niches such as closets, bays, and hutches may be the best candidates if your budget is small and you need only a minimal workspace or if you want to set up temporary office space while you are remodeling another area. Closing off a bay or hutch without compromising the adjacent room may not be possible, and you may have to make do with a dividing screen, such as a free-standing row of bookshelves.

Spare rooms are the site of choice for most home offices. As spaces already finished, they likely won't need much remodeling, and they may be about the right size for most single-person ventures. On the downside, they may not be too well situated for traffic. A remote bedroom can provide good physical separation from the house but won't be the handiest for visitors to get to.

Attics offer good isolation from the house, the potential for windows or skylights, and large, uncluttered floor areas. Their suitability as a site for a home office depends on how easy it is to get to and from the space and the amount of available headroom. Most codes require at least 7.5 feet over 50 percent of the floor space in main rooms. You may comply by installing a flat ceiling over the center (high) portion and using the space below for circulation and activity areas. A four-foot-high kneewall along the sides will define an area with less headroom, suitable for desks, tables, equipment, and storage. To gain more headroom and vertical walls for windows, consider raising a portion of the roof with a shed dormer. Other windows can be installed in separate dormers, or skylights can be built right into the roof surface. Ask an architect or builder for advice as to whether the floor is adequate to support office use—it may need structural reinforcement. You can count on extending wiring and heating lines to the space and insulating the roof, walls, and floor if it is above an unheated space.

Like attics, basements usually pose headroom problems. Though level, the basement ceiling is probably not only low but also a jumble of water pipes, heating ducts, and wiring. Hiding these unsightly necessities with a new ceiling should be done only if the ceiling would leave adequate headroom and consist of panels that can be removed to get access to the pipes and wiring. You can make the overhead stuff seem to disappear by leaving it as is, painting everything the same color, and then painting the walls a different color.

Basements are often cold and damp. Moisture seeps through porous concrete or masonry walls and floors. New stud walls built inside the original walls can solve several problems at once. Run electrical wiring through or behind the studs and then insulate the cavities with fiberglass blankets to stem heat loss. Staple four-mil poly sheeting over the face of the studs to keep moisture out and apply wallboard for a smooth, finished surface. If the floor is made of concrete and fairly level, put down another layer of poly and then a carpet, with or without a pad.

Because they are outside, porches are often overlooked as candidates for additional space. They may have potentially great views and a separate outside entrance. But turning them into a workable office isn't always easy or cheap. You may have to redirect traffic into the house if the porch leads to an entrance door. The porch may be too narrow a space to work in. Porch floors sloped to drain away from the house will require leveling. You'll have to weatherproof the floor as well as the walls and ceiling/roof. Count on new wiring, heating, and windows, too.

Garages have distinct advantages if you don't mind parking the Mercedes outside. But you may not have to if you have a two-car garage. Consider erecting a separation wall down the middle. The half not taken up by your car will probably contain around 230 square feet—ample space for an office in many cases. Remote from the house, garages also offer potential for a separate entrance. As with porches, you will need to insulate and finish floors, walls, and the ceiling. A concrete garage floor can be finished by laying down a layer of poly sheeting for moisture control, followed by two-by-fours laid flat and two feet center-to-center. Lay 1.5-

inch-thick rigid foam insulation between the two-by-fours and nail down .5-inch plywood. Finish the floor with carpet.

A new addition to one side of your house offers opportunities unmatched by converting existing spaces if you can afford it. You can create space unencumbered by a previous use, get good separation from the house, and have a separate entrance.

Separate structures built as offices reap these advantages while not being dependent on the configuration of the house's roof or problems of sharing a common wall. If you go this route, you stand to gain another plus: distance. Physical distance between home and office translates to excellent separation from the smells and sounds of the household and makes it easier to feel like you've left work when you leave the office.

Space Planning

With your list of equipment and an office location nailed down, you are ready to start laying out the space. Unless you are skilled at design, however, I strongly suggest buying a few hours of professional consulting time from an architect or designer at this point. If you choose to do your own layout, draw the outer walls of the space on a gridded sheet, with grids drawn at quarter-inch intervals. A good scale for this level of planning is to have one half-inch equal one foot (which means that four squares of the grid equal one square foot). Make cutouts of each piece of equipment to lay over the sheet. When you get the layout you want, trace around each cutout and use this as a working drawing.

If possible, locate your main working desk near a window. This aids natural lighting and gives you a chance to look outdoors to rest your eyes. Locate your computer in the darkest part of the office, away from windows, to minimize glare and contrast between the screen and bright daylit surfaces.

Wiring for your office should provide power for outlets, lighting, and equipment. Computers should connect, if possible, to their own circuit to prevent danger from power surges. If you can't run a new separate circuit from the main panel, at least make sure the computer doesn't share a circuit with a motor appliance such as a refrigerator or well pump that cycles on and off. If you need additional wiring, consider running it through surface-type conduits such as those made by the Wiremold Corp. rather than ripping walls apart to get into the studs.

Good office lighting contains general lighting and lighting directed at specific—or task—areas. For general lighting, first make the most of natural sunlight coming through windows or skylights. Slat blinds are a good way to control glare and ensure privacy. Ceiling-mounted fluorescent fixtures are the most cost-effective light source for dark days and at night. My favorite fixtures for task lighting are swing-arm lamps that clamp on to almost any surface. Costing around $20, they use 60- or 75-watt standard incandescent or low-wattage high efficiency bulbs and throw light in any direction you want.

Heating and cooling may require no additional work if your office is in a converted, finished space. For additions and space carved out of unfinished, unheated areas, try first to extend the heating ducts or piping from the house—but don't try too hard. Consider installing a separate device in the office. Electric strip heaters are cheap and easy to install but the most costly to operate, particularly if you live in a region with high electric rates. Unit heaters that use natural gas or propane cost around $1,000 but save money over time. Installed next to an outside wall, they draw combustion air and vent exhaust gases directly through the wall, without a flue or chimney.

Finishing Touches

One of the best things about having your own office is that you can decorate it to suit your own tastes. But if clients will be visiting, bear in mind how they will respond to the ambiance. A warm, homey feeling may suit a catering service but might send the wrong message to business clients visiting you on your home turf. And don't build in permanent features that will get in the way of converting the space back to residential use when you move your office or sell the house.

A One-Person Firm in the Boonies

The sudden isolation that comes when fast-lane urban professionals set up shop in the outland can affect their business, family relationships, and mental state. Some find the transition impossible. Others have learned how to cope. We'll look at some of the ways but first consider what working from home implies.

Can You Run a Real Business from Your Home?

Home-based occupations are not new. Until the 1950s it was common for medical doctors and dentists to have their offices in their homes (of course, they still made house calls then, too). In time, they moved into clinics, group practices, and hospitals, presumably for better access to increasingly sophisticated equipment. For the most part, the businesses that stayed in the home were those run by women, usually on a part-time basis, such as piece-work sewing and beauty shops. The home as a business site with any status became tainted and lost prestige. Professionals who chose to base their operations at home faced the prospect of not being taken seriously by their peers or the public.

The perception lingers, but a countertrend is underway, driven by the changing economy and the tools that make it possible to locate an office anywhere near a phone jack or electrical outlet. But you may still have to battle to establish the legitimacy of your home-office site.

Legitimacy begins with self-image. If you think of yourself as a serious professional, the feeling broadcasts to others. Start with a professional workspace, as was described earlier. Next, do what you must to become professionally legitimate. If you are a real estate broker, get certified as a Realtor™. Join the American Society of Landscape Architects (ASLA) if you are a landscape architect or the American Institute of Architects (AIA) if you are an architect. Besides the advertised benefits, letters behind your name will give you status in the eyes of the public. Barbara Blackburn advises her small business clients to get visibility by joining service clubs (Elks, Kiwanis, Rotary) and the chamber of commerce.

Loneliness

So there you are, installed in your home office and ready for action. Your spouse has gone off to work. The kids are in school. You immerse yourself in work for a few hours, then take a coffee break. There's no one to share it with. You return to your work, eventually stopping for a lunch that you make and eat alone. By midafternoon, you welcome the distraction of the kids returning from school. Eventually, your spouse returns, and you are again surrounded by people. With the passage of many more such days, you realize that you really miss the crunch of humanity you were so happy to leave behind. At its worst, loneliness can lead to depression and inability to function.

You can still work alone and not be lonely. Many home-based professionals link up with others through computer modem networks that have "chat" capabilities. Others get out of their home offices one or more times a week to meet friends for lunch. If you belong to service organizations, you will likely attend lunchtime meetings.

I work best in the mornings and slack off in the early afternoon. I often leave the office during this time to drive five miles to Keene, the nearest service town. There I do business errands, get supplies, and go to the YMCA to work out for an hour. These trips accomplish a variety of logistical needs and give me a chance to maintain my physical and mental health.

Discipline

If self-employment is new to you, you may find it hard to produce outside the structure of your former workplace. I have no problem when a pile of work sits waiting, but it's often a struggle in slow times—particularly if my work consists of going after new projects. On a warm spring day, it's so easy to give into the urge to go outside and putter in the yard. After all, someone does have to pull those weeds, right?

One of the perks of working for yourself is the very opportunity to work when, how, and if you like. But without enough drive it's all too easy to play games with yourself to the point of accomplishing nothing and then feeling guilty about it. Most successful home-based professionals I have talked to concur on certain points:

- Set up and adhere to a regular work schedule. You don't have to be a slave to long hours, but do commit a minimum number of hours each day to work.
- Dress for work. This reinforces your self-perception as a professional at work.
- Get an answering machine for your phone and let it defer calls during your most productive periods.
- Don't give into distractions in or outside of the house.
- Plan your workweek and workday and try to adhere to the plan.

As an architect, I can't help but note that some of these points have to do with physical rather than emotional factors and that the most important cluster of physical influences over your work habits lies in the workplace itself. Good physical separation between the office and the home means more than not being distracted by the smell of toast in the kitchen or your daughter practicing her guitar. These reminders of home life should also be out of sight when you are in your home office.

After isolating your office from your home physically, finish the space in a way that will trigger "work," rather than "home," associations. For me, it meant following a color scheme of cool blue-greens. These are office colors to me—a sharp break with the warm off-white and earth tones that predominate in my home.

Audiovisual producer Jim Jones uses goal setting to maintain his work discipline. He sets long-term goals for six months or a year and then works backward in weeks to the present. Each night when he wraps it up, he knows what he will be doing the next day.

Businessperson or Housespouse?

So you are up and running in your home office, but it will take a while before the receipts start rolling in. Fortunately, your spouse's job will underwrite your family in the meantime. Unfortunately, because he or she is the one with the full-time job on the outside and you are home, you end up being responsible for the majority of the household chores, which can include any or all of the following baggage: cleaning, maintenance, meal preparation, shopping, and possibly looking out for children. Instead of "businessperson," you fall heir to the title of "housewife" or "house-husband," or worse still, "homemaker." The stigmas attached to these titles are enough to do you in even if the extra chores don't impede your struggle to establish a business enterprise. So what's the answer?

First, decide jointly just how serious your enterprise is to be. If you and your partner agree that it is to be more than a hobby, then sit down together to schedule household chores.

Second, if the lion's share of keeping the home together still falls into your lap, at least try to organize your day to allow a minimum number of uninterrupted hours "in the office." Value this time every bit as much as the surgeon who couldn't possibly disturbed while "in surgery" (I wish I had the chutzpah to tell callers I couldn't be disturbed because I was "in design").

Children are the thorniest part of the problem. One of the motivations that attract many entrepreneurs—women, mostly, but increasingly men—to work out of the home is the opportunity to be around their children. Unfortunately, they fall into a trap when they discover they can't spread themselves thin enough to cover all the bases. The result is an unfortunate compromise all around. The kids don't get quality attention, you can't get your work done, and clients regard you as unprofessional. One solution is to find in-home care for preschool children. Another is to drop them off at a daycare center. Both cost money, but so does the time you need to run your business.

And how you can better spend your time was really the point of this book. Finding a better balance between work and family really comes down to how you allocate your time. Much of the gain of relocating out of the big city is the time you gain when you are freed from the long hours wasted just getting to and from work.

We live in a time when many of us are reexamining the values that underpinned the consumer society, values that put workers on an unending cycle of work, spend, work, spend. We are searching for alternatives. Whether the alternatives you quest for include trees and green grass or the chance to regain control over your work, I hope this book has given you an insight into the alternatives to the urban rat race and fast-track career that are open to you.

For the track I think we should seek, as this millennium draws to a close, is the track to a more humane existence.

Appendix:
References and Resources

Books and Periodicals about Specific Businesses

Advertising/Public Relations
Advertising Age, 740 Rush Street, Chicago, IL 60611.

Adweek, 820 Second Avenue, New York, NY 10017.

Public Relations Journal, 845 Third Avenue, New York, NY 10022.

Accounting
Journal of Accountancy, AICPA, 1211 Avenue of the Americas, New York, NY 10036.

National Public Accountant, 1010 N. Fairfax Street, Alexandria, VA 22314.

Bed-and-Breakfasts/Inns
Notarius, Barbara and Brewer, Gail Sforza. *Open Your Own Bed & Breakfast*, 2nd edition. New York: John Wiley & Sons, Inc., 1992.

Commercial Art
Artist's Market (directory), Writer's Digest, 9933 Alliance Road, Cincinnati, OH 45242.

Art Direction, Advertising Trade Publications, 10 E. 39th Street, New York, NY 10016.

Communications (Business)
Directory of Business and Organizational Communications, 870 Market Street, San Francisco, CA 94102.

Journal of Organizational Communications, 870 Market Street, San Francisco, CA 94102.

Computers
Computerworld, 375 Cochituate Road, Framingham, MA 01704.

Copreneuring (Spouse as Business Partner)
Sommer, Elyse and Mike. *The Two-Boss Business: The Joys and Pitfalls of Working and Living Together—and Still Remaining Friends*. New York: Butterick, 1980.

Consulting

Holtz, Herman. *How to Succeed as an Independent Consultant,* 3rd edition. New York: John Wiley & Sons, 1993.

Karlson, David. Ph.D. *Consulting for Success: A Guide for Prospective Consultants.* Los Altos, CA: Crisp Publications, Inc., 1991.

Direct Mail

Simon, Julian L. *How to Start and Operate a Mail-Order Business.* 4th ed. New York: McGraw-Hill, 1987.

Direct Mail Marketing Magazine, 224 S. Seventh Street, Garden City, NY 11530.

Directory of Mailing List Houses, B. Klein Publications, Inc., P.O. Box 8503, Coral Springs, FL 33065.

Environmental Enterprises

Bennett, Steven J. *Ecopreneuring.* New York: John Wiley & Sons, Inc., 1991.

Franchises

Franchising World (trade journal) and *Franchise Opportunities Guide* (directory), IFA Publications, P.O. Box 1060, Evans City, PA 16033. Phone: (800) 543-1038.

Sherman, Andrew J. *Franchising & Licensing: Two Ways to Build Your Business.* New York: AMACOM, 1991.

Information-based Enterprises

Shenson, Howard L. *How to Develop & Promote Successful Seminars & Workshops: The Definitive Guide to Creating and Marketing Seminars, Workshops, Classes, and Conferences.* New York: John Wiley & Sons, Inc., 1990.

Weitzen, H. Skip. *Infopreneurs: Turning Data Into Dollars.* New York: John Wiley & Sons, Inc., 1988.

Mail Order

Simon, Julian L. *How to Start and Operate a Mail-Order Business.* 4th ed. New York: McGraw-Hill, 1987.

Market Research

Journal of Market Research, 250 S. Wacker Drive, Chicago, IL 60606.

Photography

Photo Weekly, Billboard Publications, 1515 Broadway, New York, NY 10036.

Photographic Trade News, 101 Crossways Park W., Woodbury, NY 11797.

Sales and Sales Management

Opportunity Product Guide and Directory, 6 N. Michigan Avenue, Chicago, IL 60602.

Sales & Marketing Management, 633 Third Avenue, New York, NY 10017.

Success Magazine, 342 Madison Avenue, New York, NY 10173.

Travel Agencies
Lehmann, Armin D. *Travel and Tourism: An Introduction to Travel Agency Operations.* New York: Bobbs-Merril, 1978.

ASTA Travel News, 488 Madison Avenue, New York, NY 10022.

Travel Trade Magazine, 6 E. 46th Street, New York, NY 10017.

Writing/Editing
Editor and Publisher Syndicate Directory, 11 W. 19th Street, New York, NY 10011.

Literary Market Place, R.R. Bowker Co., 205 E. 42nd Street, New York, NY 10017.

Editor & Publisher Market Guide, 11 W. 19th Street, New York, NY 10011.

Writer's Digest (periodical) and *Writer's Market* (annual directory of market prospects), P.O. Box 10996, Des Moines IA 50347-0996.

Books on Career Change and Small Business Topics

Career Change/Self-discovery
Applegath, John. *Working Free: Practical Alternatives to the 9 to 5 Job.* New York: Amacom, 1982.

Bolles, Richard Nelson. *What Color Is Your Parachute: A Practical Guide for Job-Hunters & Career Changers.* Berkeley, CA: Ten Speed Press, 1991.

Cameron, Charles, and Elusorr, Suzanne. *Thank God It's Monday: Making Your Work Fulfilling and Finding Fulfilling Work.* New York: Jeremy P. Tarcher, Inc., 1986.

Gale, Barry and Linda. *Stay or Leave.* New York: Harper & Row, 1989.

Gale, Barry and Linda. *Discover What You're Best At.* New York: Fireside Div., Simon & Schuster, Inc., 1990.

Laurance, Robert. *Going Freelance.* New York: John Wiley & Sons, Inc., 1988.

Morin, William J., and Cabrera, James C. *Parting Company: How to Survive the Loss of a Job and Find Another Successfully.* New York: Harcourt Brace Jovanovich, 1982.

Robbins, Paula I. *Successful Midlife Career Change: Self-Understanding and Strategies for Action.* New York: AMACOM, 1978.

Demography Urban-Rural Migration
Garreau, Joel. *Edge City.* New York: Doubleday, 1991.

Heenan, David A. *The New Corporate Frontier: The Big Move to Small Town USA.* New York: McGraw-Hill, 1991.

Herbers, John. *The New Heartland.* New York: Times Books Div., Random House, 1986.

Nichols, Judith E. *By the Numbers: Using Demographics and Psychographics for Business Growth in the '90s.* Chicago: Bonus Books, 1990.

Economic Trends
Boyett, Joseph H., and Conn, Henry P. *Workplace 2000: The Revolution Reshaping American Business.* New York: Dutton, 1991.

Celente, Gerald, with Milton, Tom. *Trend Tracking: The System to Profit from Today's Trends.* New York: John Wiley & Sons, Inc., 1990.

Naisbitt, John. *Megatrends: Ten New Directions Transforming Our Lives.* New York: Warner Books, 1982.

Naisbitt, John, and Aburdene, Patricia. *Megatrends 2000: Ten New Directions for the 1990's.* New York: William Morrow, 1990.

U.S. Dept. of Commerce. International Trade Administration. Superintendent of Documents. *1990 U.S. Industrial Outlook: Prospects for Over 350 Manufacturing and Service Industries.* Washington, D.C.: Government Printing Office, 1990.

Entrepreneuring/Small Business/Self-Employment
Birch, David. *Job Creation in America.* New York: The Free Press, 1987.

Drucker, Peter F. *Innovation and Entrepreneurship: Practice and Principles.* New York: Harper & Row, 1985.

Galbraith, Oliver, III. U.S. Small Business Administration. Office of Business Development. *Starting and Managing a Small Business of Your Own.* Starting and Managing Series, vol. 1. Washington, D.C.: Government Printing Office, 1986.

Harper, Stephen C. *The McGraw-Hill Guide to Starting Your Own Business: A Step-by-Step Blueprint for the First-Time Entrepreneur.* New York: McGraw-Hill, 1991.

Hawken, Paul. *Growing a Business.* New York: Simon and Schuster, 1987.

McKeever, Mike. *How to Write a Business Plan.* Berkeley, CA: Nolo Press, 1989.

Paradis, Adrian A. *The Small Business Information Source Book.* White Hall, VA: Betterway Publications, Inc., 1987.

Resnik, Paul. *The Small Business Bible.* New York: John Wiley & Sons, Inc., 1988.

Rosefsky, Robert S. *Getting Free: How to Profit Most out of Working for Yourself.* New York: Quadrangle/The New York Times Book Co., 1977.

Stevens, Mark. *36 Small Business Mistakes—And how to avoid them*. West Niyack, NY: Parker Publishing Company, 1978

Stevens, Mark. *The Macmillan Small Business Handbook*. New York: Macmillan, 1988.

Stolze, William J. *Startup: An Entrepreneur's Guide to Launching & Managing a New Venture*. Rochester, NY: Rock Beach Press, 1989.

Fact-finding/Research

Horowitz, Lois. *Knowing Where to Look: The Ultimate Guide to Research*. Cincinnati: Writer's Digest Books, 1988.

Mann, Thomas. *A Guide to Library Research Methods*. New York: Oxford University Press, Inc., 1987.

Todd, Alden. *Finding Facts Fast: How to find Out What You Want and Need to Know*. Berkeley, CA: Ten Speed Press, 1979.

Home-based Businesses, Home Offices

Arden, Lynie. *The Work at Home Sourcebook*. Boulder, CO: Live Oak Publications, 1990.

Kishel, Gregory and Patricia. *Start, Run & Profit From Your Own Home-Based Business*. New York: John Wiley & Sons, Inc., 1991.

Relocating

Boyer, Richard, and Savageau, David. *Places Rated Almanac: Your Guide to Finding the Best Places to Live in America*. New York: Prentice Hall, 1980.

Connoly, William G. *The New York Times Guide to Buying or Building a Home*. New York: Times Books, 1978.

Honychurch, Reginald R., and Battles, Howard K. *The Complete Relocation Kit: Everything You Need To Know about Changing Homes, Jobs and Communities*. Chicago: Dearborn Financial Publishing, Inc., 1991.

Kleeberg, Irene Cumming. *The Moving Book: How Not to Panic at the Thought*. New York: Butterick, 1978.

Thomas, G. Scott. *The Rating Guide to Life in America's Small Cities*. New York: Prometheus Books, 1990.

Spouse/Family

Sommer, Elyse and Mike. *The Two-Boss Business: The Joys and Pitfalls of Working and Living Together—and Still Remaining Friends*, New York: Butterick, 1980.

General Data about the United States

The Rand McNally 1991 Commercial Atlas & Marketing Guide. New York: Rand McNally, 1991.

The National Atlas of the United States of America. U. S. Dept. of the Interior Geological Survey. Washington, D.C.: Government Printing Office, 1970.

Atlas of the United States: A Thematic and Comparative Approach. New York: Macmillan, 1986.

Magazines about Small Business

Entrepreneur Magazine, P.O. Box 19787, Irvine, CA 92713-9734. Good source for new businesses, but lacks the depth of *In Business.*

In Business, J.G. Press, 419 State Avenue, Emmaus, PA 18049. Good bi-monthly source of information for startups.

Inc., P.O. Box 1534, Boulder, CO 80321-1534. Primarily oriented toward small- and mid-sized businesses.

Money, P.O. Box 6001, Tampa, FL 33660-0001. Mostly about personal money management, but much in the way of small businesses coverage.

Mother Earth News. Good source for socially conscious, ecology, and renewable-energy businesses.

Directories

Directory of Directories, Book Tower Building, Detroit, MI 48226.

Encyclopedia of Associations, Gale Research Co., Book Tower, Detroit, MI 48266.

Guide to American Directories, B. Klein Publications, P.O. Box 8503, Coral Springs, FL 33065.

Sources of State Information and State Industrial Directories, State Chamber of Comnmerce Dept., Chamber of Commerce of the U.S., 1615 H Street, NW, Washington, D.C. 20006.

Standard & Poor's Register of Corporations, Directors and Executives, 345 Hudson Street, New York, NY 10014.

Thomas Register of American Manufacturers, Thomas Publishing Co., One Penn Plaza, New York, NY 10001.

Computer Software

Online Networks

Delphi, 3 Blackstone St., Cambridge, MA 02139. (800) 544-4005; (617) 491-3393.

Dialog, 3460 Hillview Ave., Palo Alto, CA 94304. (415) 858-2700.

Quantum Link, 8620 Westwood Center Drive, Vienna, VA 22180. (800) 392-8200.

Job Search, Resume Writing, Cover Letter Writing
The Perfect Career, Mindscape, 3444 Dundee Road, Northbrook, IL 60062.
(708) 480-7667.

BetterWorking Resume Kit, Spinnaker Software, One Kendal Square, Cambridge, MA 02139. (617) 494-1200.

The Career Management Partner, Scientific Systems, 5 Science Park, New Haven, CT 06511. (203) 786-5236.

ResumeMaker, Individual Software, 125 Shoreway Road, Suite 3000, San Carlos, CA 94070-2704. (415) 595-8855.

Professional Organizations and Trade Associations

Accounting
National Society of Public Accountants, 1010 N. Fairfax Street, Alexandria, VA 22314.

Advertising/Public Relations
American Association of Advertising Agencies, 666 Third Avenue, New York, NY 10017.

Public Relations Society of America, 845 Third Avenue, New York, NY 10022.

Bookstores
American Booksellers Association, 122 E. 42nd Street, New York, NY 10168.

Association of American Publishers, One Park Avenue, New York, NY 10016.

Commercial Art
Society of American Graphic Artists, 32 Union Square, New York, NY 10003.

Communications (Business)
International Association of Business Communicators, 870 Market Street, San Francisco, CA 94102.

Computers
Association of Computer Programmers and Analysts, 2108 Gallows Road, Vienna, VA 22180.

Crafts/Hobbies
Hobby Industries of America, P.O. Box 348, Elmwood Park, NJ 07407.

Direct Mail Enterprises
Direct Mail Marketing Association, 6 E. 43rd Street, New York, NY 10017.

American Mail Order Merchants Association, 222 So. Riverside Plaza, Chicago, IL 60606.

Franchises
International Franchise Association, P.O. Box 1060, Evans City, PA 16033. For information on franchise exhibitions, phone the Blenheim Group at (407) 647-8521.

Home Businesses
American Home Business Association, 397 Post Road, Darien, CT 06820. (800) 433-6361; (203) 655-4380.

Inns
Independent Innkeepers Association, P.O. Box 150, Marshall, MI 49068. (800) 344-5244.

Marketing/Market Research
American Marketing Association, 250 South Wacker Drive, Chicago, IL 60606.

Marketing Research Association, 111 E. Wacker Drive, Chicago, IL 60601.

Llamas
International Llama Association, 2755 Locust Street, Suite 114, Denver, CO 80222. (303) 756-9004.

Ostriches
American Ostrich Association, 3840 Hulen Street, Suite 210, Fort Worth, TX 76107. (817) 731-8597.

Photography
Photographic Society of America, 2005 Walnut Street, Philadelphia, PA 19103.

Professional Photographers of America, 1090 Executive Way, Des Plaines, IL 60018.

Sales and Sales Management
Sales & Marketing Executives International, 6151 Wilson Mills Road, Cleveland, OH 44143.

Travel Agencies
American Society of Travel Agents, 4400 MacArthur Blvd., NW, Washington, DC 20007.

Association of Retail Travel Agents, 8 Maple Street, Croton-On-Hudson, NY 10520.

Writing and Editing
American Society of Business Press Editors, 4196 Porter Road, North Olmstead, OH 44050.

Miscellaneous Support Organizations

Job Sharing/Alternative Working Arrangements
Association of Part-Time Professionals, Crescent Plaza, Suite 216, 7700 Leesburg Pike, Falls Church, VA 22043. (512) 734-7975.

Focus, 509 Tenth Avenue, E., Seattle, WA 98102. (206) 329-7918.

Workshare, 311 E. 50 Street, New York, NY 10022. (212) 832-7061.

U.S. Government Sources and Agencies

Agriculture

U.S. Department of Agriculture, Office of Information, Washington, DC 20250.

Soil Conservation Service, U.S. Dept. of Agriculture, Washington, DC 20250.

United States Geological Survey, Department of the Interior, Washington, DC 20242.

Branch offices:

United States Geological Survey, 345 Middlefield Road, Menlo Park, CA 94025.

United States Geological Survey, Federal Center, Building 25, Denver, CO 80225.

Maps distribution for areas west of the Mississippi River:

Distribution Section, United States Geological Survey, Federal Center, Building 41, Denver, CO 80225.

Maps distribution for areas east of the Mississippi River:

Distribution Section, United States Geological Survey, 1200 South Eads Street, Arlington, VA 22202.

Notes

Part One

Introduction
1. Janice Castro, "The Simple Life," *Time*, 8 April 1991, 58.
2. Seymour Martin Lipset, "The Work Ethic—Then and Now," *The Public Interest* (Winter 1990): 63.
3. Joseph H. Boyett and Henry P. Conn, *Workplace 2000: The Revolution Reshaping American Business* (New York: Dutton, 1991).
4. Peter F. Drucker, *Innovation and Entrepreneurship: Practice and Principles* (New York: Harper & Row, 1985).
5. Noel Perrin, "So Much Information, So Little Comprehension," review of *Technopoly: The Surrender of Culture to Technology,* by Neil Postman, *USA Today,* 23 April 1992.
6. Marvin Cetron and Owen Davies, "50 Trends Shaping the World," *The Futurist* (September–October 1991): 12–17.
7. John Naisbitt and Patricia Aburdene, *Megatrends 2000: Ten New Directions for the 1990's* (New York: William Morrow, 1990).
8. John Herbers, *The New Heartland* (New York: Times Books Div., Random House, 1986).
9. Judith E. Nichols, *By the Numbers: Using Demographics and Psychographics for Business Growth in the '90s* (Chicago: 1990), 63–65.
10. *Ibid.* 91.
11. Cetron and Davies, "50 Trends Shaping the World," 12.
12. Nichols, *By the Numbers,* 256.
13. Cetron and Davies, "50 Trends Shaping the World," 13.
14. "Outlook '92 and Beyond," *The Futurist* (November–December, 1991): 54.
15. Naisbitt and Aburdene, *Megatrends 2000,* 217.
16. "Outlook '92 and Beyond," 59.
17. William Dunn, "Survival by the Numbers," *Nation's Business* (August 1991): 17.
18. "Outlook '92 and Beyond," 59.
19. John Naisbitt, *Megatrends: Ten New Directions Transforming Our Lives* (New York: Warner Books, 1982).
20. Naisbitt and Aburdene, *Megatrends 2000,* 96–97.
21. Gerald Celente with Tom Milton, *Trend Tracking: The System to Profit from Today's Trends* (New York: John Wiley & Sons, Inc., 1990).

Part Two

Chapter 1
1. Doris B. Matthews, "A Comparison of Burnout in Selected Occupational Fields," *The Career Development Quarterly* (March 1990): 230–231.

2. Amy Saltzman, *Downshifting: Reinventing Success on a Slower Track* (New York: Harper Perennial, 1990), 17.
3. Charles A. Reich, *The Greening of America* (New York: Random House, 1970).
4. *Ibid.,* 273.
5. *Ibid.,* 194.
6. John Applegath, *Working Free: Practical Alternatives to the 9 to 5 Job* (New York: Amacom Div., American Management Associations, 1982), 23.
7. Dr. Joyce Brothers, *How to Get Whatever You Want Out of Life* (New York: Simon and Schuster, 1978), 19–34.
8. Richard K. Irish, *If Things Don't Work Improve Soon I May Ask You to Fire Me* (New York: Anchor Press/Doubleday, 1975), 56.
9. Rosabeth Moss Kanter, *The Change Masters: Innovation for Productivity in the American Corporation* (New York: Simon and Schuster, 1983), 149.
10. Donald Sanzotta, *Motivational Theories & Applications for Managers* (New York: American Management Association, 1977), 19.
11. *Ibid.,* 161.
12. Carole Hyatt, *Shifting Gears: How to Master Career Change and Find the Work That's Right for You* (New York: Simon and Schuster, 1990), 22.
13. Brothers, *How to Get Whatever You Want Out of Life,* 35-49.

Chapter 2
1. Richard Nelson Bolles, *What Color is Your Parachute: A Practical Guide for Job-Hunters & Career Changers* (Berkeley, CA: Ten-Speed Press, 1991).
2. Barry and Linda Gale, *Discover What You're Best At* (New York: Fireside Div., Simon & Schuster, Inc., 1990).
3. William J. Morin and James C. Cabrera, *Parting Company: How to Survive the Loss of a Job and Find Another Successfully* (New York: Harcourt Brace Jovanovich, 1982).
4. James Cotham, as quoted by Paula Mergenhagen, "Doing the Career Shuffle," *American Demographics* (November 1991): 44.
5. Betsy Jaffe, *Altered Ambitions: What's Next in Your Life?* (New York: Donald I. Fine, Inc., 1991).
6. John Applegath, *Working Free: Practical Alternatives to the 9 to 5 Job* (New York: Amacom Div., American Management Associations, 1982), 145.
7. Alvin Toffler, *The Third Wave* (New York: Morrow, 1980).
8. Robert Woessner, "Delivering Doctors on Demand," *USA Today,* 7 April 1992.

Chapter 3
1. George Harris and Robert Trotter, in Seymour Martin Lipset, "The Work Ethic—then and now," *The Public Interest* (Winter 1990): 63. Quotes from Harris and Trotter originally from a March 1989 article in *Psychology Today.*
2. John Robinson, in Marlys Harris, "What's Wrong with This Picture?" *Working Woman* (December 1990).
3. Brad Schept, "The Best Opportunities For Telecommuters," *Home Office Computing* (October 1990).
4. Robert Laurance, *Going Freelance* (New York: John Wiley & Sons, Inc., 1988).
5. Steve Bergsman, "Part-Time Professionals Make the Choice," *Personnel Administrator* (September 1989).
6. William Atkinson, "Temporary Employees: the Demand Exceeds the Supply," *Office* (May 1990).
7. Robert Woessner, "Delivering Doctors on Demand," *USA Today,* 7 April 1992.
8. Donald Pizzi, "The Job Search Can Be Enriching," *Retail Control* (March, 1990).
9. James H. Lane, "Building Your Own Network," *Computerworld,* 4 June 1990.

10. Ed Brandt with Leonard Corwen, *Fifty and Fired: How to Prepare For It, What to Do When it Happens* (Bedford, MA.: Mills & Sanderson).
11. Mike McKeever, *How to Write a Business Plan* (Berkeley, CA: Nolo Press, 1989).
12. Stephen C. Harper, *The McGraw-Hill Guide to Starting Your Own Business: A Step-by-Step Blueprint for the First-Time Entrepreneur* (New York: McGraw-Hill, 1991).
13. Walter Szykitka, ed., *How to Be Your Own Boss: The Complete Handbook for Starting and Running a Small Business* (New York: NAL, 1978).
14. Ken Prigal, "6 Ways to Generate New Business Ideas," *Home Office Computing* (November 1991): 26.
15. Gerald Celente with Tom Milton, *Trend Tracking: The System to Profit from Today's Trends* (New York: John Wiley & Sons, Inc., 1990).
16. Calvin Reynolds and Rita Bennett, "The Career Couple Challenge," *Personnel Journal* (March 1991).
17. Naomi Gerstel and Harriet Gross, *Commuter Marriage: A Study of Work and Family* (New York: The Guilford Press, 1984).
18. Uma Sekaran, *Dual Career Families* (San Francisco: Jossey-Bass, 1986), 74.
19. Kevin D. Thompson, "Married . . . With Business," *Black Enterprise* (April 1990).
20. Dyan Machan, "My Partner, My Spouse," *Forbes,* 14 December 1987.

Part Three

Chapter 4
1. David A. Heenan, *The New Corporate Frontier: The Big Move to Small Town USA* (New York: McGraw-Hill, 1991), 5.
2. Marvin Cetron and Owen Davies, "50 Trends Shaping the World," *The Futurist* (September–October 1991).
3. Steven J. Bennett, *Ecopreneuring* (New York: John Wiley & Sons, Inc., 1991).
4. "Outlook '92 and Beyond," *The Futurist* (November–December, 1991).
5. John Naisbitt and Patricia Aburdene, *Megatrends 2000: Ten New Directions for the 1990's* (New York: William Morrow, 1990), 64.
6. "Crafts are big business as U.S. extols simple life," *Ogden Standard-Examiner,* 8 March 1992. Originally written for the *Chicago Tribune.*

Chapter 5
1. John Herbers, *The New Heartland* (New York: Times Books Div., Random House, 1986).
2. Alvin Toffler, *The Third Wave* (New York: Morrow, 1980).
3. Lisa Carlson, *Caring For Your Own Dead* (Hinesburg, VT: Upper Access, Inc., 1987).
4. Steve Carlson, *Your Low-Tax Dream House* (Hinesburg, VT.: Upper Access, Inc., 1989).
5. Steve Carlson, *The Best Home for Less* (New York: Avon Books, 1992).
6. Mary Carse, *Herbs of the Earth* (Hinesburg, VT.: Upper Access, Inc., 1989).
7. Mary Blount White, *Letters from the Other Side* (Hinesburg, VT: Upper Access, Inc., 1987).
8. Pat Edwards, *Cheap Eating* (Hinesburg, VT: Upper Access, Inc., 1993).
9. Moroni Leash, M.S.W., *Death Notification* (Hinesburg, VT: Upper Access, Inc., 1993).
10. Joseph H. Boyett and Henry P. Conn, *Workplace 2000: The Revolution Reshaping American Business* (New York: Dutton, 1991).
11. John Naisbitt and Patricia Aburdene, *Megatrends 2000: Ten New Directions for the 1990's* (New York: William Morrow, 1990).

12. Gerald Celente with Tom Milton, *Trend Tracking: The System to Profit from To-day's Trends* (New York: John Wiley & Sons, Inc., 1990), 224.
13. Howard L. Shenson, *How to Develop & Promote Successful Seminars & Workshops: The Definitive Guide to Creating and Marketing Seminars, Workshops, Classes, and Conferences* (New York: John Wiley & Sons, Inc., 1990).
14. Heenan, David A., *The New Corporate Frontier: The Big Move to Small Town USA* (New York: McGraw-Hill, 1991), 104.

Chapter 6
1. John Naisbitt and Patricia Aburdene, *Megatrends 2000: Ten New Directions for the 1990's* (New York: William Morrow, 1990), 305.
2. Marvin Cetron and Owen Davies, "50 Trends Shaping the World," *The Futurist* (September–October 1991).

Part Four

Chapter 7
1. Stephen C. Harper, *The McGraw-Hill Guide to Starting Your Own Business: A Step-by-Step Blueprint for the First-Time Entrepreneur* (New York: McGraw-Hill, 1991).
2. Oliver Galbraith III, *Starting and Managing a Small Business of Your Own,* U.S. Small Business Administration, Off. of Business Development, Starting and Managing Series, vol. 1. (Washington, D.C.: Government Printing Office, 1986).
3. Judith E. Nichols, *By the Numbers: Using Demographics and Psychographics for Business Growth in the '90s* (Chicago: Bonus Books, 1990).

Chapter 8
1. John Herbers, *The New Heartland* (New York: Times Books Div., Random House, 1986).
2. Mark Baldassare, "Residential Satisfaction and the Community Question," *Sociology and Social Research* (January, 1986).
3. Joel Garreau, *Edge City* (New York: Doubleday, 1991).
4. George Gallup Jr., *The Gallup Poll: Public Opinion 1990* (Wilmington, Delaware: Scholarly Resources, Inc).

Chapter 9
1. *The Comparative Climatic Data for the United States, National Climatic Data Center* (Washington, D.C.: Government Printing Office, annual).
2. *Statistical Abstract of the United States,* U.S. Bureau of the Census (Washington, D.C.: Government Printing Office, annual).
3. *Almanac of the Fifty States* (Palo Alto, CA: Information Publications, annual).
4. *State and Local Statistics Sources* (Detroit: Gale Research, annual).

Part Five

Chapter 12
1. Sharon Donovan, "Buying Business Fraught with Risk," *USA Today,* 11 May 1992.
2. Blair Walker, "Health-Insurance Challenge," *USA Today,* 11 May 1992.
3. William Mueller, "Beyond Blue Highways," *Venture* (August 1988).
4. Joan Warner, "Adventures in the On-Line Universe," *Business Week* 17 June 1991.

Chapter 13
1. Judith Schroer, "Author Makes Mark as Small-Business Owner," *USA Today,* 11 May 1992.

2. Jane Applegate, *Succeeding in Small Business: The 101 Toughest Problems and How to Solve Them* (New York: Plume, 1992).

3. Paul and Sarah Edwards, *Working From Home: Everything You Need to Know about Living and Working under the Same Room* (Los Angeles: Jeremy P. Tarcher, Inc., 1990).

Index

If you're not looking here, you're hardly looking.

There are lots of publications you can turn to when you're looking for a job. But in today's tough job market, you need the National Business Employment Weekly. It not only lists hundreds of high-paying jobs available now at major corporations all across the country, it also gives you valuable strategies and advice to help you land one of those jobs. NBEW is a Wall Street Journal publication. It's the leading national job-search and career guidance publication and has been for over ten years. Pick it up at your newsstand today. Or get the next 12 issues delivered first class for just $52 by calling toll-free...

800-367-9600

National Business Employment Weekly

If you're not looking here, you're hardly looking.